SUPPLEMENT TO THE HANDBOOK OF MIDDLE AMERICAN INDIANS
Volume 2 Linguistics

SUPPLEMENT TO THE HANDBOOK OF MIDDLE AMERICAN INDIANS

VICTORIA REIFLER BRICKER, General Editor

VOLUME TWO

LINGUISTICS

MUNRO S. EDMONSON, Volume Editor

With the Assistance of Patricia A. Andrews

UNIVERSITY OF TEXAS PRESS, AUSTIN

Copyright © 1984 by the University of Texas Press
All rights reserved
Printed in the United States of America

First edition, 1984

Requests for permission to reproduce material
from this work should be sent to:
    Permissions
    University of Texas Press
    Box 7819
    Austin, Texas 78712

LIBRARY OF CONGRESS CATALOGING IN PUBLICATION DATA
Main entry under title:
Linguistics.
    (Supplement to the Handbook of Middle American
Indians; v. 2)
    Bibliography: p.
    1. Indians of Mexico—Languages—Addresses, essays,
lectures.   2. Indians of Central America—Guatemala—
Languages—Addresses, essays, lectures.   I. Edmonson,
Munro S.   II. Andrews, Patricia A.   III. Series.
PM3008.L5 1984   497   83-23562
ISBN 0-292-77577-6

CONTENTS

GENERAL EDITOR'S PREFACE

This is the first of two volumes edited by Munro S. Edmonson. The original plans called for a single volume with grammatical sketches of six Middle American Indian languages and six articles on the Native American literatures of the area. The publisher later decided to divide that volume into two parts. Volume 2 supplements the coverage of Middle American languages in Volume 5 of the *Handbook of Middle American Indians*. Volume 3 of the *Supplement* will contain articles on the literatures of the aboriginal peoples of Middle America.

The five grammatical sketches in this volume provide a fair sampling of the most important languages not included in the *Handbook*: Tarascan, Mixe, Chichimeco Jonaz, Huastec, and Classical Choltí. Future linguistics volumes of the *Supplement* will contain grammatical sketches of additional languages and, from time to time, bibliographic updates of research on Middle American languages.

V.R.B.

This volume differs both in scope and in content from its forerunner, Volume 5 of the *Handbook of Middle American Indians* (McQuown 1967). That work contained treatment of the history of Middle American linguistics, bibliographies of descriptive and classificatory studies, treatment of lexicostatistics, dialectology, comparative and historical linguistics, and language-in-culture, and sketches of Classical Nahuatl, Yucatec, and Quiché and modern Popoluca, Zapotec, Mazatec, Pame, and Chontal de Oaxaca.

The aim of this work is to add sketches of five additional languages: Mixe, Chichimeco Jonaz, Choltí, Tarascan, and Huastec. We had planned to include a sixth sketch grammar, on Chontal de Acala, but the author was unable to complete it in time for inclusion.

No attempt was made to coerce the authors into any particular format nor to dictate scope or method of presentation. Restrictions of space have regrettably forced some cutting of the original drafts in some instances.

In selecting the languages to be included we have tried for diversity, but could not attain quite the coverage of the original *Hand-book* volume. We have added one more Mixe-Zoque-Popoluca language (Coatlán Mixe), one more Otomanguan one (Chichimeco Jonaz), two more Mayan ones (Choltí and Huastec), and one isolate (Tarascan). All of the grammatical sketches deal with the phonology, morphology, and syntax of the languages treated, and most also cover discourse. John Fought has tried to make his sketch accessible and nontechnical. Paul Friedrich has written his "backward," i.e., from meaning to sound, and begins with style. Norman A. McQuown's is rather more than a sketch, since it is in effect an outline of and introduction to a very much larger and more comprehensive body of work. It is also distinguished by time depth, so that while we may never know about Classical Huastec directly (as we do Nahuatl, Quiché, and Yucatec), we have here a good sketch of Colonial as well as modern Huastec.

Naturally the categories of analysis and description must reflect the distinctiveness of the various languages, causing Searle Hoogshagen to become involved with "syllable onset and coda," Yolanda Lastra de Suárez with "pattern of stem variation," Friedrich with "the conditional and the three subjunctives," Fought with "primary and secondary stems," McQuown with the complexly compounded Huastec pronominal system. The sketches present clearly the differences among the Middle American languages by not having indulged in excessive idiosyncrasy of theoretical vocabulary or style of description. The differences that emerge are thus more those between the languages than those between the linguists. The results are illuminating at a comparative level, aided perhaps by the outline of subheadings that precedes each chapter.

M.S.E.

SUPPLEMENT TO THE HANDBOOK OF MIDDLE AMERICAN INDIANS

Volume 2 Linguistics

1. Coatlán Mixe

SEARLE HOOGSHAGEN

0. INTRODUCTION. This chapter describes the principal features of the phonology and grammar of the Coatlán dialect of Mixe.[1]

1. PHONOLOGY includes segmental phonemes, syllable phonology, word phonology, and morphophonemics.

1.1. SEGMENTAL PHONEMES include consonants and vowels.

1.1.1. CONSONANTS are presented in Table 1-1. The consonants *p*, *t*, and *k* are aspirated word finally after all syllable nuclei except *Vh*. Otherwise they are unaspirated. The consonants *c* and *š* have voiced allophones (*ʒ* and *ž*) following nasals and between vowels within words. All consonants except *f*, *s*, *l*, *ř*, and *ŋ* have palatalized allophones when they occur after *y*. The palatal effect differs from consonant to consonant according to the phonetic character of the consonant. A general characteristic of palatalized consonants is a slight palatal onglide. Palatalization of stops and *n*, *m*, and *w* actualizes as palatal offglide, except that *w* is not palatalized syllable finally and *m* has no palatal offglide word finally. The consonants *h*, *c*, and *š* shift to a palatal point of articulation when palatalized. When the glottal stop is palatalized syllable initially the tongue is in a palatal position. When the glottal stop is part of a short syllable nucleus (*V*ʔ) which has *y* in the coda, it is released as *i* or *y*.[2]

1.1.2. VOWELS. Coatlán Mixe has six vowels,[3] as follows:

$$i \qquad ɨ \qquad u$$
$$e \qquad a \qquad o$$

The vowels *i* and *e* are lax [ɪ] and [ɛ], except when followed by *y* in the same syllable, when they are realized as [i] and [e].

1.2. SYLLABLE PHONOLOGY. A Mixe syllable is composed of a nucleus with obligatory onset and optional coda. All three parts—onset, nucleus, and coda—can be either simple or complex.

1.2.1. SYLLABLE NUCLEUS. Vowels as syllable nuclei can be followed by glottal stop ʔ or aspiration *h*. Syllable nuclei are then: *V*, *V*ʔ, and *Vh*. To all of these nuclei a feature of length may be added: *V·*,[4] *V*ʔ*V* (realized as a laryngealized vowel), and *Vh·* (realized as an extra long vowel). These may be illustrated by: *pet* 'climb', *pe·t* 'broom', *huʔk* 'owl', *huʔuky* 'cigarette', *pahk* 'bone', and *mah·p* 'is sleeping'.

1.2.2. SYLLABLE ONSET AND CODA. The syllable onset[5] can be any consonant except *ŋ*, or any of the following consonant clusters which occur word initially only: *n* or *m* followed by any one of the other syllable onset consonants, except *p*, *t*, or *k*; also *y* or *yš* followed by any other consonant, except *b*, *d*, *g*, or *ŋ*.

The syllable coda can be any consonant, except ʔ and *h*, or any of the following clusters of consonants: *pc*, *pcy*, *pcp*, *pcpy*, *pš*, *pšy*, *pšpy*; *tp*, *tpy*; *kp*, *kpy*, *kc*, *kcy*, *kcp*, *kcpy*, *kš*, *kšy*, *kšp*, *kšpy*; *cp*, *cpy*; *šp*, *špy*; *nc*, *ncy*, *ncp*, *ncpy*.[6]

1.3. WORD PHONOLOGY. Every word begins with a consonant or a consonant cluster. Any single consonant can begin a word, except *b*, *d*, *g*, and *ŋ*.[7] A word may close with a vowel, a consonant, or a consonant cluster. Permitted consonant occurrence and permitted clusters are described in section 1.2.2.

Word initially and medially in consonant clusters with *y* as a member, the position of the *y* as first or last member of the cluster has differing effects on the other consonants present. If *y* is the first member of the cluster or is a member of a syllable coda cluster, the palatalized allophones of the other consonants will occur (e.g., [m̃]). If *y* is the last member of a non-word-final cluster, the palatalized allophones of the other consonants will not occur. This is illustrated by: *mo·k* 'corn', *ymo·k* [m̃ok^h] 'his-corn'; *yo·ok* 'mother-in-law', *myo·ok* [myo·ok^h] 'your-mother-in-law'; *yoʔoy* 'to-walk', *co·n* 'to leave', *yoʔoyco·n* [yoʔoyčo·n] 'to leave walking'; *ka·p* 'take-

TABLE 1-1. Consonants

Voiceless stops	p		t			k	ʔ
Voiced stops	b		d			g	
Affricate			c				
Fricatives		f	s		š	h	
Lateral				l			
Nasals	m		n		ŋ		
Vibrant					r̃		
Semi-vowels	w				y		

hold-of-it (a spoon)', *ka·pyoʔoy* [*ka·pyoʔoy*] 'to-move-it-with-a-spoon'; *hikšy* 'food', *hikšy-tuk* [*hik̃š̃ʔuk^h*] 'food-scraps'.

Stress occurs on the last syllable of an uninflected word that ends in a consonant or a long vowel and on the next to the last syllable of an uninflected word that ends in a short vowel. Stress occurs on the last syllable of the stem of an inflected word unless a stress-carrying suffix is present, in which case the suffix will carry the stress. The stress-carrying suffixes are *-yi·* (object person focus), *-i·* (nominalizer), and *-oʔk* (repetitive action).[8]

1.4. MORPHOPHONEMICS. Morphophonemic variations can be explained by the following rules:

(1) The phoneme *n* is replaced by *m* preceding a bilabial stop, except word initially.

(2) The phoneme *p* is lost word finally if preceded by *m*.

(3) The phoneme *n* is replaced by *ŋ* when followed by a velar stop.

(4) The phoneme *k* is lost word finally following *n*.

(5) The phoneme *w* is lost root finally when followed by a suffix beginning with a consonant.

(6) Voiceless stops are replaced by their voiced counterparts following a nasal, or between vowels.[9]

2. GRAMMAR. A brief description is given here of the grammatical structure of words, phrases, clauses, sentences, and discourse.

2.1. WORDS. Word classes (parts of speech) included in this description are verbs, nouns, pronouns, adjectives, adverbs, connectives, clause subordinators and introducers, and sentence introducers. Verbs and nouns exhibit complex morphological structures including roots, stems, derivational affixes, and inflectional affixes. The remaining word classes are less complex morphologically.

2.1.1. VERBS are composed of stems plus affixes. Verb stems can be inflected for person, tense, and aspect. Most verbs have two or more forms for each stem.

2.1.1.1. VERB STEMS are of three types: simple, compound, and derived. Simple stems are composed of a single root: *tun* 'to work or do'.

Compound stems are composed of two or more root morphemes: either verb root plus verb root, or noun root plus verb root. In a compound stem of verb root plus verb root, the first root is basic, and the second one modifies it: *tun* 'to work', *tigoy* 'to lose', *tundigoy* 'to do wrong'. In a compound stem of noun root plus verb root, the verb root is basic, and the noun root modifies it: *hot* 'liver', *ʔambihk* 'to get hot', *hotʔambihkp* 'to become angry'. In some Mixe clause nuclei the object is incorporated into the verb stem. In these constructions also, the noun root precedes the verb root: *ni·* 'water', *ʔu·k* 'to drink', *ni·ʔu·kp* 'water-drinking'. The same sense can be expressed by a different clause construction in which the object is not in-

5

corporated into the verb stem: *yɨ̀ʔ ʔuˑkp niˑ* 'he is drinking water' (subject plus verb plus object).

Derived stems are formed by four different kinds of affixation:

(1) Suffix morphemes that convert a stem from one word class to another, such as: adjective or noun to verb, intransitive verb to transitive verb, or a borrowed word into a Mixe verb. These suffixes are *-iʔi*, *-iʔɨy*, or *-ɨˑy*; *-ʔat* or *-ʔaht*; and *-iʔik*: *poˑp* 'white', *poˑbiʔi* 'whiten-it'; *hɨˑt* 'saw', *ʔahɨdiʔi* 'saw-it'; *nikš* 'to go', *nikšɨˑy* 'go-by-way-of'; *kuhkšiˑ* 'mid-day', *kuhkšiˑʔahtp* 'eating-mid-day-meal'; *ganar* (Spanish) 'to win', *ganarʔahtp* 'is-winning'; *peˑt* 'broom', *pediʔik* 'sweep-it'.

(2) Suffix morphemes that add a dimension of meaning to the root morphemes. These are *-aˑn*, *-aʔny*, or *-aˑm* (desiderative future), and *-taʔa*, *-taʔay*, or *-taˑy* 'all': *pediʔigaˑm* 'will sweep-it' (*pediʔik* 'to sweep'), *pediʔik-taʔa* 'sweep all of it'. When they both occur in the same clause, the *-aˑm* suffix occurs last: *pediʔiktaʔawaˑm* 'will-sweep-all-of-it'.

(3) Adverb-like prefixes that indicate direction of movement. These occur with verb roots whose meaning has a potential for movement. They add a dimension of meaning to the basic root morpheme that is different from that of aspect and tense. They occur adjacent to the root of the stem. These prefixes are: *ni-* 'movement downward', *nɨdih* 'to push-downward' (*tih* 'to push'); *yuhk-* 'movement-upward', *yuhktih* 'to push-upward'; *paˑ-* 'follow after', *paˑdih* 'push-it-forward'; *hɨˑ-* 'reverse movement', *hɨˑwaʔak* 'back-away-from-it' (*waʔak* 'to move the feet'); *mɨh-* 'movement toward', *mɨhwaʔak* 'move-up-to-it'; *huʔu-* 'movement around it', *huʔuwaʔak* 'move-around-it'; *kuy-* 'movement along a line', *kuywaʔak* 'move-along-the-line'; *naˑ-* 'enclose something', *naˑwɨˑt* 'enclose-it with poles' (*wɨˑt* 'tie poles together'); *koʔo-* 'movement off the top of', *koʔogaʔanahš* 'fall-off-the-top-of-it', (*kaʔaw* 'to fall', *nahš* 'to pass-it'); *niʔi-* 'movement on the surface of', *niʔinahšp* 'passing-over-it'; *win-* 'movement over the surface', *wimbuhšp* 'cutting (grass off the surface)' (*puhšp* 'cutting

with a machete'); *ʔɨš-* 'movement to dispose of something', *ʔɨškaʔac* 'throw-it-away' (*kaʔac* 'to throw'); *nahc-* 'to free something', *nahmaciʔi* 'to-free-it' (*mac* 'to grab something').

(4) Derivational prefixes that indicate relations among participants in a clause nucleus, or of a participant to the verb action. Each prefix occurs with a limited number of verb roots whose semantic properties are compatible with the prefix. These prefixes are: *yah-* (causative), *yahnikš* 'have-it-taken' (*nikš* 'to go'), *yahwoy* 'have-him-summoned' (*woy* 'to summon'); *mɨˑ-* (associative), *mɨˑnikš* 'take-it-with-you'; *mɨˑt-* (associative, person with person), *mɨˑtnikš* 'go-with-him'; *niˑ-* 'for' or 'in behalf of', *niˑnikš* 'go-for-something'; *win-* 'in respect of', *wingay* 'to-eat-in-respect-of-something' (*kay* 'to eat'); *koˑ-*[10] (permanence), *koˑhuy* 'pay-for-something-to-keep' (*huy* 'to buy'); *ʔaˑ-* (nonpermanence), *ʔaˑhuy* 'pay-for-something-to-resell'.

Verb stem alternation occurs in the nucleus of the last syllable of the verb stem (either the root or a derivational suffix). There are five types of root alternants: *Vh* and *V* (*peht* and *pet* 'to climb'); *Vˑ* and *VʔV* (*moˑy* and *moʔoy* 'to give'); *Vʔ* and *VʔV* (*haʔt* and *haʔat* 'to arrive'); *V* and *Vˑ* (*tun* and *tuˑn* 'to work'); *Vˑ* and *Vhˑ* (*hɨˑn* and *hɨhˑn* 'to swallow'). One set of roots has no alternants: *nikš* 'to go'. There are four derivational suffixes which have syllable alternants: *-ʔaht* and *-ʔat* (verbalizer); *-ɨˑy* and *-iʔɨy* (verbalizer); *-taˑy* and *-taʔay* 'all'; and *-aˑn* and *-aʔny* (desiderative).

The first member of each set of alternants is called the basic stem. It expresses present[11] and past nonconjunct relation and past conjunct relation.[12] The second member of each set is called the alternate stem. It expresses present conjunct relation.

In the forms that use the basic stem, the difference between nonconjunct and conjunct is shown by a difference of person marker and by the presence or absence of *-y*. The choice of person marker depends on subject focus and tense as well as on conjunctivity.

Intransitive subject in both present and

TABLE 1-2. Person Markers for Nonconjunct/Conjunct Predicate Types

	Tense	Person	Nonconjunct		Conjunct	
Intransitive	Present		Basic stem		Alternate stem	
		1st	Ø-		n-	-y
		2nd	m-		m-	-y
		3rd	Ø-		y-	-y
	Past		Basic stem		Basic stem	
		1st	Ø-		n-	-y
		2nd	m-		m-	-y
		3rd	Ø-		y-	-y
Transitive	Present		Basic stem		Alternate stem	
		1st	n-	-y	n-	-y
		2nd	m-	-y	m-	-y
		3rd	y-	-y	Ø-	-y
	Past		Basic stem		Basic stem	
		1st	n-		n-	-y
		2nd	m-		m-	-y
		3rd	y-		Ø-	-y

Note: See section 2.1.1.3 for plural person markers.

past nonconjunct has *Ø-* (third person) and no *-y*. Note, for example: *Ø-ʔihšp* 'he-sees'; *Ø-ihš* 'he-saw'.

Transitive subject in present nonconjunct has *y-* (third person) plus *-y*. In past nonconjunct it has *y-* (third person) and no *-y*. In past conjunct it has *Ø-* (third person) plus *-y*. Note, for example: *y-ʔihšp-y* 'he-sees-it'; *y-ʔihš* 'he-saw-it'; and *tɨ Ø-ʔihš-y* 'he-had-seen-it'.

Present conjunct forms use the alternate stem. Intransitive subject has *y-* (third person) plus *-y*. Transitive subject has *Ø-* (third person) plus *-y*: *tɨ y-ʔiš-y* 'he-does-see'; and *tɨ Ø-ʔiš-y* 'he-did-see-it'.

Some factors governing verb stem alternation are: (1) types of words in the predicate periphery, (2) word order, and (3) inflection of the verb.

(1) Certain adverbs trigger conjunct forms, such as: *tɨ* (completed action), *kaʔ* (negative action), *ma* 'where', and *mina·* 'when'.

(2) When adverbs of time precede the predicate, the predicate is conjunct, for example: *habo·m ynɨkšaʔny* and *nɨkša·m*

habo·m 'tomorrow he-will-go' and 'he-will-go-tomorrow'.

(3) When the verb is inflected by *-kiš* (plural), *ʔok-* (definite), *-ni* (definite action), *-p* (action in progress), or *-im* (plural inclusive) the nonconjunct present form occurs. Note, for example: *peht-p* 'he is climbing'.

2.1.1.2. VERB INFLECTION. Verbs are inflected for person focus, tense, and aspect. In any given clause in a Mixe text there is one principal participant. This participant is either the subject of an intransitive predicate, the subject of a transitive predicate, or the direct or indirect object of a transitive predicate. The Mixe verb is inflected by sets of person subject affixes and object orienter affixes to indicate the role of the principal participant in the action. This we call person focus. It is one of the factors in determining clause predicate types. The principal participant of a clause nucleus is determined in part by hierarchical ranking of importance and in part by relative importance. The ranking of importance is first person over second person and second person over third person. Among

7

third persons, rank is determined by relative importance.[13] For example, if a first person is involved in the action of a clause, then the verb is inflected to indicate the role of the first person whether it is subject of intransitive action, subject of transitive action, or object of transitive action. The same is true of second or third person if they are in focus in the clause.

2.1.1.3. PERSON MARKERS. The affixes indicating subject are: *n-* or *Ø-* plus *-icy*[14] (first person); *m-* (second person); and *y-* or *Ø-* (third person). Their use is illustrated by: *Ø-pehtp-icy* 'I am climbing' (*peht* 'to climb'); *ti n-bety-icy* or *ti-cy n-bety* 'I-finished-climbing'; *m-behtp* 'you are climbing'; and *Ø-pehtp* 'he-is-climbing', *ti y-pety* 'he-finished-climbing'.

The affixes indicating object focus are: *nay-* (reciprocal), *yš-* (first or second person object, declarative mode), *-k* (first person object, imperative mode), and third person object markers *-i* (with nonconjunct and conjunct past tense predicates), *-ip* (with non-conjunct present tense predicates), *-ih·p* (with nonconjunct future tense predicates), and *-yi·* (with conjunct present tense predicate). The *nay-* (reciprocal) coordinates with third person object markers. The usage of these affixes is illustrated by: *nay-ʔihš-ip* 'seeing-one-another' (*ʔihš* 'to see'), *ti yš-ʔišy-icy* 'he-saw-me', *ʔ·cy mahc-k* 'grab-me', *Ø-ʔihš-i* 'it-saw-him', *Ø-ʔihš-ip* 'it-sees-him', *ti y-ʔiš-yi·* 'it-does-see-him'.

Person plural exclusive is indicated by the verb suffix *-kiš*. It represents first, second, or third person plural in either subject or object oriented predicates. Note, for example: *ti y-peht-kiš-y* 'they-finished-climbing-it' (*peht* 'to climb'). Person plural inclusive is indicated by the verb suffix *-im*. Note, for example: *cok pehtim* 'let-us-(inclusive) climb-it'.

There is a verb suffix *-y* that functions in coordination with the sets of person affixes. Its meaning is difficult to ascertain. In some predicate constructions it seems to be associated with transitivity. Note, for example: *y-ʔihšp-y* 'he-sees-it' (transitive), and *ʔihšp* 'he-sees' (intransitive). In other predicate constructions it seems to be associated with conjunctivity. Note, for example: *kaʔ y-nikšaʔn-y* 'he will not go' (conjunct present tense) and *nikša·m* 'he-will-go' (nonconjunct present tense).

The only inflectional affix for tense is *-ipy* (future), for example: *tunipy* 'he-will-work' (*tun* 'to work').

The verb inflection for aspect includes both prefixes and suffixes. The prefixes are: *ha·-* (frustrated action), *ha·tuhy* 'he shot at it (but didn't hit it)' (*tuh* 'to shoot'); *ka·-* (negative/dubitative), *y-ka·tuny cuendi* 'he-paid-no-attention' (*tuny cuendi* 'to pay attention'); *ʔok-* (limited period of time), *ʔokmin* 'come' (*min* 'to come').[15]

The aspect suffixes are: *-p* (action in progress), *pehtp* 'he-is-climbing' (*peht* 'to climb'); *-ni* (definite action), *ti yʔokpehtni* 'he-has-climbed-it', *-ko* (immediate action), *pehtko* 'climb-it-immediately', *-oʔk* (repetitive action), *pehtoʔk* 'he-climbs-it-repeatedly'; *-ity* (stative [nontransitive action]), *yticyity* 'it is cold' (*ticy* 'cold'); *-ik* (disclaimer of authorship), *peda·mik* 'he-will-climb-it (he says)' (*peda·m* 'will-climb').

A verb word may be expanded to include some of the adverbs of manner, such as *ʔoy* 'very', *ca·cy* 'very', *tim* 'very', *niʔik* 'more', and *hak* 'more'. Note, for example: *n-ca·cy-hiwiʔiy-icy* 'I-feel-it-very-much' (*hiwiʔiy* 'to feel'). It may also be expanded to include a noun object, for example: *n-ca·cyʔukha·tuh-yicy* 'I-shot-at-the-dog (but missed)' (*ʔuk* 'dog', *tuh* 'to shoot').

The order in which inflectional morphemes occur with stems is shown in Table 1-1. The morphemes illustrated in the table occur in declarative clauses.

2.1.2. NOUNS are words that function grammatically as subjects or objects in clause nuclei, as locative expressions, and as temporal expressions. They have a complex structure developed by compounding and affixation.

2.1.2.1. NOUN STEMS may be simple, compound, or derived. Simple stems are composed of a single root, for example: *tihk*

TABLE 1-3. Person Focus Markers

Person	Subject Focus	Object Focus	
		Declarative	Imperative
1st	n-~Ø- + -ɨcy	yš- + ɨcy	-k
2nd	m-	yš-	
3rd	y-~Ø-	-ɨ~-ɨp~-ɨhˑp~-yiˑ[a]	
		nay-[b]	

[a] See text for distribution of third person object focus markers.
[b] Reciprocal *nay-* coordinates with third person object markers.

TABLE 1-4. Order in Which Inflectional Morphemes Occur

Person prefixes	n- ~ Ø- (1st person)
	m- (2nd person)
	y- ~ Ø- (3rd person)
	yš- (1st ~ 2nd person object)
Adverbs of manner	ʔoy 'very'
	tɨm 'very'
	caˑcy 'very'
Noun object	noun
Aspect	haˑ- (frustrated action)
	ʔok- (definite action)
	kaˑ- (negative/dubitative action)
Verb stem	verb
Object focus	-ɨ
	-ɨp
Person plural	-kɨš
Aspect	-nɨ (definite action)
	-p (action in progress)
Conjunct	-y
Object focus	-yiˑ
Tense	-ɨpy (future tense)
Stative	-ɨty (nontransitive action)

'house', *ʔɨcɨm* 'pig'. Compound stems are composed of two or more roots, which may be noun plus noun: *puhštɨk* 'jail' (*puhš* 'iron' and *tɨhk* 'house'); adjective plus noun: *mɨhtɨhk* 'big house' (*mɨh* 'big'); or adverb plus adjective plus noun: *ʔoymayhaʔay* 'very-many-people' (*ʔoy* 'very', *may* 'many', *haʔay* 'people').

Noun stems are derived from other words by the following derivational suffixes: *-pɨ*, *pohcpɨ* 'a mason' (*pohc* or *poc* 'to construct walls'); *-ɨˑ*, *pociˑ* 'the trade of a mason'; *-ɨn*, *kayɨn* 'a meal' (*kay* 'to eat'); *-k*, *kaˑyk* 'tortilla'; and *-y*, *cɨmy* 'a back pack load' (*cɨm* 'to carry on the back').

Noun roots also may be modified by certain affixes to indicate location: *-paʔa* 'the edge of', *tuʔubaʔa* 'roadside' (*tuʔu* 'trail or road'); *-ʔay* 'along side of', *tuʔuʔay* 'alongside-of-the-road'; *-ʔam* 'place of', *tuʔuʔam* 'road place'; -*kuhk* 'the middle of', *tu*ʔ*uguhk* 'the-middle-of-the-road'; -*pa*ʔ*t* 'underside of', *kihšpa*ʔ*t* 'underside-of-the-bed' (*kihš* 'bed'); -*in* 'place at', *ma tihkin* 'where house-at' (*tihk* 'house'); and -*hoty* 'inside of', *ni·hoty* 'in-the-water' (*ni·* 'water').

Noun roots may also be modified by certain affixes which occur on verbs (section 2.1.1.1): *ko·-* (permanent relationship), *ko·dihk* 'owner of the house' (*tihk* 'house'); ʔ*a·-* (non-permanent relationship), ʔ*a·meh·ny* 'a greedy person' (*meh·ny* 'money'); *mi·-* (associative), *mi·dihk* 'neighbor'.

Nouns are inflected for possession by person prefixes: *n-* (first person), *m-* (second person), *y-* (third person). Note, for example: *ndihk* 'my-house', *mdihk* 'your-house', *ytihk* 'his-house'.

Nouns are not inflected for plural, except for a suffix -*tihk* which means 'as a whole': *mihha*ʔ*aydihk* 'elderly people as a whole' (*mihha*ʔ*ay* 'elderly people').

2.1.3. PRONOUNS. Pronouns function as subjects and objects of clauses and as members of noun and adverb phrases. They are divided into personal, demonstrative, and relative/interrogative pronouns.

(1) The personal pronouns are ʔ*i·cy* 'I or me': *mi·cy* 'you'; *yi*ʔ 'he, she, him, her, or it (nearby)', *he*ʔ 'he, she, him, her, or it (distant)'. The pronouns *yi*ʔ and *he*ʔ have abbreviated forms which occur in phrases: *he* and *yi*. Note, for example: *he tihk* 'the house'.

The pronoun *he*ʔ can be inflected by the verb affixes *ni·-* 'for' and -*ity* (stative). Note, for example: *ni·he*ʔ*ehity* 'some of them'. It can also be inflected by -*yi* (meaning undetermined). Note, for example: *he*ʔ*eyi* 'only they'.

Personal pronouns are pluralized by forming a phrase of the pronoun plus ʔ*ahkšy*[16] for exclusive plural and ʔ*aht* for inclusive plural: ʔ*i·cy* ʔ*ahkšy* 'we (exclusive)', ʔ*i·cy* ʔ*aht* 'we (inclusive)', and *yi*ʔ ʔ*ahkšy* 'they, them'.

The plural morpheme ʔ*ahkšy* also pluralizes nouns, as in *he ha·ay* ʔ*ahkšy* 'the people'. It sometimes occurs as a pronoun: *wa*ʔ*ac*ʔ*ago·c* ʔ*ahkšy hih·py ynaywingowa*ʔ*a·gi·yi* 'in-the-darkness they there encountered-one-another'.

(2) The demonstrative pronouns are *hada·* 'this', *hadaya·bi* 'this-one', *yihimbi* 'that-one-there', and *yihih·bi* 'that-one-there (out of sight)'.

(3) The relative/interrogative pronouns are *pin* 'who', *ti* 'what', *widi·bi* 'which', and *na·k* 'how many'.

There are other words that can serve as pronouns, such as: *tigati* 'all kinds of things', *wenti* 'anything', *may* 'many', and numerals (*tu*ʔ*uk* 'one', *mec* 'two', etc.).[17] Note, for example: *tu*ʔ*uk hakwi*ʔ*imy* 'one stayed-on'.

2.1.4. ADJECTIVES are words that function principally as attributes to nouns. Adjective stems are usually composed of single roots, but they can occur with derivational affixes which convert them to other classes of words, such as nouns, stative verbs, or adverbs. Included in adjectives are numerals: *tu*ʔ*uk* 'one', *mec* 'two', etc.; words for color: *po·p* 'white', *capc* 'red', etc.; and generic attributes: *mih* 'big', *hemy* 'new', etc.

The words for color and the generic adjectives can occur with affixes for both noun derivation: -*pi* (nominalizer), *mihpi* 'big-one'; and verb derivation: -*i*ʔ*iy*, -*i·y* (verbalizer), *ti ypo·bi*ʔ*iy* 'it-is-whitened'.

The numerals can occur with the verb-derivational affixes: ʔ*a·-* (nonpermanence), ʔ*a·du*ʔ*uk* 'alone'; *mi·-* (associative), *mi·mec* 'the-second-one'; *ni·-* 'for', *ni·mec* 'between-the-two-of-them'; *ha·-* (frustrative, additional), *ha·mec* 'another-two'; and -*pi* (nominalizer), *he mecpi* 'the second-one'.

The numerals can also occur with adverbial affixes -ʔ*ok*, -*teky*, -*pahk*, and *ki*ʔ*iy*. The usage and meaning of these affixes are illustrated by *mec*ʔ*ok* 'two-times', *tu*ʔ*ukteky* 'once-only', *tu*ʔ*ukpahk* 'only-one', and *tu*ʔ*ukki*ʔ*iy* 'once-for-all'.

2.1.5. ADVERBS are semantically distinct words that function as modifiers of the verb. They give information such as time, location, manner, etc. Most of them consist of single morphemes which cannot be inflected. Each class of adverbs has its own distribution pattern in the clause (see section 2.3). The categories of adverbs are as follows:

(1) Words of affirmation, such as *hadu*ʔ*n*

'like-this-it-is', *hancy* 'it-is-true', *he²ep* 'it-is-OK', and *hadih·p* 'it-is-enough'.

(2) The negative word, *ka²* 'no'. It can be inflected with the verb affixes *-p* and *-ity*, as in *ka²p* 'no', and *ka²hity* or *ka²ydi* 'it-is-not'.

(3) Words of quantity, such as *hak* 'more', *nah·k* 'how many', *we·ny* 'a little bit', and *hawe·nhaty* 'almost'.

(4) Words of comparison, such as *ni²ik²oy* 'better' and *ni²ikhibik* 'worse'.

(5) Words of location, such as for distance: *higem* 'far away' and *wingon* 'close by'; general location: *windu·* 'in front of' and *tigiš* 'in back of'; and demonstratives of place: *him* 'there', *ya* 'here', and *hih·py* 'there (out of sight)'.

(6) Words indicating time, such as demonstratives of time: *ycam* 'now' and *habo·m* 'tomorrow'; hours of the day; *hopy* 'early forenoon', *kuhkši·* 'mid-day', and *ko·c* 'night'; and time in general: *mik²amy* 'right away' and *namni* 'just a little while ago'.

(7) The word *²anahty* (time nonpresent). This word differs from the other time words in that it does not initiate clauses and occurs only with nonconjunct predicate forms or with the stative. It has considerable freedom of position within the clause.

(8) Words of manner, including words that intensify the verb action: *²oy* 'very', *ca·cy* 'very', and *tim* 'very'; and other words of manner, such as: *²abuky* 'apart from', *timeti·ni* 'suddenly', and *²acip* 'forcefully'. Adverbs that intensify the verb action are sometimes incorporated into the predicate (see 2.1.1.2 and Table 1-4).

(9) The word *²iyšipy* (conditional mode). It occurs only in conditional sentences.

2.1.6. CONNECTIVES. The words *²e·* 'and' and *²o·* 'or' (from Spanish *y* and *o*) connect coordinate clauses or phrases. The word *²ec* 'and' connects the last two words or phrases in a string.

2.1.7. CLAUSE SUBORDINATORS introduce dependent clauses. They include *ko* 'that' or 'because', *ko* 'when', *mina·* 'when', *hayge²e* 'so that', *higiš* 'for this reason', *pah·ky* 'so that', *ma* 'where', *win²it* 'then', and *²išti ko·n* 'until'.

2.1.8. CLAUSE INTRODUCERS introduce various types of clauses. *Cok* 'let's' introduces an independent hortatory clause. *Pen* 'if', *²oy* 'even though', and *wen* (permissive) introduce dependent conditional, concessive, and permissive clauses respectively.

2.1.9. SENTENCE SEQUENCE INTRODUCERS are *yci·* or *yci· hada²* 'and then'. They introduce non-initial sentences in narrative discourse and show narrative sequence.

2.2. PHRASES are groups of words that form a grammatical unit which is less than a clause. There are verb phrases, noun and pronoun phrases, and adverbial phrases.

2.2.1. VERB PHRASES. There are four basic types of verb phrases: (1) adverb plus verb, (2) auxiliary verb plus main verb, (3) semantically matching dual verbs, and (4) multiple coordinate verbs.

(1) Type (1) verb phrases are introduced by the adverbs *ti* (completed action) or *ka²* (negative). The verb has a conjunct stem form and is inflected for person focus, tense, and aspect. Note, for example: *ti ypety* 'he-has-climbed-up', and *ka² ypety* 'he-has-not-climbed-up' (*peht* 'to climb').

(2) The main verb of verb phrase type (2) carries primary stress and is inflected for person, tense, and aspect. The auxiliary verb precedes the main verb (not necessarily contiguously) and is inflected with suffix *-y*: *nikš-y widihtp* 'go walking'; and *poyi²ik-y ti ynikš-y* 'running he-went'. In the first phrase *nikš* 'to go' is the auxiliary verb; in the second phrase it is the main verb.

(3) Semantically matching dual verbs in a predicate are very common in Mixe texts. Each verb carries primary stress and can be inflected for person, tense, and aspect: *He² ²ahkšy ni²igi y-²ok-wam-giš-ni y-²ok-hiwi·y-giš-ni* 'they more they-milled-around they-felt-excited' (dual verb stem *wam* [action based on emotion] and *hiwi·y* 'to feel').

(4) Occasionally a clause will have a coordinate series of verbs in the predicate. Each verb is inflected for person, tense, and aspect and carries primary stress: *Pah·ky he² yca·y²u²uky ytigoy²u²uky y²awa²n²u²uky* 'For-this-reason they sip-drink lose-drink

fight-drink' (*ca·y* 'to sip', *ʔuʔuk* 'to drink', *tɨgoy* 'to lose', *ʔawaʔn* 'to fight').

2.2.2. NOUN AND PRONOUN PHRASES. Noun phrases function as subject, object, temporal, and locational expressions. Pronoun phrases function as subject and object expressions. There are three basic noun phrase types: (1) head plus modifier, (2) coordinate, and (3) appositional. Pronoun phrases can be of types (1) and (3).

(1) Head word plus modifier phrases consist of pronouns *he* 'the' or *yɨ* 'the' plus noun head: *he tɨhk* 'the house'; demonstrative pronoun plus noun head: *hada· tɨhk* 'this house'; numeral plus noun head: *tuʔuk tɨhk* 'one house'; pronoun *he* plus noun head plus adverb or verb modifier: *he sera tuʔukhaty* 'the candles one-each' (adverb *tuʔukhaty* 'one-each'), and *he ca·y ʔabuguky* 'the coiled rope' (*ʔabuguhk* 'to coil'); head word noun or pronoun plus *ʔahkšy* (plural). The pluralizer can occur noncontiguous to its head word: *yci· he soldadtɨhk yahʔɨ·cy ʔahkšy yʔuʔuky* 'the soldiers boiled they their drink (*yahʔɨ·cy* 'to boil').

(2) Coordinate noun phrase constructions are composed of a string of nouns with *ʔec* connecting the last two: *mo·k, šɨhk, ʔec paʔak* 'corn, beans, and cane-sugar'.

(3) Appositional phrases consist of noun plus noun: *tɨhk tɨhk* 'house-to house', *habo·m habo·m* 'morning by morning', *tuʔukkapšhaty yʔɨ·y* 'one-stanza his-song'; two noun phrases: *he tɨhk he mɨhpɨ* 'the house the big-one'; numeral plus noun or pronoun phrase: *tuʔuk he mɨhʔanaʔakpɨ* 'one the elderly-one', *nidugɨ·k yɨʔ ʔahkšy* 'three-of-them they'; pronoun phrase plus noun or noun phrase: *yɨʔ ʔahkšy ypudunɨh·py* 'they his-helpers'; plural plus pronoun with verb affixes: *ʔahkšy niheʔehity* 'they some-of-them'; pronoun plus pronoun: *niheʔe niheʔe* 'each-one each-one'.

2.2.3. ADVERBIAL PHRASES are divided semantically into locative, temporal, manner, and instrument phrases.

(1) Relator axis locative phrases have *ma* 'where' or 'at' as the relator with nouns or noun phrases as the axis: *ma he tɨhk* 'at the house'. Some speakers attach a locational suf-

fix *-in* on the end of the phrase: *ma he tɨhkin* 'at the house'.

Appositional locative phrases are initiated by a demonstrative adverb of location which is in apposition with a noun or relator axis phrase: *hɨm kahphoty* 'there in-village', *hɨm ma he tɨhk* 'there at the house'. The two parts of the appositional phrase can be noncontiguous in some clauses.

(2) Temporal phrases may consist of modifier plus head construction: *tuʔuk tiempo* 'one time' or 'once upon a time'. Or they may be composed of duplicated adverbs: *na·kʔok na·kʔok* 'each-time, each-time'.

(3) Manner phrases are relator axis phrases with *haduʔn neh* 'like/as' as the relator and a noun phrase as the axis: *haduʔn neh he capcpɨ* 'like/as the red-one'.

(4) Instrument phrases are relator axis phrases with *mɨh·t* 'with' as the relator and nouns or noun phrases as the axis: *mɨh·t he ca·y* 'with the rope'.

2.3. CLAUSES are discussed in terms of clause nucleus and periphery and clause types (Hoogshagen 1974).

2.3.1. CLAUSE NUCLEUS AND PERIPHERY. A clause nucleus consists of a predicate plus or minus a subject expression, plus or minus an object expression. The predicate may consist of a verb stem plus affixation, a verb phrase, or a nonverb root with verb affixes. Verb phrases are discussed in section 2.2.1. Nonverb predicates are discussed under stative clauses in section 2.3.2.1.1(5). Predicates consisting of verb stem plus affixation are affixed for subject and object focus and for tense and may exhibit alternation of verb stem type (see section 2.1.1.2).

The subject and object expressions may consist of nouns, pronouns, noun phrases, or a noun or pronoun plus a relative or appositional clause.

The clause periphery consists of expressions for time, location, and manner. Time and location are expressed by adverbs or nouns, adverb or noun phrases, or clauses. Manner is expressed by adverbs, adverb phrases, clauses, or the auxiliary verb of a verb phrase. Note, for example: *poyɨʔɨky tɨ yntikšy* 'running he-went' (auxiliary verb *poyɨ ʔik* 'to run').

Mixe clauses exhibit variety in the order of their constituents. Some factors influencing order are discourse structure, sentence types, clause types, and emphasis.

In discourse structure the order of constituents of a clause depends on the part the clause plays in the discourse. The first clause in narrative discourse usually begins with a temporal expression followed by a subject expression, to introduce the time setting and the participants.

Different types of clauses or sentences exhibit different ordering of constituents. For example, imperative and coordinate dependent clauses are usually initiated by predicates, while declarative and main clauses are not.

Word order is sometimes shifted for the sake of emphasis. This shift moves the emphasized word to a position where it receives the rhythm group stress. This can be illustrated by: *yɨ ʔ nikša·m* 'he will-go' (rhythm group stress on the *-ša·m*) and *nikša·m yɨ ʔ* 'will-go he' (rhythm group stress on the *yɨ ʔ* 'he').

In declarative independent or main clauses, time and subject expressions normally precede the predicate; object and location expressions normally follow it. The words *ʔahkšy* (plural) and *ʔanahty* (time nonpresent) do not initiate clauses but have considerable freedom of occurrence within the clause.

2.3.2. CLAUSE TYPES. Clauses are divided into two types: independent and dependent.

2.3.2.1. INDEPENDENT CLAUSES are divided into declarative, imperative, hortatory, and interrogative.

2.3.2.1.1. DECLARATIVE CLAUSES include (1) intransitive, (2) transitive, (3) ditransitive, (4) reciprocal, and (5) stative. The predicates of declarative nonstative clauses can be nonconjunct or conjunct, present or past tense. The predicates of stative clauses do not have conjunctivity; past tense is expressed by *ʔanahty*.

(1) Intransitive clauses require a predicate inflected for intransitive subject focus: *∅-ʔišpihkp* 'he-is-learning'.

(2) Transitive[18] clauses require a predicate inflected for transitive subject or object person focus, as in: *y ʔihšpy* 'he-sees-it' and *ʔihšip* 'it-sees-him' (*ʔihš* 'to see').

(3) Ditransitive clauses require a predicate inflected for transitive subject or object person focus. Both direct and indirect object are either expressed or understood from context. Ditransitivity is an inherent characteristic of the verb root. Note, for example: *He ʔuŋdeh·ty tɨ ymo ʔoy y ʔuŋ he ʔi·k* 'The father gave his son the toy' (*mo ʔoy* 'to give'), and *Tɨ yšmo ʔoyɨcy he ʔi·k* 'he gave-me the toy'.

There can be as many as four participants in a ditransitive clause: subject, subject's agent or associate, direct object, and indirect object or instrument. This can be illustrated by: *He tatpi·t he pi ʔk ʔana ʔak he kišy yahmo ʔoy he kway* 'The older-man caused the boy to give the girl the horse' (*yahmo ʔoy* 'cause-to-give').

(4) Predicates of reciprocal clauses have the *nay-* prefix and the third person object suffix (*-i, -ip,* or *-yi·*). Note, for example: *nayyah ʔihšpihkip* 'teaching one another' (*yah ʔihšpihk* 'to teach').

(5) Stative clauses have a subject but may or may not have a predicate. In those with predicates, the predicate is an adverb, adjective, noun, pronoun, or intransitive verb. The predicate is inflected by *-ity* (state) and may also have a prefix *y-* (third person). An adverb of manner may be incorporated into the predicate. There is usually no periphery: *y-ʔoy-ticy-ity* 'it is very cold' (*y-* 'it', *ʔoy* 'very', *ticy* 'cold', *-ity* [state]), or *šihk ka·ka ʔhity* 'there are no beans' (*šihk* 'beans', *ka ʔ* 'not', *h* added for syllable onset, *-ity* [state of]).

Stative clauses without inflected predicates are illustrated by *kišy ʔoy he tihk* 'the house is very high' (*kišy* 'high', *ʔoy* 'very', *he tihk* 'the house'); *we ʔe he ʔe ʔanahty yhimiht ʔi·pš* 'he was twenty years old' (*we ʔe he ʔe* 'he', *ʔanahty* (time past), *yhimiht* 'his-years', *ʔi·ps* 'twenty'); and *yɨ ʔ yšɨ· Juan* 'his name is John' (*yɨ ʔ yšɨ·* 'his name').

2.3.2.1.2. IMPERATIVE CLAUSES. There are

four types of imperative clauses: (1) intransitive imperative, (2) transitive or ditransitive imperative with third person object, (3) transitive or ditransitive imperative with first person object, (4) immediate action imperative.

(1) The predicate of type (1) initiates the clause. The predicate may be a single or compound verb stem, a verb phrase with the negative *ka*ʾ, or a verb phrase with auxiliary verb: *nikš* 'go', *ka*ʾ *mnikš* 'don't go', *nikš poyɨ*ʾ*iky* 'go running' (*poyɨ*ʾ*ik* 'to run'). In the negative form the verb is inflected with *m-* (second person). The verb can also be inflected with *-kiš* (plural): *nikškiš* 'you-all-go'.

The periphery may or may not be expressed, as in *nikš* 'go' and *nikš ma mdihk* 'go to your-house'.

(2) The predicate of type (2) also initiates the clause. The predicate may be a single conjunct verb stem or a verb phrase with the negative *ka*ʾ and second person subject prefix *m-* on the verb: *koš* 'punch him', *ka*ʾ *mgoš* 'don't punch-him'; *mo*ʾ*o* 'give (it to him)', *ka*ʾ *mmo*ʾ*oy* 'don't give (it to him)'. The direct and indirect objects can be overtly expressed as in *mo*ʾ*o m*ʾ*ucy he pa*ʾ*ak* 'give your brother the candy' (verb, indirect object, direct object). The verb can be inflected with *-kiš* (plural): *moh·ygiš* 'give it to them'.

(3) The imperative clause with first person object begins with the first person pronoun *ʾɨ·cy*. It requires a nonconjunct transitive predicate inflected by the suffix *-k* or *-ik* 'me': *ʾɨ·cy moh·ky* 'give it to me', *ʾɨ·cy mahcik* 'grab me' (*mo*ʾ*o* 'to give', *mahc* 'to grab').

(4) Immediate action imperatives require a nonconjunct form and are inflected with the suffix *-ko*: *we·ygo* 'lick-it [ice cream cone] immediately' (*we·y* 'to lick').

2.3.2.1.3. HORTATORY CLAUSES are initiated by *cok* 'let's' and terminated by the verb suffix *-im* (inclusive first person). The predicate requires a nonconjunct present tense stem: *Cok pehtim* 'Let's climb it' (*peht* 'to climb').

2.3.2.1.4. INTERROGATIVE CLAUSES are of two types: (1) information questions, and (2) yes/no questions.

(1) Information questions begin with an interrogative adverb or pronoun and end with question intonation. The interrogative adverbs are *ma* 'where', *mina·* 'when', and *na*ʾ*amy* 'why'. Note, for example: *Ma mnikša*ʾ*ny?* 'Where are you-going?'; *Mina· mnikša*ʾ*ny?* 'When are you-going?' Interrogative adverbs require a conjunct verb stem.

The interrogative pronouns are: *pin* 'who' (*Pin nikša·m?* 'Who is going?'; *ti* 'what' (*Ti mimšɨ·?* 'What is your-name?'); *widi·* 'which' (*Widi· tihk mi·cy mhe*ʾ*e?* 'Which house is yours?'). They can occur with either nonconjunct or conjunct form.

The question intonation is a rising inflection on the last syllable of the clause.

(2) Yes/no questions begin (optionally) with *neh* (question indicator) and end with question intonation. Note, for example: *Neh tɨ m*ʾ*oy tigam?* or *Ti m*ʾ*oy tigam?* 'Did you go to town?'

2.3.2.2. DEPENDENT CLAUSES are divided into subordinate, coordinate, conditional, concessive, permissive, and appositional. Unless otherwise specified, these clauses are unrestricted as to conjunctivity.

2.3.2.2.1. SUBORDINATE CLAUSES. A subordinate clause is initiated by a subordinator which relates it to another clause or phrase. The types include relative, temporal, locative, manner, purpose, result, cause, and indirect discourse clauses. Temporal, locative, cause, and indirect discourse clauses require conjunct forms; the others, except purpose, are unrestricted. Purpose clauses introduced by *higiš* require conjunct forms; those introduced by *hayge*ʾ*e* are unrestricted.

2.3.2.2.1.1. RELATIVE CLAUSES. There are three introducers of relative clauses: (1) *widi·* 'which', *ʾɨštah·ybicy he kway widi· yo*ʾ*oydigoy ʾɨšɨ·y* 'I am looking for the horse which strayed yesterday'; (2) *ti* 'what', *Ka*ʾ*p n*ʾ*okha*ʾ*aymehcnicy ti partido he*ʾ *ʾahkšy* 'I don't remember what political party they were'; and (3) *pin* 'who', *Cok ʾihšim, pin nikša·m habo·m* 'Let's see who will go tomorrow'. There is also a pronoun phrase *we*ʾ*e he*ʾ*e* 'he or which' that sometimes introduces relative clauses. This is illustrated by *Yci· he sera ykohy ʾe· we*ʾ*e he*ʾ*e yahtihy*: *Nayga*ʾ*ac*

14

sera 'Then the candles are made which are known as: Throw-at-one-another candles'.

2.3.2.2.1.2. TEMPORAL CLAUSES are introduced by *ko* 'when', *mina·* 'when', *win?it* 'then' or 'at that time', and *?išti ko·n* 'until'. Introducers *ko*, *mina·*, and *win?it* are illustrated in the sentence *Ko he merdombi nigapšy, mina· he ha?ašy yha?ada?ny, win?it he pudunih·yp ynayni? iši?iyi mih·t ni· hu?uky* 'When the mayordomo speaks of when the firewood will arrive, at that time the helpers prepare-themselves with (supplies of) liquor and cigarettes' (*kapš* 'to speak', *ha?at* 'to arrive', and *ni?iši?i* 'to prepare'). *?išti ko·n* is illustrated by *Cuend?at n?un ?išti ko·n nwimbityicy* 'Take care of my child until I-return' (*wimbiht* 'to return').

2.3.2.2.1.3. LOCATIVE CLAUSES are introduced by *ma* 'where'. They require a conjunct present predicate: *Ykahppicim ?ahkšy ma yi Mitla tu?u ynikšy* 'They left the village where the trail goes to Mitla'.

2.3.2.2.1.4. MANNER CLAUSES are introduced by *hadu?n neh* 'like/as': *Hada· pi?k?ana?ak tim yo?oy hadu?n neh mihha?ay ?ahkšy yo?oy* 'This child walks just like old-people walk'.

2.3.2.2.1.5. PURPOSE CLAUSES are introduced by *higiš* 'so that' and *hayge?e* 'so that'. They are illustrated by *Ti kafe· toh·ky, higiš kway huya?ny* 'He sold his coffee, so that he could buy a horse' and *Nikš cohk widit, hayge?e ya hadu?uk?ok mdunipy* 'Go quickly on your errand, so that you can return again to your work'.

2.3.2.2.1.6. RESULT CLAUSES are introduced by *pah·ty* 'for this reason': *Pihkip y?un, pah·ty nikši coydumbi ?ištah·yp* 'His-son is sick, for this reason he is looking for a doctor'.

2.3.2.2.1.7. CAUSE CLAUSES are introduced by *kom* 'because' or *kom ko* 'because that': *Aktim soldado yi cahtihk kop, kom ko?owa?ac ?anahty yi cahtihk* 'Soldiers were on the church roof, because it was uncovered' and *Kom ho ?amišanbu?uc ?anahty y?ok?amayity, ka?p nyajnikšibicy ma nrancho* 'Because smallpox is an awesome disease, I didn't take him to my ranch'.

2.3.2.2.1.8. INDIRECT DISCOURSE CLAUSES

are introduced by *ko* 'that' and follow verbs of saying, reporting, or perceiving: *He kapšy ymina·ny ko he soldado ti yha?aty* 'The word was out that the soldiers had arrived' and *Hadu?n he ?ahcytihk ?ihšy nehwi·y ?ahkš, ko he cip ytuni yhahti* 'Like this the elders saw (and) knew that the fighting happened'.

2.3.2.2.2. COORDINATE DEPENDENT CLAUSES. There are two types of coordinate dependent clauses. Type (1) consists of two or more clauses of parallel structure that have semantic interdependence and share constituents. They may or may not be joined by *?e·* 'and' or *?o·* 'or'. In the following example the two clauses have only one predicate expression and one object expression: *Nihe?ehity ?oy?amy tihaty pihkcoy, ?e· nihe?ehity ?acip ?a?ek* 'Some of them in a nice manner asked for things, and some of them forcefully' (*pihkcoy* 'to ask for' and *tihaty* 'things').

A type (2) coordinate dependent clause follows the main clause of a sentence and shares the subject of the main clause but has its own predicate which is inflected for subject person focus and has conjunct verb forms. The nucleus may have an object expression, and the periphery is restricted usually to manner expressions. Note, for example: *Yci· ?ahkšy nihe?ehity y?u·ktigi·y, ?e· nigo· y?okha·mnehp y?okna·šnehp, y?okkapškišni hancy hibik, ywa?n yhiwi?iy ?oy ka?ʔoy, ymicip ytah yteh·ty yahmidoy* 'Then some of them began-to-drink, and how they-kicked-up-lime, they-kicked-up-dust; they-talked foul language, they-showed ill will, their enemies' parents they-cursed' (*?u·ktigi·y* 'began to drink', *ha·mnehp na·šnehp* 'to kick up dust', *kapš* 'to talk', *wa?n hiwi?iy* 'to feel', *yahmidoy* 'to cause to hear').

2.3.2.2.3. CONDITIONAL CLAUSES. There are two types of conditional clauses. Type (1) is initiated by the adverb *pen* 'if': *Pen mnikša·m, wen nikš* 'If you-want-to-go, you can go'.

Type (2) incorporates the adverb *?iyšipy* (conditional). It may or may not be introduced by *pen* 'if': *Pen ka? ?iyšipy ti m?oy, ka? ?iyšipy ti y?oyi?iy* 'That if you hadn't gone, nothing would have been arranged'. The conditional *ʔiyšɨpy* is required in both clauses.

2.3.2.2.4. CONCESSIVE CLAUSES are introduced by the adverb *ʔoy* 'even though': *ʔoy mgaˑnikša ʔny, kopɨty ko mnikšɨp* 'Even though you-don't-want-to-go, it is necessary that you-go'. They require a conjunct predicate.

2.3.2.2.5. PERMISSIVE CLAUSES are introduced by the adverb *wen*: *Pen nikšaˑm, wen nikš moˑkmaˑkp* 'If she wants to go, let her go wash corn'.

2.3.2.2.6. APPOSITIONAL CLAUSES occur in apposition to a subject or object expression. They are parallel to relative clauses introduced by *widiˑ*. This type is illustrated by: *He pohcpɨ, he tɨgambɨ cinaˑyp, tum ycam ma he escuela* 'The mason, the one living in the village, is working today at the school'. In Coatlán this clause type is not common, but in some Zoquean languages it is very common (Elson 1980).

2.4. SENTENCES. A sentence may be composed of a word, a phrase, one clause, or a number of clauses. In certain types of discourse, sentences have introducers (section 2.1.9). The usual intonation pattern is a high tone on the stressed syllable, falling to a low tone at sentence end. Infrequently the op₇ posite pattern has been observed, in which the stressed syllables have a low tone followed by a rising intonation. The latter pattern appears to connote excitement.

Sentences that are composed of a single word or a phrase are usually in answer to questions. In Mixe the negative *ka ʔ* is used for negation. For affirmation a number of words are possible, such as *haduˑʔn* 'like this', *he ʔep* 'all right', and *hadihˑp* 'it is enough'.

Sentences composed of more than one clause have different ways in which these clauses interrelate. They are divided into complementary clause sentences, subordinate clause sentences, and coordinate clause sentences.

2.4.1. COMPLEMENTARY CLAUSE SENTENCES are made up of two clauses that complement each other. They are divided into conditional, concessive, dubitative, and comparative sentences.

2.4.1.1. CONDITIONAL SENTENCES. There are two conditional sentence types:

(1) The condition expressed in the first clause sets up a contrary-to-fact statement in the second clause. Both clauses have the adverb *ʔiyšɨpy* (conditional verb action): *Pen ka ʔ ʔiyšɨpy tɨ m ʔoy, ka ʔ ʔiyšɨpy tɨ y ʔoyɨ ʔiy* 'If you had not gone, this would not have been arranged'.

(2) The condition expressed in the first clause sets the stage for the action of the second clause. The conditional morpheme is *pen* 'if': *Pen tɨ mgu ʔušyiˑ, pɨdɨ ʔikni* 'If you are full, get up'.

2.4.1.2. CONCESSIVE SENTENCES. The first clause begins with the adverb *ʔoy* 'even though' and is the condition for the action of the second clause: *ʔoy mgaˑnikša ʔny, nikšaˑmicy ʔɨˑcy* 'Even though you are not going, I am going'.

2.4.1.3. DUBITATIVE SENTENCES. The doubt expressed in the first clause leads to a statement of doubt in the second clause. Doubt is expressed by the verb prefix *kaˑ* (negative of doubt) in both clauses: *Kaˑnanhancyity, ko miˑcy mgaˑnikša ʔny haboˑm* 'It is not (doubt) true, that you are not (doubt) going tomorrow'.

2.4.1.4. COMPARATIVE SENTENCES. The first clause has the adverb *ni ʔik* 'more (of quality)' or *hak* 'more (of quantity)', and the second clause has a form of the negative *ka ʔ* 'not' as predicate. For example: *Ni ʔik ycam ʔambiky, ka ʔhity ʔɨšɨˑy* 'It is hotter today than yesterday (more hot today, was-not yesterday)' and *Hak mɨh miˑcy m ʔuk, ka ʔhity ʔɨˑcy n ʔuk* 'Your dog is bigger than my dog (more big your-dog, is-not my dog)'.

2.4.2. SUBORDINATE CLAUSE SENTENCES consist of a main clause with one or more clauses subordinated to it. They are divided into two classes. In class (1) the subordinate clause or clauses are embedded in the main clause. In class (2) the subordinate clause follows the main clause.

(1) In the first class, the subordinate clauses function as part of a subject, object, temporal, locative, or manner expression of another clause. The subordinators of these

16

clauses are *wïdi·* 'which', *ko* 'when', *mïna·* 'when', *ma* 'where', and *hadu²n neh* 'like/as'. All of these are illustrated in sections 2.3.2.2.1.1–2.3.2.2.1.4. Note also: *He Judïs he² ²ahkšy pïda·kkïšy ma he wïttïhk ²agu·hïn ma he santi ²anahty* 'Judas they put at the entrance of the tent where the saint was' (object, subject, predicate: *pïda·k* 'to put', locational phrase, locational clause).

In class (2) the clauses are distinct though related by the subordinator. The subordinators are *win²ït* 'then, at that time', *²išti ko·n* 'until', *hïgïš* 'so that', *hayge²e* 'so that', *pah·ty* 'for this reason', *kom ko* 'because', and *ko* 'that (indirect quote)'. These are illustrated in sections 2.3.2.2.1.2 and 2.3.2.2.1.5–2.3.2.2.1.8. Note also: *Ka² mo·k nhuya²nyïcy, ²išti ko·n he hemy mo·k ypïcïmy* 'I am not going to buy corn until the new corn is harvested' (*²išti ko·n* 'until' relates the second clause to the first one).

2.4.3. COORDINATE CLAUSE SENTENCES are divided into three classes:

Class (1) consists of two or more coordinate independent clauses, sometimes connected *²e·* or *²o·*, sometimes juxtaposed. These are illustrated by *Yci· he maysoldadi ypa²ttïgi·y ²e· kuhkwa²akš ynïkš tun hïhp²am* 'Then the many-soldiers came-up (the main trail) and half-of-them went-along the ridge'; *Neh mcohkpy cahmuny ²o· mcohkpy šihk?* 'Do you want potatoes or do you want beans?'; and *Yci· ²ahkšy yhakke·k ni-may ykahppïcïm ²ahkšy ma he mïhtu²u* 'Then many fled, they left the village on the main trail'[19] (*hak* 'more', *ke·k* 'to flee', *ni-may* 'many of them', *kahppïcïm* 'to-leave-the-village').

Class (2) consists of a main clause plus one or more dependent clauses that share the predicate of the main clause: *Nihe²ehïty ²oy²amy tihaty pïhkcoy, nihe²ehïty ²acïp ²a²ek* 'Some (soldiers) in a nice manner asked for things, some forcefully' (subject *nihe²ehïty* 'some', adverb *²oy²amy* 'in a nice manner', object *tihaty* 'things', predicate *pïhkcoy* 'to ask for', adverb *²acïp ²a²ek* 'forcefully').

Class (3) consists of a main clause plus one or more dependent clauses that share the subject of the main clause. The main clause usually opens the sentence: *Yci· ²ahkšy*

nihe²ehïty y²u·ktïgi·y, ²e· nigo· y²okha·mnehp y²okna·šnehp, y²okkapškïšni hancy hïbïk, ywa²n yhïwï²ïy ²oy ka²²oy, ymïcïp ytah yteh·ty yahmïdoy 'Then some of them began-to-drink, and how they-kicked-up-lime, they-kicked-up-dust; they-talked foul language; they-showed ill will, their enemies' parents they-cursed' (*²u·ktïgi·y* 'began to drink', *ha·mnehp na·šnehp* 'to kick up dust', *kapš* 'to talk', *wa²n hïwï²ïy* 'to feel', *yahmïdoy* 'cause to hear, curse').

2.5. DISCOURSE STRUCTURE. A detailed analysis of discourse is beyond the scope of this chapter. A few salient features may be noted. Discourse is of two major types, monologue and dialogue; but even in narrative monologue discourse, audience participation and response are expected, usually in the form of a word of agreement, such as *hadu²n* 'that's how it is'.

Monologue discourse is usually narrative, either of folklore or of more recent history. It can also be didactic. Folklore is marked by frequent use of *yci·* or *yci· hada²* 'then' (denotes chronological sequence). Also the suffix *-ïk* (disclaimer of authorship) is used in folklore texts. Sometimes it occurs affixed to the *yci·* (*yci·k*).

Both folklore and historical narrative make frequent use of past tense verb stem forms and of the adverb *²anahty* (time nonpresent). The initial clause or sentence in a discourse gives the time and location setting and introduces the major participants. Only one participant is in focus in any given predicate. Other participants are referred to by nouns or pronouns. The most frequent referents used to denote subjects and objects are *he²* (third person) and *²ahkšy* (plural). The use of these referents can be illustrated by *Ypïda·k ²ahkšy mo·kkam* 'They planted corn' (*ypïda·k* 'they-planted', subject *²ahkšy*, object) and *Tïm he²eyï he² yha²ty ma ykahp, yci· ²oy²o²kni* 'And just like this he arrived at his village, then died' (*ha²t* 'to arrive', *²o²k* 'to die', *he²* 'he').

In narrative texts the narrator can "zero out"[20] a participant by inflecting a transitive verb for subject intransitive focus. This can

17

be illustrated by *Kom he merdombɨ yˀanuˑkšpy yɨˀ ymɨˑkpɨ ˀoˑy he mɨˀɨky ykohy yˀabadɨˀɨy* 'Because the mayordomo contracts for his tamale makers, the tamales are made'. The predicate of the last clause of this sentence *ˀoˑy he mɨˀɨky ykohy yˀabadɨˀɨy* 'the tamales are made' is conjunct, intransitive subject focus present. This in effect zeroes out the subject 'the tamale makers'.[21]

Didactic discourse makes frequent use of the imperative mode. This can be illustrated by *Naycohkɨgiš nayhɨwɨˑyɨgiš nɨduˀuk nɨduˀuktɨ* 'Love-one-another each-one each-one'.

Dialogue involves conversational interchange of varying length. A typical opening interchange would be: *Hɨhˑpy mɨˑcy?* 'Are you in there (in the house)?'. *Ycehˑbyɨch* 'I am in here'. *Tɨ mdumy?* 'What are you doing?' *Kaˀtɨ, pokšpɨcy* 'Nothing, I am resting'.

This is followed by further conversation leading up to the principal topic. If one has come to seek help or some needed item, the other person must give the opportunity by saying: *Tɨ ˀanahty?* 'What was it?'. The response would be something like this: *Weˀe coˑy nhuyaˑmybɨcy* 'I want to buy medicine'.

NOTES

1. Coatlán is located in the district of Tehuantepec, in the state of Oaxaca, Mexico. In phonology and grammar, Coatlán Mixe has much in common with the dialects of other Mixe towns, but it also has its distinctive characteristics. Other dialects of Mixe are described in Crawford 1963; Elson 1960, 1967, personal communication (1980); D. Lyon 1967; S. Lyon 1967; Nordell 1962; A. Schoenhals 1962, 1979; Schoenhals and Schoenhals 1965; and Van Haitsma and Van Haitsma 1976. One distinctive characteristic of Coatlán Mixe is that vowels exhibit a three-way length contrast (Hoogshagen 1959). In this paper, the extra-long vowel is analyzed as *Vhˑ*.

2. The consonant phonemes *f*, *s*, *l*, and *r̃* are found only in Spanish loan words. In purely Mixe words [*s*] is an allophone of *c* following *k* syllable finally.

3. Some Mixe languages have as many as seven, eight, or nine contrastive vowels. The extra vowels have developed from the effect of the palatalization of the syllable border on the syllable nucleus.

4. In some Mixe languages syllable nuclei are also found with *Vˑ* followed by *h* or *ˀ*.

5. Word-medial syllable onsets are restricted to single consonants.

6. The consonant *p* does not occur as the second or third member of a word-medial syllable coda cluster.

7. Van Haitsma and Van Haitsma (1976:7) note that initial *d* is found in elliptical speech, where *haduˀn* 'like this' is shortened to *duˀn*.

8. Under certain as yet undefined conditions *-ɨpy* (future tense) may also carry stress.

9. This voicing replacement does not occur following the verb prefixes *haˑ-* (frustrative) and *kaˑ-* (negative).

10. The derivational affixes *koˑ-* and *ˀaˑ-* have different meanings in different contexts. No one meaning fits all contexts.

11. Julia and Willard Van Haitsma (1976:59) and some other Mixe grammarians use the term *timeless tense* for what is here called *present tense*.

12. Alvin Schoenhals (1979) describes Totontepec Mixe clauses in terms which he calls *stage* and *event*. The clause types he sets up for stage and event roughly parallel the clause types set up by Shirley Lyon (1967) and the Van Haitsmas (1976) as nonconjunct and conjunct clauses. In this chapter I have dealt with nonconjunct and conjunct as relations expressed in the predicate rather than setting up nonconjunct and conjunct clauses. I have indicated, however, where clause types are restricted or nonrestricted in relation to conjunctivity.

13. Working out the relative importance of multiple third persons pertains to discourse and is outside the scope of this paper.

14. The morpheme *-ɨcy* indicates first person involvement, as subject or object. This

morpheme is enclitic to the verb or to some other word preceding the verb.

15. Mixe grammarians have assigned a variety of glosses to ʔok-, but its basic meaning remains uncertain. An example of use: ya ʔokmin 'here come', meaning 'come here for just a minute'. The idea of 'just a minute' is expressed by ʔok-.

16. In some neighboring dialects this word is ʔahtkišy.

17. A complete list of pronouns is given in Van Haitsma and Van Haitsma (1976:45–47).

18. Some verbs are basically transitive, others are made transitive by derivational affixes, and still others are used either intransitively or transitively. Intransitive or transitive use is shown by inflection for person.

19. In this example, the word order (predicate-subject) of the second clause indicates that it is part of a sentence. If it were a separate sentence it probably would be introduced by yciˑ and the word order would be subject-predicate.

20. Benjamin F. Elson (1980) discusses this phenomenon in relation to Sierra Popoluca, where verb suffixes "zero out" one of the participants in a verb construction. Coatlán Mixe does not have special affixes for this, but handles it as shown here.

21. The zeroing out of the subject results in a construction that appears in its English translation to be passive voice. Voice was not considered to be a useful category in the organization of Mixe grammar. Nevertheless there are some constructions that have passive voice implications. The zeroing out of the subject is one. Another is the use of the causative verb prefix yah- with a verb root that implies the use of an instrument: n-yah-wohp-y-ɨcy 'he is hitting me' or 'I am being hit'. A third construction with passive voice implications in some usages is the object focus verb suffix -yiˑ: tɨ y-paˑd-yiˑ 'he has been found' (tɨ [completive action], paˑt 'to find').

Mood, like voice, was not considered a useful category in the organization of this Mixe grammar. Some Mixe grammarians have used the term *mood* when referring to conjunct and nonconjunct predicate types (S. Lyon 1967). I considered the term *mood* confusing when applied to these concepts, since it usually is associated with such terms as *declarative, conditional*, and *subjunctive*. In this chapter the terms *imperative, declarative*, and *conditional* occur in the description of clause types as part of the overall description of clause types (see sections 2.3.2.1.1 and 2.3.2.2.3).

2. Chichimeco Jonaz

YOLANDA LASTRA DE SUÁREZ

0. INTRODUCTION. Chichimeco is an Otomanguean language spoken in Misión de Chichimecas, an *ejido* east of the town of San Luis de la Paz in the municipality of the same name in the state of Guanajuato, Mexico. The 1970 census gives a total of 495 speakers of Chichimeco, although the true number may be slightly higher. Some Chichimeco children are still learning the language, while others are brought up speaking only Spanish. Most Chichimecos are bilingual.

Previous studies of the language include Angulo 1933, Soustelle 1937, Romero Castillo 1960, and Lastra de Suárez 1969. Ethnographic information on the Chichimecos is provided by Driver and Driver 1963 and Lastra de Suárez 1971.[1]

1. PHONOLOGY.

1.1. CONSONANTS.

Chichimeco has twenty consonants. They include the voiceless obstruents, /p, t, c, č, k, ʔ/; the voiced obstruents, /b, d, ǰ, g/; the voiceless fricatives, /s, h,/; the voiced fricative, /z/; the fortis nasals, /m, n/; the lenis nasals, /m̥, n̥/; the lateral, /l/; the vibrant, /r/; and the semi-vowel, /w/.

/c/ has a voiced variant after /n/: [sándzeɸ] 'eight'.

/b/ is a stop in initial position and after /m/; a voiceless fricative [ɸ] in final position; and a voiced fricative with not much friction [β] elsewhere: [beʔé] 'hot pepper', [námba] 'my hat', [saküsɸ] 'seven', [uβa̧ʔ] 'day'.

/g/ is a stop in initial position and after /n/; a voiceless velar fricative with a labial release [xʷ] in final position; and a voiced fricative elsewhere: [gásá] 'I will win', [kánga] 'child', [ikáxʷ] 'I', [ikáγos] 'we' (dual inclusive).

/r/ is a flap in initial position and intervocalically; a voiced trill when followed by /ʔ/; and voiceless when followed by /h/ and in final position: [rímóʔ] 'peel', [kúrí] 'water', [kárʔá] 'skunk', [úřháʔ] 'pulque', [riméř] 'potato'.

/d/ and /ǰ/ only occur after /n/, but /t/ and /č/ contrast with them: kíndo 'hail', ninthé 'root', pínǰaʔ 'bones', činče 'small'.

Lenis nasal /m̥/ is a bilabial pronounced without the lips coming into contact; it is similar to a [β] but strongly nasalized. /n̥/ sounds like a nasalized alveolar flap. /m̥/ and /n̥/ contrast both with their fortis counterparts and with /b/ and /r/: kúmóʔ 'turtle', ku̧m̥ṳr 'spider', kanú 'my nose', ku̧n̥í 'my heart', kara̧ 'fly', min̥a̧ 'lime', ṳba̧ 'when', ku̧m̥á 'badger'.

The following consonants occur initially: /p, t, c, č, k, b, g, s, z, m, n, r/. All consonants occur medially. The following ones occur finally: /ʔ, b, g, s, m, n, r/. Table 2-1 illustrates their occurrence in initial, medial, or final position:

/l/ occurs in very few words: in the word for 'grandmother,' in kuléʔ 'turkey', and in Spanish loans such as málí 'Mary'. Other Otomanguean languages have words for 'turkey' similar to kuléʔ, which seems to be a loan.

/m/ is always flanked by nasal vowels; /n/ can occur between nasal vowels, but it can also be preceded by /n/ or followed by /h/.

/w/ only occurs in the medial clusters /ngw/ and /nkh/.

Table 2-2 shows the two-consonant clusters that have been found. The disyllabic ones are indicated by hyphens. Examples of the clusters follow:

p ʔ	úpʔoho 'prickly pear cactus'
ph	íphér 'fireworks'
t ʔ	katʔí 'young man'
th	kíthæ 'oven'
c ʔ	etṷcʔ 'candle'
ch	táchénʔ 'rattle'
č ʔ	čičʔé 'wing'
k ʔ	úkʔi 'gnat'
kh	úkhe 'ant'
ʔ-p	ínoʔpí 'that one'
ʔs	íno̧ʔs 'they (dual)'
ʔm	tiʔeʔm 'we say goodbye (dual exclusive)'
ʔn	zizéʔn 'clean'
ʔr	íriʔr 'good'
s-t	místoho 'cat'
sb	saküsb 'seven'
sg	čʔímahasg 'I am tall'
s-h	koʔóshṷʔ 'our house (plural exclusive)'
m ʔ	emʔá̧ʔ 'sour prickly pear'
m-b	émbó 'hill'
m-h	emhá̧ 'a prickly shrub'
n-t	kuntár nizé 'organpipe cactus'
n-č	čínče 'small'
n ʔ	kanʔí 'his hand'
n-d	nándeʔ 'big'
n-ǰ	pínǰa 'bones'
n-g	kánga 'boy'
n-h	unhí̧ 'his body'
n̥-h	ta̧nhénes 'two'
n-z	sánzeb 'eight'
n-n̥	símaʔann̥ó 'dog'
r-ʔ	urʔós 'their house'
r-h	urhṵs 'salt'

Three-consonant clusters (and one cluster of four consonants) are all disyllabic. The first member of such a consonant cluster is /s, r,

TABLE 2-1. Consonant Positions

	Initial	Medial	Final
p	pahá 'evil'	pipʔé 'barrel cactus'	——
t	tásǽ 'my comb'	satű 'new'	——
c	cúzoʔ 'ribs'	tucá 'I made'	——
č	číporí 'right now'	ičí 'now'	——
k	kúrí 'their water'	píkú 'sweet potato'	——
ʔ		kánʔí 'his hand'	zímboʔ 'dark'
b	beʔé 'hot pepper'	númbeʔe 'my hunger'	sakűsb 'seven'
d	——	nándeʔ 'big'	——
ǰ	——	pinǰaʔ 'bones'	——
g	gátuʔu 'I will sow'	egú 'his foot'	ikág 'I'
s	satű 'new'	suséʔ 'my arm'	meʔés 'sour'
h	——	káhó 'shaman'	——
z	zizéʔn 'clean'	názạ 'my tongue'	——
m	maréʔ 'old'	nímbeʔe 'his hunger'	mísóguʔm 'we are brothers' (dual exclusive)
n	názạ 'my tongue'	kankhé 'bean'	karéʔn 'coward'
m̥	——	sịm̥ás 'his mat'	——
n̠	——	mą́n̠ę́ 'soon'	——
l	——	nalé 'my grandmother'	——
r	rinʔe 'church'	míroʔ 'avocado'	rimér 'potato'
w	——	tangwé 'rabbit'	

TABLE 2-2. Two-Consonant Clusters

	p	t	c	č	k	ʔ	b	d	ǰ	g	s	h	z	m	n	m̥	n̠	l	r	w
p						pʔ						ph								
t						tʔ						th								
c						cʔ						ch								
č						čʔ														
k						kʔ						kh								
ʔ	ʔ-p										ʔs			ʔm	ʔn				ʔr	
b																				
d																				
ǰ																				
g																				
s		s-t					sb			sg		s-h								
h																				
z																				
m						mʔ	m-b					m-h								
n		n-t		n-č		nʔ		n-d	n-ǰ	n-g		n-h	n-z				n-n̠			
m̥																				
n̠												n̠-h								
l																				
r						r-ʔ						r-h								
w																				

TABLE 2-3. Paradigm for Inflection of Possessive for 'House'

Person	Singular	Dual	Plural
1st	koʔós	koʔós-umʔ (excl.)	koʔos-hų́ʔ (excl.)
		koʔós-és (incl.)	koʔos-ín (incl.)
2nd	utʔós	utʔós-és	utʔós-ín
3rd	utʔís	utʔís-és	urʔós

m, n/, the second is /m/ or an obstruent, the third is /w/, /h/, or the glottal stop, and the fourth is /w/. The following examples illustrate three- and four-consonant clusters in Chichimeco:

s-kʔ	cʔimaháskʔun 'you are tall (plural)'
smʔ	koʔósmʔ 'our house (dual exclusive)'
m-ph	zímphonʔ 'hunchback'
n-tʔ	nántʔa 'one'
n-th	nánthǽ 'meat'
n-kʔ	sinkʔén 'an edible herb'
n-kh	kankhéʔ 'bean'
n-khw	únkhwa 'yet'
n-gw	kúngwaʔ 'frog'
n-cʔ	éncʔá 'sweet'
n-čʔ	ínčʔes 'mosquito'
r-kʔ	pimbérkʔún 'you are fat (plural)'

1.2. VOWELS. Chichimeco has seven oral vowels and the same number of nasal ones: /i, ü, u, e, o, æ, a, į, ü̧, ų, ę, ǫ, æ̧, ą/.

Nasal vowels always precede and follow /m/ and /n/, the second vowel sounding more nasal than the first. Vowels flanking the fortis nasals are only slightly nasalized and are here transcribed as oral vowels. At any rate, vowels do not contrast in nasalization in the environment of nasal consonants.

2. MORPHOLOGY.

2.1. NOUNS. Noun possession is indicated in one of two ways, by a change in the form of the noun or by its association with one of four sets of classifiers. Variable nouns may undergo tone or segmental changes or outright suppletion, or they may have special syllables prefixed to them. The first, second, and third persons are marked, along with the distinction between the inclusive and exclusive in both dual and plural.

2.1.1. VARIABLE NOUNS. The inflection for possession of the noun meaning 'house' is shown in Table 2-3. The paradigm suggests that the dual forms and those of the first and second person plural are based on the singular forms; the third person plural is typically different, although sometimes -r (or -er in consonant-final stems) is added to the third person singular as, for example, in urá 'his face', urá-r 'their face'. The morpheme alternants when the noun stem ends in a vowel are -s, first person inclusive, second and third person, -mʔ, first person exclusive for the dual, and -n first person inclusive and second person plural.

The independent pronouns, which can occur optionally with variable nouns, are shown in Table 2-4. Examples of these pronouns with variable nouns are ikág katá 'my face', ihékʔ útá 'your face', ígoʔr urán 'their face', ikág kundí 'my water'.

Table 2-5 illustrates the types of changes that variable nouns can undergo.

2.1.2. NOUNS WITH CLASSIFIERS. Nouns which do not undergo changes when possessed occur with one of the classifiers in Table 2-6.

A complete paradigm for 'rock' is given in Table 2-7.

Other examples include: nantʔé kankhé 'my beans'; nirʔű pʔán 'your shirt'; úngwæʔæ kazų́ 'his cow'; úpʔihi maréʔ 'their story'.

2.1.3. THE DUAL IN NOUNS. The dual of nouns is -s (-és with consonant-final stems):

23

TABLE 2-4. Independent Pronouns Which Can Occur with Variable Nouns

Person	Singular	Dual	Plural
1st	ikág	ikágumʔ (excl.)	ikághý̨ʔ (excl.)
		ikagos (incl.)	ikágun (incl.)
2nd	ihékʔ	ihékʔos	ihekʔun
3rd	íno̜ʔ	íno̜ʔs	ígoʔr
	(n)igoʔ		

TABLE 2-5. Types of Changes in Variable Nouns

Tone changes:

'sister-in-law'	ka̜mý̨	ká̜my̨	ka̜mý̨	ka̜mý̨r
'tail bone'	kúmoʔ	kumóʔ	kúmoʔ	kúmoʔr
'nose'	kanú	kánú	kanú	kanúr
'shoulder'	sángwæʔæ	sangwǽʔæ	sángwæʔæ	sángwæʔæ
'knee'	námenʔ	naménʔ	naménʔ	naménʔ

Vowel changes (with or without tone changes, depending on the noun):

'blood'	kukhé	kíkhe	kikhé	kikhér
'lip'	suní	síni	síni	sinír
'nixtamal'	ruké̜	riké̜	riké̜	riké̜
'dish'	numáha	nímaha	nimáha	nimáha
'sling'	tahǘr	tíhür	tahǘr	tarhür

Voicing:

'pants'	ruкǘʔ	rúküʔ	rugǘʔ	rukhǘʔ

Prefix-like changes:

'neck'	kútún	utún	útun	kutún
'tail'	túmbiʔir	nímbíʔir	nímbiʔir	nímbiʔir
'fire'	nápa	unápa	unípa	mápá

Prefix-like changes and additional changes:

'friend'	nahí	únho	enhí	búnho
'body'	nahí̜	únha̜	unhí̜	unhí̜r
'husband'	naʔú	unʔú	únʔu	burʔú
'belt'	tásócʔ	kisócʔ	tásócʔ	tachócʔ

Prefix-like changes plus voicing:

'foot'	nakú	úku	egú	ekhúr
'food'	náca	ucá	úza̜	úcʔa
'sandal'	nápa̜cʔ	upá̜cʔ	úba̜cʔ	úpa̜cʔ
'ear'	suká̜	síka̜	sigá	sikhá

Prefix-like changes and lenition:

'carrying rack'	namá	é̜ma̜	emá	emhá
'mat'	sumás	sí̜ma̜s	si̜más	simhás

Prefix-like changes and alternation of /r/ and /t/:

'face'	katá	úta	urá	urhá
'knife'	taté	kíte	kíte	narhé
'work'	natánʔ	utánʔ	úranʔ	úrhanʔ
'clothing'	nuntʔǘʔ	nírʔüʔ	nintʔǘ	urʔǘʔ

TABLE 2-5 (continued)

Prefix-like changes and alternation of /r/ and /n/ and of /nd/ and /r/:

'mouth'	*katí*	*úti*	*uní*	*unír*
'father-in-law'	*úrí*	*éṇi*	*urí*	*bárir*
'water'	*kúndí*	*kirí*	*kíndí*	*kúri*
'money'	*túndehenˀ*	*kiréhenˀ*	*níndehenˀ*	*úrehenˀ*

Alternation of labials:

'hat'	*nambá*	*úngwa*	*uṃá*	*upˀá*
'horn'	*námbahanˀ*	*úmahanˀ*	*úmahanˀ*	*úpˀahanˀ*
'thirst'	*numbǘ*	*níbü*	*nimbǘ*	*upˀǘ*
'hunger'	*númbeˀe*	*níbeˀe*	*nímbeˀe*	*úbeˀe*
'sons'	*rungwǽr*	*ríngwær*	*ripǽr*	*burˀǘr*
'land'	*kúmboˀ*	*kibóˀ*	*kimbóˀ*	*úboˀ*

Other changes:

'hand'	*kaˀá*	*kanˀá*	*kanˀí*	*kanˀír*
'female relative'	*mánthü*	*manthǘ*	*éngü*	*bǘnthü*

Suppletion (first person):

'wife'	*masṳ́*	*uniˀí*	*úniˀi*	*buráˀa*
'father'	*táta*	*úngwæ*	*émǽˀ*	*úngwæ*
'grandmother'	*naléˀ*	*utǘ*	*erǘ*	*butǘr*

TABLE 2-6. Classifiers for Nouns

'food'	*nantˀé*	*útˀe*	*utˀé*	*úcˀa*
'clothing'	*nuntˀǘ*	*nírˀü*	*nintˀǘ*	*urˀǘ*
'animals'	*námbæˀæ*	*ungwǽˀæ*	*úngwæˀæ*	*úbæˀæ*
'things'	*námbihi*	*úngwihi*	*úṃịhị*	*úpˀihi*

TABLE 2-7. Paradigm for 'Rock'

Person	Singular	Dual	Plural
1st	*námbihi kúroho*	*námbihi kúroho-mˀ* (excl.)	*námbihi kúroho-hụˀ* (excl.)
		námbihi kúroho-s (incl.)	*námbihi kúroho-n* (incl.)
2nd	*úngwihi kúroho*	*úngwihi kúroho-s*	*úngwihi kúroho-n*
3rd	*úṃịhị kúroho*	*úṃịhị kúroho-s*	*úpˀihi kúroho*

kánga-s 'two boys', *síma ?an-és* 'two dogs'. Thus the dual possessor and the dual possessed are ambiguous. 'My two dogs' and 'our (dual inclusive) dogs' are both *námba ?a síma ?anés*.

The dual may not be marked if the noun is preceded by the numeral 'two': *tanhé síma ?an* 'two dogs'.

2.1.4. THE PLURAL IN NOUNS. Nouns are seldom pluralized. A singular noun with a plural verb, for instance, is quite common. If it is marked, the plural is *-r* (*-er* if the stem is consonant final): *kánga-r* 'boys', *ríkúr-ér* 'tortillas', *umhą́ síngwun ? egą́* 'the sheep are in their pen'. The verb *egą́* is plural; the noun *umhą́* is singular.

2.2. VERBS.

2.2.1. TENSES. There are eight tenses in Chichimeco: present; future; three past tenses, one of which, however, may refer to events in the immediate future; a negative; and what Jaime de Angulo (1933) calls contemporaneous and potential. The first five are more properly tenses; the other three could also be called modes.

The *present* tense is used in expressions which refer to the present or which are continuative or habitual. When they are habitual they may be located in the past and in translation are rendered by 'used to', 'would', etc. This tense is also used in expressions which are represented in English by gerunds, even if the first verb is past (see section 2.2.2). Examples:

kíkú títá étu ?u
here town I-come
'I come to the market.'

ko ?ós énu ?u
my-house I-look-at
'I am looking at my house.'

enero be ?é er ?ų́
January peppers they-plant
'In January they plant peppers.'

įnǫ ? éce úra étan ?
he comes his-work he-works
'He comes to work.'

ubengí éndü
every-day he-goes
'He went every day.'

sa ? úzạ énas
already food (3rd person) they-eat (dual)
'They would both eat.'

ut ?é ríkhúr
3rd person classifier for food tortilla

   é ?ür
   she-sells

'She used to sell tortillas.'

ú ?uhun mu éņeheb
he-arrived only he-runs
'He came running.'

The *future* tense refers to future events. It is used in objective clauses with the main verb meaning 'want', 'expect', or the like. It is also used in sentences meaning 'if' or 'when' (cf. contemporary and potential), and to give commands instead of the imperative. Examples:

síni ?i tátá ganú
tomorrow my-father I-will-see
'Tomorrow I will see my father.'

gátehe ubés
he-will-come later
'Is he coming later?'

ikág é ?i máņ́ę gúrho
I I-want soon I-will-finish
'I want to finish soon.'

ikág épihi tá ?uhun
I I-expect I-will-come
'I expect to come.'

málí ndi gá ?uhun po
Mary when she-will-come then

   gúndürín
   we-will-go (plural)

'When Mary comes we will go.'

26

sakhá gasán ígo? úrehen   níhü
if   we-win they their-money middle

gísa?an
you (plural)-will-distribute

'If we win you will split the money.'

kítehe
you-will-come
'Come!'

The *anterior past* refers to past events which took place more than a few hours before. Examples:

kimbáre   úkhar
compadre he-had
'He had a compadre.'

nábą̧   tupą̧k?
yesterday I-saw-you
'I saw you yesterday.'

úne̯ kánga íru   umą̧   rábó
that child man his-hat cut-off

kazá-símó? únhín egú   er?ér
his-head   put-on his-foot cloth

egú   únhín rígu̯ ki ų̧mi̯hi
his-foot put-on stick and he-took

ki úndü   úne̯heb
and he-went he-ran

'That young man put on the cut-off hat, put the sock on his foot, took the stick and ran away.'

The *recent past* refers to events which took place a few hours before. Examples:

ígo? kúntho   be   sa?
they they-finished then already

sáteher
they-left

'They finished and left.'

ka?á kusék?
who told-you

mi?ík?
you-might-come (contemporaneous)

'Who told you to come?'

The *immediate* tense refers to events which either took place a few minutes before or will take place in a short time. It is often used for accidental happenings. Examples:

námbihi   suerte mą̧
1st person classifier for things luck time

zúc?eg
he-spoiled-for-me

'He just spoiled my luck for me.'

čičá epó?   sa? ki
arch it-goes-down already and

záno̯
it-approaches

'The fiesta is fast approaching.'

úc?é itó?
pot it-broke
'The pot broke.'

The *contemporaneous* tense expresses wishes and doubts. It is used in what are translated as if-clauses to express conditions. It is also used in dependent clauses with verbs of wishing, telling, and the like, and to recount sequences of events in stories. Examples:

ikág párámá rúrho
I   perhaps I-might-finish
'Perhaps I will finish.'

man?í máre?-ne̯ rapíb
what old   I-might-tell-her
'What story shall I tell her?'

ohalá   ų̧ne̯ rá?uhun
would-that that-one he-might-come
'I hope he comes.'

úrehen   ndi rúkhar
their-money when I-might-have

27

nándü   kúrihü
I-might-go Mexico

'If I had money I would go to Mexico.'

anteske   kúrí   rukég
before   their-water it-might-get-me
'Before the rain gets me.'

kaʔá   kusékʔ   miʔíkʔ
who   he-told-you you-might-come
'Who told you to come?'

ntʔa   úrehenʔ mapé rupás   ntʔa
one   money a-lot they-might-find one

úcʔé ndeʔ úrehenʔ rupás
pot large money   they-might-find

rúkeheʔs
they-might-take-it-away

'They both found lots of money, they found
a large pot of money and took it away.'

simæʔǽthǽ sáʔ   gíʔe rúcehe
coyote   already also they-might-tell
'So they told the coyote.'

The *potential* tense usually occurs in dependent clauses; it is also found after verbs of
motion and sometimes in contrary-to-fact expressions. Examples:

bueno ígoʔ nehé eʔí   nusékʔ
well   that only I-want I-may-tell-you
'OK, that's all I want to tell you.'

uség   m̩á maʔí
he-told-me time I-may-come
'He told me to come.'

nábą́ urı́g   para síniʔi
yesterday he-asked-me for   tomorrow

maʔį̃
I-may-come

'Yesterday he asked me to come
   tomorrow.'

úphü   kándü múgüč
excrement I-went I-may-pour
'I went and poured excrement.'

ndi péló ráʔuhun   párámá
when Peter he-might-arrive perhaps

mukǽhǽgun
he-may-take-us

úm̩ihį
3rd person classifier for things

tárhǽr
car

'If Peter came perhaps he could take us in
   his car.'

In general, it is hard to tell the difference
between the potential and the contemporaneous tenses, and this is a topic which requires further study.

The *negative* is used to express negation,
regardless of what tense one would use in the
affirmative; *siʔán* is used with the negative
when referring to future events. In the following examples, the name of the tense in
parentheses indicates which one would be
used in the affirmative:

tátá   utʔís
my-father his-house

singwǽhǽme (present)
he-is-not

'My father is not at home.'

síniʔi   siʔán   sándüme
tomorrow negative I-won't-go

títá (future)
town

'Tomorrow I won't go to town.'

mapáb   sųn̩úkʔme (immediate)
a while ago I don't-see-you
'A little while ago I didn't see you.'

suʔí   unʔú   urá
she-doesn't-want her-husband her-face

28

sųnų́ʔume (potential)
he-doesn't-see

'She didn't want her husband to see her face.'

2.2.2. RELATIVE USE OF TENSES. As mentioned above, the present tense is used in expressions that refer to the past but were present from the point of view of the event itself. In the sentence

úʔuhun   *ungwǽhæ*   *ésų́ʔ*
he-arrived his-song   he-sings
'He came singing.'

the subject was singing as he came.

2.2.3. PREFIX CLASSES. The tenses whose meanings have been briefly characterized and illustrated are formed with prefixes. Each of the three persons usually has a different prefix. The third person plural has a different prefix in some cases, but in other cases a single form is used for third person singular, dual, and plural. Verbs take the same suffixes as those added to nouns to form the dual and the first and second person plural (section 2.1.1). The third person plural stem is usually somewhat different. The six classes of verbs that are defined by the prefixes they take are given in Table 2-8.

The fifth class contains reflexive verbs. The sixth class has mostly verbs of movement, but not all verbs of movement belong to it. It has some prefixes for dual and plural which differ from the singular; they are listed in the table. In addition, the verbs in this class have the following peculiarities in the plural: -*rín* is added to the stem of the first person plural inclusive of all tenses, except the continuative and negative, and to second person plural anterior past, present, and future. In addition -*rkʔún* is added to the second person plural recent past, immediate, potential, contemporaneous, and negative forms, and -*gos* is added to the first person dual inclusive negative. Examples:

gu-ndü-rín   'We (inclusive) went.'

kí-ndü-rkʔún   'You (plural) went (Recent Past, Immediate).'
sí-ndü-gos-me   'We (dual inclusive) don't go.'

2.2.4. IRREGULAR VERBS. There are also some irregular verbs. The most common ones are 'to be' (which also means 'to sit') and 'to walk around'. Partial paradigms of these verbs appear in Table 2-9.

2.2.5. PATTERNS OF STEM VARIATION. Verb stems have different patterns of variation. Some have only one form to which the various prefixes and suffixes are attached; others have a different form for the third person plural; still others have as many as six forms. Very often more than one form is used for a given person depending on the tense. In Table 2-10 the numbers refer to different forms; there are at least thirteen major patterns of variation, and within some of these (for instance patterns VIII–XII which undergo tone variation), there are also subvarieties.

Examples of the stem forms for each pattern follow, with their prefix classes in parentheses.

    I. -*pánʔ* 'heat' (3)
    II. -*sür*, -*chür* 'peel' (1)
    III. -*neheb*, *ņeheb* 'run' (1)
    IV. -*ga*, -*nga* 'greet' (2)
    V. -*ndá*, -*tá*, -*rá*, -*rhá* 'buy' (1)
    VI. -*ʔán*, -*táʔn*, -*ndáʔn*, -*rʔánʔ* 'ask' (1)
    VII. -*há*, -*nháʔ*, -*rháʔ* 'drink' (1)
    VIII. -*sé*, -*se*, -*ché* 'open' (1)
    IX. -*ndza*, -*cá*, -*ca*, -*zá*, -*cʔá* 'try' (1)
    X. -*ʔí*, -*ʔi*, -*tʔí*, -*ndi*, -*rʔí*, -*rʔi* 'want' (1)
    XI. -*ʔoʔ*, -*ʔóʔ*, -*tʔiʔ*, -*ndíʔ*, -*rʔó*, -*rʔo* 'hear' (1)
    XII. -*tan*, -*tán*, -*ran*, -*rhan* 'work' (1)
    XIII. -*pihi*, -*ngwihi*, -*ṃįhį*, -*mbihi*, -*bihi* 'spy' (1)

Table 2-11 presents partial paradigms for verbs with patterns V, VII, X, and XIII, with four, three, six, and five forms respectively.

2.2.6. THE IMPERATIVE is used for commands in the second person or as a sort of

TABLE 2-8. Prefix Classes

Class	Person	Present	Anterior Past	Recent Past	Immediate	Future	Potential	Contemporaneous	Negative
1	1st	e-	tu-	ku-	u-	ga-	nu-	ra-	su-
	2nd	ki-	ki-	ki	i-	ki-	mi-	gi-	si-
	3rd	e-	u-	ku-	zu-	ga-	mu-	ra-	su-
	3rd pl.						mi-		
2	1st	tu-				gu-		ru-	
	2nd	su-						gi-	
	3rd	u-		Same as Class 1				ru-	
	3rd pl.	e-						ra-	
3	1st	tu-	tu-			gu-			
	2nd	su-	su-						
	3rd	u-	u-		Same as Class 1				
	3rd pl.	e-	e-						
4	1st	tu-	tu-	ku-	u-	gu-	mu-	ra-	su-
	2nd	ka-	ka-	ka-	e-	ka-	ma-	ga-	sa-
	3rd	u-	ku-	ku-	e-	ga-	ma-	ru-	sa-
5	1st	ti-	ta-	sa-	i-	ta-	na-	Same	si-
	2nd	si-	sa-	sa-	i-	sa-	za-	as	si-
	3rd	i-	ta-	sa-	i-	ta-	na-	Potential	si-

6

Singular

Class	Person	Present	Anterior Past	Recent Past	Immediate	Future	Potential	Contemporaneous	Negative
	1st	e-	ta-	ka-	Same	ta-	ma-	na-	sa-
	2nd	ki-	ki-	ki-	as	ki-	mi-	mi-	si-
	3rd	e-	u-	ku-	Recent Past	ga-	mi-	ra-,ma-	si-

Dual

Class	Person	Present	Anterior Past	Recent Past	Immediate	Future	Potential	Contemporaneous	Negative
	1st			ki-		ti-	ma-	ma-	si-
	2nd								
	3rd		Same as Singular						

Plural

Class	Person	Present	Anterior Past	Recent Past	Immediate	Future	Potential	Contemporaneous	Negative
	1st	u-	ti-,-gu	ki-		gu-	mi-	ma-	su-
	2nd								
	3rd		Same as Singular				ra-		

exhortative in the first person. It has the same stem as the potential. The prefixes and suffixes are shown in Table 2-12. Examples: *ucá izą* 'Eat!'; *i-čǽn-sé* 'Pay! (dual)'; *ti-thǽr-nhé̜* 'Let's play! (plural)'; *ucánhé̜* 'Let's do it! (plural)'.

The negative imperative is formed with the particle *inhé* and the prefix *na-*; *-sé* and *-nhé̜* are added to the dual and the plural respectively. Example: *inhé ucá nazą́* 'Don't eat!'

2.2.7. AUXILIARIES. The most frequent auxiliaries are *-ndü* 'go', *-tu³u* 'walk around',

and *-mǽhǽ* 'to be' (see section 2.2.4). When *-ndü* is used as an auxiliary, the main verb occurs with special prefixes as shown in Table 2-13. (The future and the negative use prefixes of class 1.) The auxiliaries *-tu³u* and *-mǽhǽ* do not cause any modifications in the prefixes of the main verb. Examples: *tándü pútá* 'I went to buy'; *man³í kitu³u sucáge* 'What are you doing?'; *émǽhǽ énu³u* 'I am looking'.

2.2.8. VERBS WITH PLURAL OBJECT. There are cases where the same gloss can be expressed by two different verbs in Chichimeco

TABLE 2-9. Partial Paradigms of Irregular Verbs

Present	Anterior Past/ Future	Recent Past/ Immediate	Potential/ Contemporaneous	Negative
		'To be' Singular		
é-mǽhæ	ta-ngwǽhæ	sa-ngwǽhæ	na-ngwǽhæ	si-ngwǽhæ-u-mehe
kí-mǽhæ	sa-ngwǽhæ	sa-ngwǽhæ	za-ngwǽhæ	si-ngwǽhæ-kʔ-mehe
é-mǽhæ	ta-ngwǽhæ	sa-ngwǽhæ	na-ngwǽhæ	si-ngwǽhæ-mehe
		Dual		
é-mǽhæ-s	ti-ngwǽhæ-s	si-ngwǽhæ-s	ni-ngwǽhæ	si-ngwǽhæ-gus-mehe
kí-mǽhæ-s	ti-ngwǽhæ-s	si-ngwǽhæ-s	za-ngwǽhæ	si-ngwǽhæ-kʔos-mehe
é-mǽhæ-s	ti-ngwǽhæ-s	si-ngwǽhæ-s	na-ngwǽhæ	si-ngwǽhæ-s-mehe
		Plural		
u-gǽ	ti-ngwǽhæ-n	si-kán	ni-kán	si-ngwǽhæ-gu-mehe
ki-gán	sa-ngwǽhæ-rín	sa-kán	za-kán	si-ngwǽhæ-kʔu-mehe
e-gǽ	ta-kǽ	sa-kǽ	na-kǽ	si-ngwǽhæ-mehe
		'To walk around' Singular		
é-tʔu	ta-tʔú	sa-tʔú		sá-nʔú-mehe
kí-tʔu	sa-tʔú	sa-tʔú		sí-nʔú-mehe
é-tʔu	ta-tʔú	sa-tʔú		sí-nʔú-mehe
		Dual		
é-tuʔus	ti-tʔús	si-tʔús		sí-nʔú-s-mehe
kí-tuʔus	sa-tʔús	sa-tʔús		sí-nʔú-s-mehe
é-tuʔus	ta-tʔús	sa-tʔús		sí-nʔú-s-mehe
		Plural		
ú-turín	ti-turín	ti-turín		sú-nʔú-r-gu-mehe
kí-turín	sa-túrín	sa-turín		sí-nʔú-r-kʔ-mehe
é-tʔur	ta-tʔúr	ta-tʔúr		sí-nʔú-r-mehe

TABLE 2-10. Verb Patterns Showing Number of Forms Schematically

Patterns	First Person	Second Person	Third Person Singular	Third Person Plural
I	1	1	1	1
II	1	1	1	2
III	1	2	2	1
IV	1	1	2	2
V	1,2	2	2,3	4
VI	1	2	1,3	4
VII	1	1,2	1,2	3
VIII	1	2	1	3
IX	1,2	3	2,4	5
X	1,2	1,3	1,2,4	5,6
XI	1,2	1	1,2,3	4,5
XII	1,2,4	2	1,2,4	5
XIII	1,2,4	2,1	1,2,3	4,5

Table 2-11. Stem Variation in Four Selected Verbs

Person	Present	Anterior Past	Recent Past	Imme- diate	Future	Potential	Contem- poraneous	Negative
			'To buy' (Pattern V, Prefix Class 1)					
1st	é-tá	tú-tá	kú-ndá	ú-tá	gá-tá	nú-tá	rá-tá	sú-tá-me
2nd	kí-tá	kí-tá	kí-tá	í-tá	kí-tá	mí-tá	gí-tá	sí-tá-me
3rd	é-tá	ú-rá	kú-rá	zú-tá	gá-rá	mú-tá	rá-rá	sú-tá-me
3rd pl.	é-rhá	ú-rhá	kú-rhá	zú-rhá	gá-rhá	mú-rhá	rá-rhá	su-rhá
			'To drink' (Pattern VII, Prefix Class 1)					
1st	é-háʔ	tú-háʔ	kú-háʔ	ú-háʔ	gá-háʔ	nú-háʔ	rá-háʔ	sú-háʔ-me
2nd	kí-háʔ	kí-nháʔ	kí-nháʔ	í-nháʔ	gí-nháʔ	mí-nháʔ	gí-nháʔ	sí-nháʔ-me
3rd	é-háʔ	ú-nháʔ	kú-nháʔ	zú-háʔ	gá-nháʔ	mú-háʔ	rá-nháʔ	sú-háʔ-me
3rd pl.	é-rháʔ	ú-rháʔ	kú-nháʔ	zú-rháʔ	gá-rháʔ	mí-rháʔ	rá-rháʔ	sú-rháʔ-me
			'To want' (Pattern X, Prefix Class 1)					
1st	e-ʔí	tú-ʔí	ku-ʔí	ú-ʔi	ga-ʔí	nú-ʔi	rá-ʔi	sú-ʔí-me
2nd	ki-ʔí	ki-tʔí	ki-tʔí	i-ʔí	ki-tʔí	mi-tʔí	gi-tʔí	si-tʔí-me
3rd	e-ʔí	u-ndíʔ	ku-ndíʔ	zú-ʔi	ga-ndíʔ	mú-ʔi	ra-ndí	sú-ʔi-me
3rd pl.	e-rʔí	u-rʔí	ku-rʔí	zu-rʔí	ga-rʔí	mú-rʔi	ra-rʔí	sú-rʔi-me
			'To spy on' (Pattern XIII, Prefix Class 1)					
1st	é-pihi	tú-pihi	kú-mbihi	ú-mbihi	gá-pihi	nú-ngwihi	rá-pihi	sú-ngwihi-me
2nd	kí-pihi	kí-ngwihi	kí-ngwihi	í-ngwihi	kí-ngwihi	mí-ngwihi	gí-ngwihi	sú-ngwihi-me
3rd	é-pihi	ú-mjhi	kú-mjhi	zú-mjhi	gá-mjhi	mú-ngwihi	rá-mjhi	sú-ngwihi-me
3rd pl.	é-pihi	ú-mbihi	kú-bihi	zú-bihi	gú-mbihi	mú-bihi	rá-mbihi	sú-bihi-me

Table 2-12. Imperative Prefixes and Suffixes

Person	Singular	Dual	Plural
	Verbs of Prefix Class 1		
1st	tu-	tu-...-sé	u-...-nhę́
2nd	i-	i-...-sé	i-...-nhę́
	Verbs of Prefix Classes 2–4		
1st	e-...-nę́	e-...-sé	e-...-nhę́
2nd	i-	i-...-sé	i-...-nhę́
	Verbs of Prefix Class 5		
1st	ta-...-nę́	ti-...-sé	ti-...-nhę́
2nd	sa-	sa-...-sé	sa-...-nhę́
	Verbs of Prefix Class 6		
1st	e-...-nę́	e-...-sé	ú-...-nhę́
2nd	ki-	ki-...-sé	ki-...-nhę́

TABLE 2-13. Prefixes Used with Auxiliary *-ndü*

Present	Anterior Past	Recent Past/ Immediate	Potential/ Contemporaneous
u-	pu-	mu-	mu-
ku-	ku-	ku-	mi-
u-	u-	nu-	mu-
ba-	ba-	ba-	mi-

TABLE 2-14. Object Suffix Forms

Person	Singular	Dual	Plural
1st	-g	-g (u)m? (exclusive)	-gu-hú (exclusive)
		-g-os (inclusive)	-g-un (inclusive)
2nd	-k?	-k?-os	-k?-un
3rd	(-b)	(-b-os)	-r

depending on whether the verb has a singular (or dual) or a plural object. Examples:

zúngwæhæn 'He killed one just now.'
mápé zu?ü 'He killed many just now.'

nda simhæs túpęhę? 'I put something on a mat.'
é?ehe 'I put down many things.'

zúkehe 'I took something out just now.'
zukür 'I took lots of things out just now.'

2.2.9. OBJECT SUFFIXES. The object suffixes are obviously related in form to the free pronouns. They are used to mark a direct object, as in *ki-pą-g* 'you see me', or an indirect one, as in *ur?ósé gá-po-k?* 'I'll give you bread'. The forms are shown in Table 2-14.

The third person singular and dual are seldom marked; *-b* is optional in a case like *ínǫ? ríkhúr étịhị (-b)* 'she asks him for tortillas'. It is obligatory in expressions with a causative or benefactive meaning:

cúcé   ut?ís   gándéb
Joseph his-house will-enlarge
'Joseph is going to enlarge his house.'

ínǫ? uség   nánt?a ụmą́
he   asked-me one   his-hat

nutáb
I-may-buy-him

'He asked me to buy a hat for him.'

The negative *-me* follows the object suffix: *su-zą-g-os-me* 'he doesn't eat us'.

When first and third person object suffixes occur with imperatives, the forms are *-gó* and *-bó*: *iségó* 'Tell me!'; *íta?abó* 'Cut it!'

3. SYNTAX.

3.1. WORD CLASSES. Chichimeco has nouns, verbs, adverbs, adjectives, and particles.

Nouns include the personal pronouns and classifiers. They function as subjects, objects, or predicatives. Some nouns are locatives; others function as temporal adverbs. Nouns can modify other nouns. A few Chichimeco nouns, which are translated in English as prepositions, appear after the nouns they modify. Classifiers modify the nouns that follow them. Examples:

> *kánga   úrí   ubá*
> boy   man   saw
> 'The boy saw the man.'

kánga is subject and *úrí* is object.

> *kacú máli nántʔa urü-pʔan gámboho*
> Jesús Mary one   rebozo   he-will-give
> 'Jesús will give Mary a rebozo.'

máli is an indirect object.

> *ikág manuél úma-g*
> I   Manuel   son (1st person)
> 'I am Manuel's son.'

umá-g is a predicative.

> *émbó kundáhrʔer émæhæ*
> hill   eagle   is
> 'The eagle is on the hill.'

émbó is a locative in the above example.

> *ínọʔ úsa síʔühünme*
> he   night   he-doesn't-sleep
> 'He doesn't sleep at night.'

úsa is used as an adverb here.

> *kázu irú*
> cow   male
> 'bull'

The above phrase exemplifies a noun modifying another noun. The next example illustrates a noun which also modifies another noun and is translated 'around':

> *símaʔan mápá   súnga*
> dog   their-fire   edge
>
> *egá*
> be (third person plural, present)
>
> 'The dogs are around the fire.'

urʔú
3rd person plural classifier for clothing

> *mhą́*
> blanket

'their blanket'

urʔú by itself means 'cloth' or 'clothing'.

Verbs are predicates. They may be intransitive, transitive, or bi-transitive. The objective suffixes mark both direct and indirect objects and are added to the verb. Examples:

> *ripʔá   émæhæ*
> outside   he-is
> 'He is outside.'

> *péló   ínọ énuʔu*
> Peter   he   he-sees
> 'Peter sees him.'

> *ikág urʔósʔé gapo   -kʔ*
> I   bread   I-will-give   you
> 'I'll give you bread.'

> *ígoʔ upą   -kʔ*
> they   they-saw   you
> 'They saw you.'

Some transitive verbs require a cognate object or some other special object. These include 'to work', 'to eat', 'to be tired', 'to like', 'to sing', 'to run', etc. Examples: *nátanʔ étạnʔ* 'I work', literally 'I work my work'. The verb 'to run' is *-ņeheb*, and its apparent object 'race' is partially conjugated as well: *suʔí úņęhęb* 'he ran', *gaʔí gáņęhęb* 'he will run'. The verb 'to eat' does not take its cognate object if a specific object is mentioned: *úza kuzą́* 'he ate'; *beʔé mapé kuzą́* 'He ate many peppers'.

Some verbs occur with the word for 'heart' as a modifier:

> *ikág rungwǽr   kụņí   tụmą́r*
> I   my-children   my-heart   I-think
> 'I think about my children.'

Literally, 'I think in my heart.'

A verb 'to go' usually occurs with the word meaning 'face':

kúrihü   katá   ęmą́
Mexico my-face I go
'I go to Mexico.'

It may be interpreted as 'I direct my face toward'.

Words like *bésá?* 'later', *bíngi* 'every day', *kíki* 'again', *kíkú* 'here', and *mą́nę́* 'soon' are adverbs.

Adjectives include words like *(č)ínče* 'small', *ení?n* 'red', and *mapé* 'a lot', numerals like *rácoro* 'ten', and demonstratives like *kíni* 'this' (although some demonstratives are pronouns).

Particles include a few subordinating conjunctions like *ndí* 'that' or 'where' and *sakhá* 'if' and coordinating conjunctions like *por-?umhé* 'but' and *ki* 'and'. Other particles include *handa* 'lest' and *nímú* (hesitation).

3.2. ORDER. Chichimeco is an SOV language. It is the only Otomanguean language known to have this order. As predicted by Joseph H. Greenberg's (1963) work on order typology, it has no prepositions. As mentioned above, some postposed nouns have the same function as prepositions in English or Spanish. English 'with' (accompaniment) is represented by the dual in Chichimeco:

tátá   cúcé   íkehes
my-father Joseph they-are-together (dual)
'My father is with Joseph.'

The genitive precedes the noun:

cúcé   kánthe
Joseph hair
'Joseph's hair'

Adjectives occur after nouns:

narhé nánde?
knife   big
'big knife'

The verb follows its modifiers when these are not clauses:

ikág kíkú   tukhar
I   here I-have
'I have it here.'

įnǫ? nimámba?a é?ühün
he   a-lot   he-sleeps
'He sleeps a lot.'

nábą́   tupą́k?
yesterday I-saw-you
'I saw you yesterday.'

rikįs   ni   émbó mánó tápoho
thorn very deep near entered
'The thorn pricked superficially.'

Conditional clauses precede main clauses:

sakhá ganú   narhé-ndé gátįhįb
if   I-will-see machete I-will-ask-him
'If I see him I will ask him for the machete.'

Contrary to what is usual in SOV languages, purpose clauses follow main clauses in Chichimeco:

ut?ís   sátehe   kúngag
his-house he-went-out he-greeted-me
'He came out of the house to greet me.'

'When' clauses may precede or follow main clauses:

be?é   enín? i?í   ndi sá?
pepper red   it-comes that already

  matá?
  ripe

'Peppers turn red when they are ripe.'

ndí émą̈hą̈ náca   énna inhé
that I-am   my-food I-eat negative

  nandáhagó
  don't-bother-me

'Don't bother me when I eat.'

Chichimeco does not have Greenberg's possible OSV word order.

Objective clauses follow the main verb:

ikág kunú man?ígo ígo? ur?ós
I I-saw what they their-house

sanúr
happened

'I saw what happened in that house.'

Despite Greenberg's predictions, both auxiliaries and main verbs are inflected in Chichimeco, and the auxiliary precedes the main verb:

íno? e-mǽhǽ
he be (3rd person present)

é-?ühün
sleep (3rd person present)

'He is sleeping.'

Demonstratives, numerals, and classifiers precede the noun: *kíni ur?ós* 'his house'; *tín?uhun síma?an* 'three dogs'; *námbæ?æ síma?an* 'my dog'. A demonstrative can precede a variable noun: *kíni ut?ís* 'this house of his'. A classifier may be preceded by a personal pronoun: *ikághú? námbihi cuce?ehú?* 'our (plural exclusive) basket'. A demonstrative may precede a numeral: *ki?í sangwáro ur?ós* 'these five houses'.

Relative clauses do not conform to Greenberg's predictions in that they follow rather than precede nouns:

íno? úrí ndí tátehe ikág epá
that man that he-went-out I I-know
'I know the man who left.'

When adjectives follow nouns, they assume the inflection for the whole phrase:

kánga ínče -r
boy small (plural)
'small boys'

Chichimeco is like other SOV languages in this respect.

3.3. PHRASES. Noun phrases have already been treated in the section on word order above. They function as subjects, objects, or predicatives. They may also be adverbials, and they are not marked in any particular way. For instance, instrumental 'with' is simply not expressed; the instrument occurs alone without function words or particles:

inhére úc?é rígu nangwæhǽ?
negative pot stick don't-hit
'Don't hit the pot with a stick.'

3.4. CLAUSES.
3.4.1. VERBLESS CLAUSES. Chichimeco has both verbless clauses and clauses with verbs. The former may be equational:

urárimé̜ čičáha?
huitlacoche bird
'Huitlacoches are birds.'

íno? kúce?e
that basket

námbihi kúce?e
1st person classifier for things basket

'That is my basket.'

Classifiers can be used anaphorically in equational clauses:

íno? síma?an úmbó
that dog black

námba?a
1st person classifier for animals

'That black dog is mine.'

Equational clauses may consist only of nouns inflected for person:

ikág irú -g
I man (1st person)
'I am a man.'

Place names can be combined with the

noun *moʔós* 'place', inflected for person, to express one's place of origin:

ikág kúrihü   moʔós -g
I   Mexico place (1st person)
'I am from Mexico.'

Variable nouns can occur with pronouns in expressions meaning 'I am hungry', 'I am thirsty', etc.:

ikág númbeʔe
I   hunger
'I am hungry.'

Equational expressions about the weather can be formed with nouns meaning 'hot', 'cold', 'wind', etc.:

ni   kunhé
very wind
'It is very windy.'

A noun may occur by itself with the topicalizer *-nǫ* (from *inǫ* 'that') with the meaning 'It is a . . . over there':

símaʔan- nǫ́
dog   topicalizer
'It is a dog over there.'

Similarly, *-nę* (from *unę* 'that over there') serves as a topicalizer:

mu   umʔá- nę́
only moon topicalizer
'It was just the moon!'

3.4.2. INTRANSITIVE CLAUSES. Several types of intransitive clauses occur in Chichimeco. Examples follow.
Clauses with a predicative:

ịnǫʔ kábạ íta   ni   nándeʔ taʔí
that tree more very large   will-come
'That tree will become large.'

Intransitive clauses with verbs of location that require a locative (other adverbials are optional):

kacú nábạ́   rítehen tángwæhæ
Jesús yesterday Ortega was
'Jesús was at Ortega yesterday.'

A locative may precede the subject:

kíni símaʔan síkuʔur egüʔ
this dog   spots   are
'This dog has spots.'

Existential clauses occur with several locative verbs, the most frequent of which is the verb 'to be' or 'to sit' (see section 2.2.4). It is used with persons, animals, or objects:

koʔós   úrí   egạ́
my-house man   are
'There are people at my house.'

igoʔ   nántʔa símaʔan nehé émæhæ
there one   dog   only is
'There is only one dog there.'

ráncó rinʔé   émæhæ
rancho church is
'There is a church at the rancho.'

Another irregular verb meaning 'to be' (*eniʔi* 3rd person singular, *égʔü* 3rd person plural) is used mostly with objects which are lying down:

narhé-ndé mapé égʔüʔ
machete   many are
'There are many machetes.'

Other existential verbs include *emǫ́ʔ*, which is used only for liquids, and *ebóʔ*, which is used for trees. Examples:

úcʔé kúrí   emǫ́ʔ
pot   their-water is
'There is water in the pot.'

kábạ ebóʔ
tree are
'There are trees.'

Intransitive clauses with optional adverbials:

ịnọʔ nimámbaʔa ubạ́ mạ́ éʔühün
he a-lot day time he-sleeps
'He sleeps a lot by day.'

Intransitive clauses may occur with a topicalizer:
kégó bé enʔí-nẹ́
where then it-is-topicalizer
'Where is it that it is, then?'

3.4.3. TRANSITIVE CLAUSES. Some examples of transitive clauses will now be presented. The object of a transitive clause may be a free word or a suffix:

ikág ntʔá símaʔan túkhar
I one dog I-have
'I have a dog.'

nábạ́ tupá-kʔ
yesterday I-saw-you
'I saw you yesterday.'

The following transitive verb takes both direct and indirect objects:

ịnọʔ ríkhúr étịhị -g
she tortilla she-asks me
'She asks me for tortillas.'

The following transitive clause contains optional adverbs:

čígú kiki nátan gatanʔ
today again my-work I-will-work
'I will work today again.'

A special particle is used for causatives:

nantʔé ríkhúr
1st person classifier for food tortilla

émæhæ tuhű
causative I-burned

'I burned my tortilla.'

The verb 'to say, tell' is sometimes combined with a dependent clause to express causation:

ịnọʔ uség símaʔan nungwǽnʔ
he told-me dog I-might-kill
'He made me kill the dog.'

Some transitive clauses occur with topicalizers:

ntʔá mạ́ upʔá rábó
one time their-hat cut-off

úmbo-nẹ́
he-gave-topicalizer

'It was a cut-off hat that he gave him.'

Impersonal clauses may be formed in several ways, using either the second person singular or the third person plural:

kábe íʔe kankhé kítụʔu
how also bean you-sow
'How are beans sown?'

nábá núndehen úmbog
yesterday my-money they-gave-me
'I was paid yesterday.'

3.4.4. NEGATIVES. An equational clause is negated by adding the negative particle *sínhạ* and suffixing the negative suffix *-me* (*-mehe* in some pronunciations) to the predicate:

ịnọʔ kúceʔe sínhạ
that basket negative

námbihi
1st person classifier for things

kúceʔe-me
basket-negative

'That is not my basket.'

cúcé   sínhạ   kacá ?ar-me
Joseph negative carpenter-negative
'Joseph is not a carpenter.'

Verbs are negated by using a negative prefix and *-me* (see sections 2.2.1 and 2.2.6 for the formation of the negative tense, the negative future, and the negative imperative).

Existential clauses are negated by using the proper form of the negative or the special negative form *bénça ?ạn*:

igo ? ur ?ós   síma ?an bénçạ ?ạn
that their-house dog   there-is-no
'There is no dog in that house.'

kíkú ríkhúr ni   sing ạ́me
here tortilla very there-are-no
          or
kíkú ríkhúr ni   bénçạ ?ạn
here tortilla very there-are-no
'There are no tortillas here.'

kábạ símbome
tree   there-are-no
          or
kábạ bénçạ ?ạn
tree there-are-no
'There are no trees.'

In an objective clause the main verb does not take the negative suffix:

ikág supạ́   simbǽr-me
I   I-don't-know I-don't-swim
'I don't know how to swim.'

kíkú su ?í   nehé sihǽk ?-me
here I-don't-want alone you-don't-stay
'I don't want you to stay here alone.'

3.4.5. INTERROGATIVES. Yes/no questions are signaled by intonation without any change in word order:

ičí   nubạ́ rítehen émǽhǽ ↑
now day Ortega he-is

'Is he at Ortega today?'

simá ?an nímbi ?r úkhar ↑
dog   tails   they-have
'Do dogs have tails?'

Sometimes the word *parí*, which is translated as 'let's see' (*a ver*), is used, but it is optional:

parí   nábí kipạ́
let's see God you-know
'Do you believe in God?'

Interrogative words occur in initial or second position, that is, after the subject:

kégó ? úngwǽhǽ émǽhǽ
where your-father is
'Where is your father?'

cúcé   nígo ? uc ?á
Joseph what he-does
'What does Joseph do?'

ịnọ ? ur ?ós   kábe ?
that their-house how
'What is that house like?'

3.4.6. SUBORDINATE CLAUSES.

3.4.6.1. OBJECTIVE CLAUSES. Some examples of objective clauses follow:

kíkú e ?í
here I-want

  zahǽ ?
  you-may-stay (contemporaneous)

'I want you to stay here.'

The objective clause in this sentence is not independent because its verb is in the contemporaneous tense. It should be compared with the objective clause in the next example, which could stand alone:

ikág kunúk ? nehé sihé   kímǽhǽ
I   saw-you alone alone you-are

úcá   kíną
your-food you-eat

'I saw you eating by yourself.'

The first sentence below is an example of juxtaposition; the second is not:

síni?i   gúm?ab   kunú
tomorrow I-will-begin my-field

gátu?u
I-will-plant

'Tomorrow I will begin planting my field.'

ičigú kunú   gúrhó   gátu?u
today my-field I-will-finish I-will-plant
'Today I will finish planting my field.'

In the following example, the objective
clause is discontinuous and, so to speak, in-
tertwined with the main clause:

nánk?u   nimál mapé kúmba
my-road animal many I-saw

ét?ur
they-walked

'I saw many animals on the road.'

There are no verbs with the meanings 'to
be able' and 'not to be able' in Chichimeco.
These ideas are expressed by combining
words like 'easy' and 'difficult' with a verb in
the potential tense:

ma?ír   íną? kabą́ nahą́
difficult that tree I-may-climb
'I can't climb the tree.'

Chichimeco has no subjective clauses. A
sentence like "It is good to be here' is rendered as 'You probably like it here' in this
language.

3.4.6.2. ADVERBIAL CLAUSES. The following is an example of an adverbial clause:

málí ndi   gá?uhun   po   gúndurín
Mary when she-comes then we-will-go

'When Mary comes we will go.'

Next is a purpose clause:

ikág esék?   sá?   kit?i
I   I-tell-you already you-hear
'I am telling you so you will know.'

There are very few ways of expressing voli-
tion in Chichimeco, short of using 'want' with
an objective clause (see above). Another possibility is to use Spanish *ojalá* plus a verb in
the contemporaneous tense:

ohalá   íną? rá?uhun
would that he   he-might-come
'I hope he comes.'

Some concepts that are treated adverbially
in English or Spanish are expressed as verbs
in Chichimeco, although they function as adverbial clauses. 'Always' and 'slowly', for instance, are verbs:

íną? i?űc   ríkhúr erįhįk?
she she-always tortilla asks-you
'She always asks you for tortillas.'

ikág ti?űc ...
I   always

ihék? si?űc ...
you   always

tupáb   ét?u
I-slowly I-walk
'I walk slowly.'

suáb   kít?u
you-slowly you-walk
'You walk slowly.'

3.4.6.3. CONDITIONAL CLAUSES may use
future tenses in Chichimeco:

sakhá pélo   gá?uhun   unkhwa ubą
if   Peter he-will-arrive early   day

gíteherín
we-will-leave

'If Peter comes we will leave early.'

In the following example of a contrary-to-fact conditional, the verbs in both clauses are in the contemporaneous tense:

sakhá mú pélo rá?uhun
if only Peter he-might-arrive

míndü nuku?unín ránco
we-might-go we-might-arrive rancho

'If Peter came we would go with him to the rancho.'

3.4.6.4. RELATIVE CLAUSES may be formed on subjects, objects, or adverbials. The relative conjunctions themselves always follow nouns (see section 3.2 above). In the following example, *ndí* 'that' is translated as 'whose' in English:

úrí ndí úngwæ?æ
man that 3rd person classifier for animals

síma?an kúmbeb sátehe
dog I-killed he-went-out

'The man whose dog I killed, left.'

Chichimeco frequently uses relative clauses where English would use noun-noun constructions like 'coffee bag'.

íno? ur?ü
that 3rd person classifier for clothing

simbás ndi kafé égü? ni
bag that coffee is (located) very

mahǽ
heavy

'That coffee bag is very heavy.'

3.5. COORDINATION is marked by *ki* 'and', *por?umhé* 'but', and a few other conjunctions:

úndü ki sikǘme
he-went and he-did-not-return

'He went and didn't return.'

ná?u sá urǘné por?umhé
my-husband already dead but

nukhǘ sa? énó gá?uhun
my-son already soon he-will-arrive

'My husband is dead but my son will soon arrive.'

Alternative constructions are marked by *ọmẹ* or by *ni*:

úngwæ?æ urhǽ
2nd person classifier for animals horse

sínhạ úbóme ni kúnu?u
negative not-black nor white

'Your horse is neither black nor white.'

Juxtaposition is extremely frequent:

ikág námba ésụ ihek? kínẹhẹ?
I my-song I-sing you you-dance
'I sing and you dance.'

kégó? kipág man?í ubá
where you-saw-me what day

kipág
you-saw-me

'Where and when did you see me?'

Gapping is very rare in Chichimeco. The following example illustrates the absence of gapping:

cúcé be?é gáru?u ikág be?é
Joseph pepper he-will-sow I pepper

sutú?ume
I-will-not-sow

'Joseph will sow peppers but I won't.'

In the remaining examples, the translations reflect the wording used in elicitation.

The responses are just strings of phrases and have no structural relation to the constructions that were sought:

táʔühü   suṇų́gume
he-went-by   he-did-not-see-me
'He went by without seeing me.'

étʔu   úra   étan   ni   mahíb
he-walks his-work he-works very lazy
'He works without effort.'

íṇọʔ maʔí   nahé nehé nándü
he   difficult alone alone he-may-go

ni   manʔí eténʔ
very   what   he-fears

'He doesn't go alone because he is afraid.'

NOTE

1. The research reported in this chapter is based on field work in San Luis de la Paz, carried out in 1958 and for three months in 1968–1969. More work on Chichimeco was done in 1980 with Valente Mata, who is temporarily in Mexico City.

3. Choltí Maya: A Sketch

JOHN FOUGHT

1. INTRODUCTION. Choltí, an extinct language of the Cholan subgroup of the Mayan family, is known through a single document written in the Manche territory of Guatemala between 1685 and 1695, as established by dates and place names in the manuscript (Berendt 1876). This was donated to the American Philosophical Society in 1836 by the Academia de Ciencias de Guatemala and the head of state, Mariano Gálvez (1794–1855?), and it remains in the society's library in Philadelphia (Freeman 1966:111–112).

Most published accounts of the language are based wholly or in part on one or another of the relatively recent copies of the Philadelphia manuscript. These copies are very similar to each other, but omit some significant Choltí forms present in the Philadelphia version, for reasons which will become apparent. A brief account of the history of these copies is therefore in order.

Daniel Garrison Brinton (1837–1899) seems to have been the first scholar to recognize the importance of the Choltí material for Mayan studies. In 1869 he had a copy made for his own use and published a description of this and other Central American manuscripts then in the society's collection. Of the Choltí manuscript he wrote that it is "a small quarto of 92 leaves" (1869:224). Following a barely legible description of the missions of

1689–1692 to the Manche, the *Arte ‖ en lengua cholti que qui ‖ ere decir lengua de mil ‖ peros* begins on page 5 and ends on page 34. This version, which I will call P1, is written "in a clear hand, ornamented with scroll work and pen sketches of birds and grotesque animals" (ibid.); it is immediately followed by another grammar, P2, on pages 35–57, "in a cramped but legible hand" (ibid.), not ornamented. As Brinton recognized, the nature of the differences between P1 and P2, together with the references in both to Fray Francisco Moran (fl. 1625) as the author of the different parts of the book, made it evident that both versions are copies of an earlier source, now lost.

Perhaps because it comes first in the volume and has the more decorative calligraphy and ornamentation, P1 has served as the basis for the later copies and facsimiles. This is unfortunate, because, as Brinton had already noticed (1869:224), P2 is "fuller and more accurate." It contains examples and remarks, some of them crucial, that are not found in P1.

Following these two versions of the grammar is a section of doctrinal materials (pages 59–80), including Choltí translations of portions of a catechism, the rosary, some of the sacraments, and a manual for confession, this last partly in Spanish as well.

The rest of the manuscript is devoted to a Spanish-to-Choltí vocabulary of some 5,000 items, found mostly on the rectos of pages 81–181. Most entries gloss the Spanish headword with a single Choltí form; some give synonyms in one or both languages. There are very few examples of usage.

The fate of Brinton's copy is not known, but Karl H. Berendt (1817–1878) made a copy from it in 1871. To judge from that, Brinton or his copyist followed P1, despite Brinton's awareness of the superiority of P2. During a visit to Philadelphia in 1876, Berendt was able to compare his copy with the Philadelphia manuscript, and added variants and emendations of the Choltí forms from P2 to his transcript. His notebooks, one containing the *Arte* and doctrinal material and the other the vocabulary, are in the University of Pennsylvania Library's Brinton Collection together with a number of Berendt's excellent handwritten copies of other Mayan manuscripts and the rest of his linguistic and anthropological library and papers.

The next period of attention to the manuscript came about fifty years later. William E. Gates (1863–1940) sold a copy to the Latin American Library of Tulane University in 1924. It appears to be identical to the facsimile he published in 1935. Both contain a version of the *Arte* that follows P1 in almost every detail, even imitating the ornamentation, a rearrangement of the doctrinal material, and the vocabulary. Gates does not reveal the source of this copy, but its neat appearance and the handwriting suggest that it is very recent.

The most far-reaching analysis of Choltí, however, was carried out during this period by Oliver La Farge and Ernest Noyes. By 1929, La Farge had transcribed the *Arte*, following the Tulane copy but referring to Berendt as well. Soon after, he began corresponding with Ernest Noyes about Choltí, and they worked on the language together for several years. Their correspondence for 1932–1933, on file in the Peabody Museum in Cambridge, contains the transcripts, fragments of a grammatical restatement by Noyes dealing very insightfully with particular constructions and affixes, and various lists of lexical items. It had not reached a stage of overall integration, however.

Noyes then went to Guatemala, intending to take up the linguistic work on Chortí set aside by Charles Wisdom. Before his death in 1942, he had prepared two files, one a very rough reversal of the Moran vocabulary to Choltí-to-Spanish, and the other a substantial Chortí file; both were later incorporated into the University of Chicago microfilm series (Noyes 1957).

My own editing project, often interrupted, is now nearly finished. It will continue along the lines traced by Berendt, La Farge, and Noyes, establishing a critical text of the *Arte* by comparing P1 and P2, giving a modern grammatical restatement, appending the texts and translations of the doctrinal material, and giving a Choltí-to-Spanish and Spanish-to-Choltí glossary of all the forms from the grammar and texts as well as the original vocabulary items.

The object of this sketch is to make the main outlines of Choltí, as a representative of Cholan and Mayan, accessible to the widest possible circle of readers, including especially those with little or no technical linguistic background. Accordingly, the use of technical terms and comparative evidence will be kept to a minimum, and what cannot be avoided will be explained.

It seems entirely reasonable to expect linguists to make an effort from time to time to explain their findings to the widest possible audience. The claims of nonlinguist Mayanists for such help are especially pressing, considering the gains for them and for us to be expected from an eventual decipherment of the hieroglyphic writing system. The Cholan languages, with Choltí as their earliest documented representative, are now widely regarded as having a special contribution to make to the decipherment effort. Hence this sketch, presented in such a way that a persistent reader without special training in linguistics will, I hope, be able to understand Choltí morphology.

Linguistically trained readers are asked to remember that this is after all a sketch, and of a limited body of data at that. It does not aim for completeness, although the outline of the analysis is meant to be taken seriously.

2. PHONOLOGY. Some important features of Cholan phonology are not reflected consistently in the manuscript spellings. The modern Cholan languages, Chol, Chontal, and Chortí, are very similar to each other in their sound systems, and Choltí was presumably not much different. Three consonant positions are expected, with plain voiceless stops [p, t, k], glottalized stops [p', t', k'], nasals [m, n, ŋ], fricatives [s, š] in approximately the [t] position, with [š] a sibilant, and both plain and glottalized affricate clusters [ts, ts', tš, tš'], an [h] or [x] fricative in the [k] position, resonants [l] or [r] or both, and five or six vowels: [i, e, a, o, u] and possibly [ə] in contrast with [a]. The manuscript follows primarily Spanish spelling conventions, of course, rendering [k] as qu before i and e, and as c elsewhere. It does not consistently distinguish glottalized consonants from plain ones; though b is often used for [p'], there is no rendering of [t'] distinct from [t], and the symbol ε, often used in Highland Mayan documents for [k'], is here only a random graphic variant of c. Except for one instance of chh, there is no effort to distinguish [tš] from [tš']: both are ch or εh. Both [ts] and [ts'] are spelled tz or tʒ or z or ʒ; the last two, with ç and s, are used for [s].

There is no evidence in the manuscript spellings of an [a] / [ə] contrast. Since it is not found in all the modern Cholan languages, nothing more can be said about it in Choltí.

Vowel length is often not noted in the spellings of forms, but is sometimes indicated by doubling a vowel letter, or by the use of an accent mark, or by postvocalic h. This last spelling aggravates an already difficult problem of interpretation, since there was undoubtedly a real postvocalic fricative in some forms, sometimes indicated by h or j, and sometimes omitted. An h is often used between vowels in affix sequences, apparently as a merely graphic device for separating elements (e.g., cuxpahel 'alive' [P61], cuxpael 'alive' [P161]). The problem can only be dealt with form by form, and when justified, an h will sometimes be added to forms here.

Two other deviations from the Philadelphia manuscript spellings will be found: hyphens will be used whenever convenient to break up examples into constituent elements, and an apostrophe will be used after consonants known from comparative evidence to be glottalized, and occasionally after vowels known to be long. Since the manuscript used neither of these devices, all occurrences are my emendations. Otherwise, forms are cited in their original spellings.

3. PREDICATION. This section outlines

ways in which simple forms combine to make more complex propositions. The categories and combinations of roots and affixes identified here are examined and illustrated in more detail in later sections.

3.1. COORDINATE PREDICATION. There are two main types of construction in Choltí: one in which the two parts are *coordinate* with each other, and another in which one part is grammatically *subordinate* to the other. Examples of coordinate constructions follow:

(1) *utz Pedro* 'Pedro is good.' [P42]

(2) *utz-et* 'You are good.' [P42]

(3) *natz-et ca-na* 'You are our Mother.' [P65]

In the first two examples, the two constituents are on an equal grammatical footing. The personal suffix *-et* 'you (singular)' in (2) plays the same grammatical part as the name *Pedro* in (1). Just as (1) might be paraphrased in a heavily logical way as 'There is something which is good and is Pedro', so (2) might be read as 'There is something which is good and is you'. Like other Mayan languages, Choltí has no form corresponding to our verb 'be'. In (3), the first form is a demonstrative (cf. *natz-al* 'nearness'); the personal suffix here also forms the second element in a coordinate construction which in turn serves as the first element in a larger such construction. Its second part, however, is a subordinate type.

3.2. SUBORDINATE PREDICATION. Examples of subordinate constructions include:

(4) *ui-otot Dios* 'the house of God' [P44]

(5) *u-chu-ul Ah-itza-ob* 'the idols of the Itzas' [P37]

(6) *utz-il uinic* 'a good man' [P38]

(7) *inu-il-a misa* 'I saw Mass.' [P44]

(8) *Dios u-pat-a-on* 'God formed us.' [P40]

Examples (4) and (5) are similar in structure, but *otot* 'house' does not require a suffix when subordinated to a following head noun by the possessive prefix; *chu* 'idol' does require one, consisting here as usual of an echo or harmonic vowel and *l*. The *ah-* prefix is agentive when an action is involved (as in *ah-pol-on*, 'merchant'); it is often expressive of membership, as here, being quite compara-

ble to the *-er* suffix of English in both uses. Many adjectival uses of roots are organized as in (6), with a suffix, usually *-il* whatever the preceding vowel, marking the subordinate element. If (6) were changed to read *ui-utz-il uinic* it would mean 'the man's goodness'. The first element in (7) is a personal prefix; the next is the root meaning 'see', followed by a thematic (stem-forming) suffix, and the Spanish word for the Mass. A closer translation would be 'my seeing of the Mass'. The thematic suffix may be seen as a device for marking the linkage of verb and object, forming a construct which accepts a possessive prefix; (8) shows this same type of construction with an object pronoun in final position.

Personal prefixes, like the *ca-* 'our' of (3) and the first forms of examples (4), (5), and (7), are constituents of subordinate constructions, whereas personal suffixes are found in coordinate types.

4. ROOT CLASSES. The grammatical functions of Choltí roots are shown by their various patterns of occurrence with affixes. Some roots do not occur with affixes: these are the particles, including prepositions such as *ta/ti* 'to, at'. Most roots occurring without suffixes function as nouns or adjectives; with an appropriate thematic or other suffix or suffix combination, the same root may act as a verb. With still other suffixes, especially a final suffix composed of a vowel followed by *l*, the root may function as a derived noun or adjective:

(9) *utz* 'good'; *utz-t-ez* 'blessed' [P38; 89]

(10) *mem* 'mute'; *mem-l-ez* 'made mute' [P138; 113]

(11) *atzam* 'salt'; *atzam-i* 'salted' [P163]

(12) *c'ux* 'pain'; *ah-c'ux* 'biter'; *c'ux-u* 'bit' [P138; 106]

Because of their meanings, it would be tempting to consider the roots in (9) and (10) as adjectives, that in (11) as a noun, and that in (12) as a verb, and to regard uses of these roots with other grammatical functions as somehow derivative. In the long run, however, it is better to make the effort to see these functions as defined by the affix system, rather than as inhering in the individual roots. The

TABLE 3-1. Personal Prefixes and Suffixes

Person	Prefixes Singular	Plural	Suffixes Singular	Plural
1st	*inu-*	*cau-*	*-en*	*-on*
2nd	*au-*	*iu-*	*-et*	*-ox*
3rd		*ui-*		

TABLE 3-2. Independent Person Markers

Person	Demonstratives Singular	Plural	Objects of Preposition ta / ti Singular	Plural
1st	*natz-en*	*natz-on*	*t-in-tze*	*ti-ca-tze*
2nd	*natz-et*	*natz-ox*	*t-a-tze*	*t-i-tze*
3rd	*ne*	*natz-ob*	*t-u-tze*	*t-u-tze-ob*
	'me', etc.		'with me', etc.	

use of a thematic suffix in (11) is no less natural than in the last example of (12); conversely, the absence of thematics in the first forms of (11) and (12) is equally basic in the grammar.

Root and stem classes are based on *primary derivation*, that is, on the occurrence of a root with (or on the presence in a stem of) an affix in the first suffix position. *Particles* are roots which never have primary (or secondary) suffixes; *root stems* are occurrences of roots without primary suffixes—roots which occur in other environments with such primary suffixes. *Primary stems* are those made up of roots with primary (thematic) suffixes or, in a few instances to be discussed later, of roots with primary suffixes it is expedient to regard as deleted. Affixes occurring after primaries (and the stems they occur in) are secondaries. In example (9) above, the first stem is a root stem, and the second is a *secondary stem*, with thematic *t* (for *ta*) and secondary *-ez*. In (10), the only difference is that the intransitive primary stem of the second form has *l* (for *lau*) as its thematic suffix. The stems in (11) are root and primary types;

the first two in (12) are root stems and the last is a primary stem. Examples (5) and (6) begin with primary *l*-stems (noun forms derived by a vowel + *l* suffix). Most *l*-stems will be secondaries, however.

The same classification of stems into root, primary, and secondary types will serve to classify the predicates built out of the stems: examples like (1)–(3) above are root predications (or *athematic* predications); most of the examples in this paper, on the other hand, are either primary (thematic) or secondary predications.

4.1. PERSONAL AFFIXES. Choltí has a set of personal prefixes and a set of personal suffixes (Table 3-1). The last segment of each prefix is a glide element found only when the next segment, at the beginning of the stem, is a vowel. Plurality in the third person is marked by a suffix *-ob*.

These personal affixes are constituents of a number of sets of independent person markers having various functions (Table 3-2).

4.1.1. PERSONAL SUFFIXES. In all their occurrences, personal suffixes designate participants who have entered the state result-

47

ing from the predicated form. In the examples already seen, they are coordinate with adjectival predicates, and thus are appropriately translated as subjects in English sentences with predicate adjectives. If the preceding predicate is a Choltí intransitive stem composed of a root and a thematic suffix, the personal suffix will again be translatable as a subject, usually of an English intransitive verb. And if the preceding predicate is composed of a personal prefix, a root, and a thematic suffix forming a Choltí transitive expression, the personal suffix will be translated into English as the direct object of a transitive verb. Even in such cases, however, it should be interpreted as designating a participant having entered a state resulting from the subject's performance of the predicated act. Additional examples of each type follow:

(13) *tal-i-en* 'I came.' [P40]

(14) *c'ot-oi-et t-uy-otot* 'You arrived at his house.' [P67]

(15) *Dios u-col-o-et* 'God saved you.' [P40]

(16) *Dios u-pat-a-on* 'God formed us.' [P40]

The first two stems are intransitive thematics; the last two are transitive thematics with the suffixes in the direct object's role. Example (16) might be paraphrased as 'God has formed something: us.'

4.1.2. PERSONAL PREFIXES. The personal prefixes are equally consistent in their functions: they are always possessives, prefixed to the possessed element. The forms to which they are affixed are always substantive in function, even when they must be translated as transitive verbs. Examples have already been given of their use with root nouns, and with nouns consisting of a root and a *-Vl* suffix. (Chortí also provides a set of transitive formations based on verbal stems, most of them formed by adding a final *-Vl* suffix to the otherwise intransitive verbal formation.)

(17) *natz-en x-in-cal-e-n inu-otot* 'I will make my house.' [P44]

(18) *in-c'an-a x-ui-utz-t-ez-en naic Padre* 'I want the Father to bless me.' [P47]

(19) *lop-a-el u-cal-e t-u-il-al Padre* 'He came to see the Father.' [P48]

(20) *yual in-choh-b-en Dios* 'Now I love God.' [P44]

Example (17) illustrates the usual order and relationship of elements in a transitive predication. The middle element is a transitive stem composed of a root (*cal*) and a thematic suffix (*-e*), here flanked by the *x-* and *-n* affixes which together mark it as a future tense form according to the terminology of the *Arte*. The third element, *inu-otot* 'my house', is linked to this stem by the thematic suffix: together with the second element, it is part of a noun-like structure meaning approximately 'future making of my house'. It is this construction that is possessed by the speaker of the sentence, designated by *natz-en* 'me', and the possessive prefix (*inu-*) referring to that form.

In (18), the first constituent is a transitive stem made up of a root (*c'an*) and a thematic suffix (*-a*). Its "object" is everything following it. This second element is itself a transitive expression built on the root *utz* 'good' and the suffix *ta* (here without its vowel). This stem in turn bears a causative suffix *-ez*. The object of this inner transitive expression nested within the larger one is the next element, the personal suffix *-en* 'I'; its subject, to which the personal prefix *ui-* refers, is *Padre*, here displaced to the end, but retaining its relationship to the transitive stem. The form *naic* is a separable marker of the optative, as the *Arte* calls it. The *x-* prefix is the future marker again, without a corresponding *-n* here because the stem ends in a consonant.

Number (19) begins with an inversion of the more usual order of elements. The object of the transitive stem is the first element here; it is a derived form built on an intransitive stem consisting of the root *lop* 'come' and its thematic suffix, followed by the noun-deriving *-el* suffix. The second element has the same root *cal* 'do, make' fov᠁ . in example (17), again with its characteristic thematic suffix. The next element is a prepositional construction introduced by *ta/ti* 'at, to', a personal prefix referring to *Padre*, the root *il* 'see', and a primary (first-position) *-al* suffix.

This last element means approximately 'for the seeing of the Father'; the two preceding ones together amount to 'his act of arrival'. Note that the two *u*- prefixes do not refer to the same elements. The first refers to an unnamed third person 'subject'; the second refers to *Padre*. Finally, note the difference between the two derived noun formations, one based on an intransitive and the other on a transitive.

Example (20) shows the stem for 'love', lavishly used throughout the *Arte*, perhaps because its Spanish translation, *amar*, is the favorite regular verb of Spanish grammarians. The *-b-* verbs, however, have nothing like the number or regularity of the Spanish first conjugation to commend them. This example is a "present" form in the system of the *Arte* and accordingly has with it the particle *yual*, cognate with Chortí *uar* of similar function.

4.1.3. INTRANSITIVE PERSONAL PREFIXES. Of the Mayan languages, only Chortí and Choltí give evidence of a third set of personal affixes, and the Choltí evidence has been overlooked or brushed aside by the compilers of the *Arte* and all the later commentators as well.

The crucial passage in the grammatical portion of the manuscript is on page 55, where three uses of an *a*- prefix are mentioned: one makes intransitive presents into futures, but the passage is clearly defective—the illustrations have nothing to do with the rule; the second makes preterite passives into present participles, and again, the illustrations appear to have little to do with the rule. The last is omitted from P1 almost entirely, and amounts to an explanation of the loss of *h* in the agentive prefix *ah*- and a warning ascribed to Fray Moran to put the *h* in '*para quitar equivocasiones*'. All of the examples on this portion of page 55 appear to be agentives, with or without *h*.

In the doctrinal texts, however, there are a number of forms with third person *a*- in clearly intransitive constructions. Admittedly the significance of these, especially given the "explanation" in the *Arte*, would

not be easy to understand. It clearly eluded La Farge (1929:21n2), who accepted the agentive interpretation, and though Noyes refers to the good examples as third person forms, his interpretation was not explained.

The grammatical implications of this third set of pronouns are very important. In the other Mayan languages, and for the most part in Choltí too, thanks to the efforts of the compilers of the *Arte* to minimize the role of the intransitive prefixes, the "present tense" (i.e., imperfective) forms of verbs have possessive prefixes as their subject markers, and often, in the case of underlying intransitive stems, final suffixes marking them as nouns as well. Thus, Choltí *uix-i* 'he went', but *u-uix-n-el* 'he goes' (compare Chortí *ixin*, 'he went', but *a-axin* 'he goes', where the vowel change is automatic). Now, Chortí also has a form like the Choltí "present tense" form for this verb: *uu-ixn-er ʔkin* 'the going of the sun', 'sunset point', and it (I would say, *it too*) is a noun form.

The thematic system in Chortí provides distinct suffixes, in most cases, for roots used transitively and intransitively. Thus, the great majority of roots must be cited with two thematics: *ʔkux* 'bite' takes *-i* as a transitive, *-uan* as an intransitive; *kan* 'learn' takes *-i* and *-o*; *uai* 'lie flat' is an *-an* stem, but 'lay flat' is an *-i* transitive, and so on. A few roots take the same suffix in both cases: *at* 'bathe' is one of these, with *-i* and *-i*. Its third person forms are thus *ui-at-i* 'someone bathes someone' and *a-at-i* 'someone is bathing'.

Chortí roots having a transitive *-i* stem, the largest stem class, are also found with secondary *-pa*, *-ʔka*, and *-ma* suffixes as intransitive secondary forms, which take *a*- prefixes when imperfective, just like the few examples with *-pa* found in the manuscript. The *-Vi* class, in Chortí composed of most of the same roots as are found in the Choltí manuscript, also calls for *a*- prefixes in the imperfective, but these are not attested in Choltí. Indeed, it is unfortunately not possible to know just how close the parallels were between the two languages, given the scar-

49

city of examples. It is clear, however, that the *a-* prefix forms were in use, even though their functions were not understood by the compilers.

5. PRIMARY STEMS: THE THEMATIC SYSTEM. The thematic system is the key to Choltí morphology. Each root occurs with a particular subset of the affixes and affix combinations. This pattern of occurrence thus defines the grammatical potential of the root and guides interpretation of the construction where it is found. For each root, one suffix is an especially useful index of this grammatical potential, in that a knowledge of the root-plus-suffix combination allows us to predict the other affix combinations for that root. This key suffix is called the *thematic suffix*. Roots having the same thematic suffix share the same or nearly the same range of grammatical environments and functions: they form a stem class.

The thematic suffixes of Choltí are shown in Table 3-3. The *-i* and *-e* classes are either transitive or intransitive, as are the *-a* and *-o* classes, but the two groups differ in distribution from each other, and from the transitive *-u* class. The *-b-* class is best treated as a separate subsystem within the transitive system. The remaining four classes form intransitive stems. The symbol *V* here stands for an echo or harmonic vowel identical to the preceding root vowel; thus, the suffix is *-ai* after root *a*, *-oi* after root *o*, and so on.

5.1. TRANSITIVE. The primary transitive stem formations are the preterite (a past or perfective), the present, the future, the imperative, and a verbal *L*-noun, so called here because its formative suffix ends in *l*.

The vocalic stem classes form these stems as follows:

Preterite: personal prefix + root + thematic suffix

Present: *yual* + personal prefix + root + thematic suffix

Future: *x* + personal prefix + root + thematic suffix + *n*

Imperative: root + thematic suffix + *n*

L-noun: (personal prefix) + root + *l*-suffix

If any of the first three has a first or second

TABLE 3-3. Thematic Suffixes

Transitive/ Intransitive		Transitive	Intransitive	
-i	-a	-u	-Vi	-ta
-e	-o	-b-	-uan	-lau

TABLE 3-4. Transitive *-i* Roots and *-e* Roots

-i *Roots*	-e *Roots*
ahal 'conquer'	*cal* 'make, do'
c'aht 'ask'	*quex* 'swap'
il 'abhor'	*mequ* 'embrace'
ub 'hear'	*zet* 'break'

person object, the personal suffix will follow the formation shown above. A plural suffix, if any, comes after that.

Vocalic stems fall into three groups in relation to these formations: the *-i* and *-e* stems drop their thematic suffixes before secondary suffixes, and have *-Vl* as their *l*-suffix; the *-a* and *-o* stems drop their suffixes before secondaries also, and have *-al* as their *l*-suffix; and the *-u* class keeps its thematic before secondaries (except before the *l*-suffix, which is *-al* for this stem class also). Thematic suffixes in all these classes are retained before future and imperative *-n*.

The *L*-nouns bear a personal prefix only if possessed by some participant.

Example (17) above shows a future form of *cal*; there is a "negative future" formation also, with particle *el* and no final *-n*:

(21) *el a-ub-i axcil pehcahel* 'You will not hear evil words.' [P45]

The usual Mayan negative particle *ma* is also used in Choltí, and may be preposed to the ordinary future form to give the same result as the negative future of (21).

Examples (7) and (16) show transitive *-a* stems; (15) shows the *-o* stem *col-o* 'saved'. Example (12) shows an important *-u* stem *c'ux-u* 'bit', but only as a citation form.

50

TABLE 3-5. Transitive *-a*, *-o*, and *-u* Roots

-a *Roots*	-o *Roots*	-u *Roots*
cach 'tie'	*col* 'save'	*ahc'* 'give'
c'an 'want'	*tol* 'imitate'	*c'ub* 'believe'
ch'am 'take'		*c'ux* 'bite'
haz 'divide'		*nup* 'join'
il 'see'		*tuch* 'declare'
na't 'know'		*tzub* 'suck'
pat 'form'		
zat 'destroy'		
tzib 'write'		

TABLE 3-6. Suffix Combinations for the *-b-* Class

-b-in *Stems*	-b-en *Stems*	-b-un *Stems*
zuc 'calm down'	*choh* 'love'	*tzatz* 'help'
chui 'hang up'	*noh* 'help'	*hatz* 'help'
nuc 'lay face down'	*tzih* 'renew'?	*çat* 'cross'
		lech 'hang'
		ua 'accompany'

(22) *yual in-c'an-a in-c'ub-u u-pehcah-el Dios* 'I want to believe the word of God.' [P47]

(23) *tal-i-en t-uy-ac'-u-na-el ne-pa' t-u-ba ne-ba* 'I have just come from giving bread to the poor.' [P53]

Example (22) illustrates a common type of verb phrase, with the stem *c'an-a* 'want' used as an auxiliary: what is wanted is all that follows the auxiliary verb stem.

In example (23), the predication is the first element, modified by a prepositional phrase containing, as its object, a transitive predicate whose root is *ahc'* 'give', written here without the *h*, the passive *-na* suffix, and another secondary, the final *-el* called for because of the *u-* prefix. This second element, then, translates as something like 'from its having been given'; then comes a demonstrative and the *pa'* 'bread' (really 'tortilla') root, and another prepositional phrase meaning. literally 'to the persons of those poor'. Note

that the *-u* suffix is retained here before a secondary *-na*.

5.1.1. THE *b*-SYSTEM. There are primary and secondary *b*-suffixes, just as there are primary and secondary *l*-suffixes. The primary or thematic *-b-* class includes both transitive and intransitive stems with the suffix combinations shown in Table 3-6.

Note the precarious but real complementarity of the root vowels in these three subclasses: after root *u*, suffix *-in*, after root *o* or *i*, suffix *-en*, and after root *a* and *e*, suffix *-un*. The Chortí suffix corresponding to this one is *-ʔpa* or *-ʔpu*, discussed in Fought (1973:76–77). Noyes (1957: Memo 23, 5 March 1933) pointed out the remarkable correspondence between these stems and Yucatec stems in *-cin-ah* and *-cun-ah*.

When a secondary *-na* suffix follows these stems, the stem-final *n* contracts with the suffix-initial *n*: *choh-b-e-na-el* 'loved'. The stems shown in Table 3-6, with personal pre-

TABLE 3-7. Choltí and Chortí Imperative Suffixes

Choltí Thematic	Choltí Imperative	Chortí Thematic	Chortí Transitive Imperative
-i	*-i-n*	*-i*	*-V*
-e	*-e-n*	*-e*	*-V*
-a	*-a-n*	*-a*	*-a-n*
-o	*-o-n*	*-o*	*-o-n*
-u	*-u-n*	*-u*	*-u-n*

fix, serve as transitive preterites; with personal suffix instead, as intransitive preterites. Transitive present and future are formed by preposing the particle *yual* or the *x-* future marker; the bare stem is the imperative formation.

> (24) *yual i-tzatz-b-u-na-el ca-men-el* 'You are being helped by us.' [P50]

In (24) the personal prefix is the second person plural *i-*, and the stem is parallel to that of (23). The root *men*, one of the roots meaning 'do' in Yucatec Maya, is found in Chortí in just the function it has here, a dummy verb for the agent in passive constructions (cf. Fought 1973:72–73).

5.1.2. IMPERATIVE. The Choltí thematic system appears to be very similar to but more limited in scope than that of its nearest relative, Chortí, but this appearance may be deceptive, due more to the selection and arrangement of data favored by the compilers of the *Arte* than to the structure of Choltí. The *Arte* concentrates much of its attention on forms without thematic suffixes, and cites many forms, especially in the vocabulary lists but also frequently in the grammar, with a *-V* suffix or a *-Vn* suffix that suggest the imperative formations of Chortí, although only the latter type is given in the *Arte* as an imperative formation. Thus, Choltí *c'ux-u* 'bite, eat', so cited in the grammar, and used in examples, corresponds to Chortí *ʔkux-i* with the same meaning. The Chortí form has *ʔkux-u* as its imperative, as do all *-i* and *-e* thematics in that language; all the single vowel thematic

classes of Choltí are said to have imperatives marked by *-n* after the thematic suffix.

5.2. INTRANSITIVE. The primary intransitive formations are the preterite, the future, and the imperative. The present and the *l*-noun forms are transitives, bearing personal prefixes and ending in *-el*.

Preterite: root + thematic suffix + personal suffix

Future: *x* + root + thematic suffix + *(i)c* + personal suffix

Imperative: root + thematic suffix + *en*

Before the future marker *-(i)c*, the *-Vi* thematic drops. Others, such as the *-i* intransitive thematic, may be said to drop or to contract; still others, such as the *-lau* suffix, remain.

There are few examples of the intransitive imperative. One is apparently formed on the root *chu*, glossed in the *Arte* as '*estar*' ('be'), and bearing an *-l*. This form is probably cognate with Chortí *ʔtxu-ur*, literally 'hanging' or 'floating', but often used in contexts where '*estar*' is an appropriate translation. The imperative given is *chulen*, plural *chulenic*. Another, in the manual of confession, is the instruction to kneel: *xac-l-en*, apparently a *-lau* stem, but not otherwise attested.

A similar scarcity of attestation limits what can be said about the *-uan* class, quite common in Chortí and important in comparative Mayan. There are just three roots attested, as citation forms only: *tzuc* 'sit', *chun* 'stand, dwell' (perhaps another form of *chu* above), and *coi* 'lie down'.

Following are some attested examples of intransitive -*i* and -*e* roots:

-*i* roots:
c'ax 'fall'
pacx 'return'
tal 'come'

-*e* roots:
uay 'sleep'
uain 'sleep'

Another root which probably belongs here is *ahn* 'run', but it is not attested in thematic form. These classes, like their transitive counterparts, drop the thematic before secondary suffixes. These intransitive classes, however, have -*el* as the primary *l*-suffix. Examples (13) and (23) above show *tal* 'come' in context.

The only clear examples of intransitive -*a* stems are *lop* 'come'—shown in context in example (19)—and *xam* 'walk'. The one clear -*o* root is *chol* 'make milpa'.

The -*Vi* roots are as follows:
cham 'die'
c'ot 'arrive'
loc' 'leave'
em 'descend'
taab 'rise'
och 'enter'
tzam 'get wet'
pul 'burn'
putz 'flee'
uan 'sleep'

Comparable in importance on the intransitive side to the *b*-system transitives, the -*Vi* class includes a limited number of verbs of change of state, but among them are some frequent items. Like the -*i* and -*e* intransitives, these lose their thematics before secondary suffixes, and have -*el* nouns. Example (14) above shows *c'ot*. Most of these roots are attested in Chortí in the same thematic class. 'Die' appears in two forms, as *cham* and *tzam*, suggesting either dialect mixture in the community at the time of compilation of the *Arte* or an error in copying or transcription.

(25) *Ma ca taab-ai ti chan* 'Didn't he rise to the sky?' [P61]

The first two particles in example (25) are negative and interrogative; then comes the stem without personal affix, i.e., third person, and finally a prepositional phrase. The customary pattern for an affirmative answer is to repeat the verb stem; a negative answer repeats the negative particle and the verb stem.

The following -*lau* roots are attested:
bac 'become thin'
can 'become yellow'
lob 'become ugly'
noh 'become fat'

The glosses of these roots give their meanings as -*lau* stems; as root stems, they are "adjectives." This suffix, like the -*ta* to be discussed next, drops its syllabics before secondaries, but the consonant remains. Before -*el*, however, the entire thematic remains: *bac-lau-el* 'becoming thin'. Causatives on these stems are especially frequent in the *Arte*.

The -*ta* roots are:
tzac 'complete, right'
uz 'prepare, fix, create'
yep 'exert effort'
utz 'bless'

Another group of roots is attested with the *t*-form of this affix followed by the causative. This includes *uch'* 'give drink', *ue'* 'give food', and the very frequent *uix* 'go', which with -*t-ez* is translated as 'send along the road', 'direct'. To the extent one can be determined, something like "resultative" appears to be the semantic contribution of this affix. A causative form is found above in example (18).

5.3. *L*-NOUNS. Both transitive and intransitive vocalic primary stems form primary *l*-nouns by the substitution of one or another vowel-plus-*l* suffix for the thematic suffix. For the intransitive -*i*, -*e*, and -*Vi* stems, the most frequent *l*-suffix is -*el*, but that is not the only possibility: both *em-el* 'descending' and *em-al* are listed, the latter glossed as '*abajo*', or 'low'; *pul-al* 'burned' is also listed, identified as a passive participle in the *Arte*. For the transitive -*i* and -*e* stems, the most frequent formation is -*Vl*: *ue-el* 'feeding', *poch-ol* '*suelto*', that is, 'released, untied'. Again, however, that is not the only formation, since there are a number of *-el* suffixes in this class too: *uch-el* 'drinking'. The issue is further complicated by the prevalence of *a* vowels in the roots of the *-a* stem class, so that it is difficult to decide whether to treat a final primary suffix in this class as *-al* or *-Vl*. With some reservations, which it may be impossible to dissipate, I have decided on the *-al* analysis, since it covers roots like *il* 'see' (*il-al* 'seeing') and the *-u* class roots like *c'ub* 'believe' (*c'ub-al* 'believing') as well as the unclear cases just mentioned.

Athematic or root stems also form primary *l*-nouns, usually with *-il*, and a semantic change in the direction of abstractness: *utz* 'good', *utz-il* 'goodness'; *noh* 'big', *noh-il* 'bigness', etc.

6. SECONDARY STEMS. The category of secondary affixation is best regarded as a rather loose cover for the post-primary elements in a stem. It includes both transitive and intransitive secondary formations on either transitive or intransitive primaries; in many instances, a stem contains more than one secondary affix.

The most widely distributed and most frequently attested secondary formations are the *-na* passive, the *-ez* causative, the *-pa* reflexive, and the secondary *b-*, *l-*, and *-ia* noun types. Less numerous but equally important for comparative Mayan linguistics are the intransitive personal prefixes, known from Chortí and very clearly if rarely attested in Choltí, and the *-c'a* (middle) and *-ma* (customary) suffixes, also found in Chortí.

6.1. THE *-ez* CAUSATIVE is an important secondary suffix, forming transitive stems from both transitive and intransitive primary stems. It is often followed by other secondary suffixes, especially the passive *-na* and reflexive *-pa*. In a few forms where it precedes secondary *-el*, its form is *-za-*; with *-Vi* roots the thematic is dropped, and when final, the causative is *-ze*; otherwise it is *-ez*.

(26) *em-ei-et ti xibalba, a-loc'-ze ixte uy-animas, baxan ca-mi-ob* 'You descended

to Hell, you freed the souls of our first fathers.' [P70]

(27) . . . *u-zaz-l-ez-nah-el ca-puczic-al* . . . '. . . *the healing of our souls* . . .' [P64]

6.2. THE *-na* PASSIVE suffix is one of the most productive in Choltí. It comes after other secondaries (except the future marker *-c* and secondary *-el*), and may occur with the optional agent construction using the root *men* 'do'. Example (23) shows it with the root *ahc* 'give'. Often the forms are quite complex:

(28) *U-cux-p-ez-nah-el ixte ca-u-anima tama grasia* 'Its revival also of our souls in grace.' [P64]

The root of the first element is not the transitive *c'ux* 'bite', but an intransitive *cux* 'live', followed by a prevocalic form of the *-pa* reflexive, a causative, the passive, and a secondary *l*-suffix. The next element is a particle meaning 'also'; the last two elements have possessive prefix *ca* 'our' and preposition *tama* 'in'.

6.3. THE *-pa* REFLEXIVE. The interpretation of the *-pa* suffix as a reflexive, with the subject acting on itself, admittedly leans on Chortí evidence. The *Arte* treats this affix as another passive marker. In Chortí, it occurs with personal suffixes as a perfective or past form, and with the intransitive personal prefix set as imperfective or present in time reference. This is also the case in Choltí, as a few examples show very clearly:

(29) *t'ox-pa u-bulich ch'ich' u-bulich chac-pa ixte u-men-e-ob uy-ah-tza-il* . . . 'It broke out, his sweat of blood, his sweat reddened by the doing of his enemies . . .' [P72]

The root *t'ox* means 'break' literally, and is the root stem 'knife', presumably for a chipped flint. The next reflexive is based on *chac* 'red'. The agent construction here either omits the *l* of the more common *men-el* form by accident, or is parallel to the Chortí forms with *e-* as a definite article for the following form, or it may be a thematic suffix.

(30) *a-quex-pa ne-pa' ti-choh-u-ia bact-al cau-ahau-il Jesu X^to a-quex-pa ne-uino*

t-u-choh-u-ia ch'ich'-el 'The bread turns itself by love into the flesh of Our Lord Jesus Christ; the wine turns itself by love into blood.' [P63]

In example (30) the reflexive stems with root *quex* 'swap' have the intransitive prefix *a-* as found in Chortí forms comparable to these. In Chortí these prefixes mark the subjects of intransitive imperfectives. The *-u-* spellings in the *choh* stems are merely graphic variants of *b*.

6.4. THE *-c'a* OF MIDDLE VOICE. The *-c'a* suffix is attested only in citation forms. Examples like *putz-c'a* 'flee', *patz-c'a* 'become light, dawn', and *tip-c'a* 'swell up' appear to be parallel to the Chortí "middle" suffix *-ʔka*, as is the noun formation *uai-ac'* 'dream', identical in form and meaning to the corresponding Chortí form. The examples in the manuscript are consistent with the interpretation given in Fought 1973:74 as designating an act performed by the subject "in and of itself," as for instance green lumber may be said to split, or a ripe gourd (when heated) may burst.

6.5. THE *-ma* USITATIVE. The *-ma* suffix in Chortí is used with actions performed as part of an occupation, or at least with comparable frequency. The evidence of the Choltí manuscript, also attested only in citation forms, is not good, but a similar element may be behind such items as *chil-ma-n* 'torcer hilando' ('twine or twist while spinning') or *oh-ma-el* 'herber' ('weeding').

Both the *-c'a* and the *-ma* suffixes presumably belong in the same position class with the reflexive *-pa*, and presumably both may be followed by the causative, but there are no such examples.

6.6. SECONDARY *b*-STEMS. Stems belonging to the *b*-system have a verbal noun formation spelled either *-b-ia* or *-be-ia* (for *-b-en* roots). The former spelling is doubtless due to phonological raising or assimilation of the *e*. The Chortí cognate of the final suffix ends in [*h*], and the Choltí form probably did as well. This same final element occurs in both languages as a nominalizing suffix after the causative as well: *ah-cham-s-ah* or *-s-iah* 'one who kills', or *ah-choh-be-iah* 'one who loves'. Note also *can-t-ez-nah-ib* 'place where learning is caused'.

The relation of the other secondary *b*-formations to the primary *b*-system is doubtful, but most promising in the case of the "participle" *-b-il*. Both primary and secondary *-b-* elements are sometimes found in the same form: *choh-b-en-b-il in-men-el* 'loved by me'. This formation is also found with "noun" roots (*Dios mi-b-il* 'God the Father') and of course with vocalic thematic roots, such as *il-b-il* 'seen', or better, 'the seen'.

Finally, there is a verbal noun formation in *-b-a* with roots not belonging to the *b*-system, such as *quex-b-a* 'a trade', and *zat-b-a* 'loss'.

6.7. SECONDARY *L*-NOUNS. Some of the uncertainties of analysis noted for the primary *l*-formations are also found in the secondaries, particularly in the case of roots having *a* vowels and *-a* thematics, where the choice of *-Vl* or *-al* interpretations is difficult. The form *bacat* (Chortí *ʔpahkat*) is translated as 'animal flesh', and human flesh is *bact-al*. Whether this is primary *-al* (or *-Vl*) or secondary depends on the status of *bacat* in relation to *bac* 'bone' and the *-ta* suffix. A further complication is introduced by the fairly numerous forms in *-t-al* with other root vowels, such as *chun-t-al* 'seat', 'dwelling place', and *coi-t-al* 'lying down'.

The great majority of secondary *l*-nouns, however, of whatever stem class, have *-el* as a final suffix, as in examples (22)–(24), and in numerous other forms cited throughout.

4. Tarascan: From Meaning to Sound

PAUL FRIEDRICH

0. PREFATORY NOTE. This study is the gist of about 500 pages of published or at least drafted analysis which, in turn, was based on three years of field work in 1955–1956, 1966–1968, and 1970 (resulting, in part, in 300 pages of text and three feet of 3 × 5 cards with one to ten lexical entries each). From mid-1967 until 1972 I spoke Tarascan flu-

ently. My work has been mainly with northern dialects—intensively, those of Cocucho, Tiríndaro, and San José de Ocumicho, supplemented by extensive research elsewhere in the Zacapu Valley and the Eleven Pueblos. I also did a dialect survey that encompassed twenty-six towns all over the area. My northern dialects, in any case, while not constituting a linguistic region, do differ considerably from those of Lake Pátzcuaro where the bulk of anthropological and linguistic investigations have been carried out. Notable among the differences between the northern and sierra dialects in question and those from the Pátzcuaro region (and others) are the merger of /e/ and /o/ with /i/ and /u/. Three of the sierra towns have, as a diagnostic morphological peculiarity, -ku and -kuri for the practically pan-Tarascan -kwa and -kwari (a nominalizing suffix, and one denoting individual action).

The components in this sketch vary in their status. The short syntax was done for this description and is, of necessity, quite tentative. Most of the morphology, ethnography, semantics, and some of the style (e.g., in the stories) reflects a great deal of prior work by myself and others. The phonetics draws on published work by myself that still seems valid, whereas the phonology has been greatly improved from that of my 1975 monograph (e.g., away from the then fashionable versions of distinctive feature analysis and rule ordering). I have, in general, limited myself to suggesting many of the relations between lexical and grammatical structures, on the one hand, and, on the other hand, cultural ones; for example, the relation between syntactic subordination and cultural pragmatism; between body part imagery and concreteness; between distinct styles and syntactic sets and cultural sets; etc. For other "top-to-bottom" grammars, incidentally, see Henderson 1960 and Dixon 1972—to both of which I was referred by Tony Woodbury after this chapter was completed.

Aside from what is indicated in the bibliography, this chapter reflects varying debts to the comprehensive dictionaries of Maturino de Gilberti (1559), Morris Swadesh (1969), and Pablo Velázquez Gallardo (1978); to the specific grammatical insights of Mary L. Foster (1969), Morris Swadesh (1969), and Allan C. Wares (1956); to the critical comments on my earlier work by John Attinasi (personal communication, mainly on Friedrich 1969b and 1970—morphology and shape categories), Louanna Furbee (personal communication, mainly on phonology), William Labov (in Friedrich 1975, on phonological dialectology), and Michael Silverstein (in Friedrich 1971a, 1974a, and 1974b, especially on aspect and dialectology); to many valuable conversations about all levels of Tarascan with Margaret Hardin and Lisa and Max Lethrop; to the support and encouragement of Norman McQuown while I was in the field; to the native expertise and helpfulness of Gonzalo Aguilar, Feliciano Santiago, and other Tarascans too numerous to mention here; and to the critical reading of various stages of this manuscript by John Attinasi, Ranjit Chatterjee, Deborah Friedrich, Paul Lifman, Alexis Manaster-Ramer, Bruce Mannheim, and Tony Woodbury. Finally, I would like to dedicate this sketch to Norman ("Mac") McQuown, in recognition of his talent and achievements in the field of Mexican Indian languages and linguistics in general.

1. INTRODUCTION. Tarascan, like Basque, has not been related to any other language genetically—and this despite efforts by leading linguists to group it with Mayan, Mixe, Zuñi, and even Quechua (e.g., Swadesh 1966). Speakers of early Tarascan mixed with other tribes in and around what is now the state of Michoacán in southwestern Mexico about the first part of the second millennium A.D. After this there evolved a powerful and diversified empire with several capitals, the main one at Tzintzuntzan on the shores of Lake Pátzcuaro; the Tarascans defeated the Aztecs in 1424 and never paid them tribute. Since the conquest by the Spaniards in the 1520s, Tarascan has been maintained as a

language island due to the cold, mountainous terrain, the Tarascans' ability to defend themselves, and their attachment to what is felt to be a more beautiful sounding language than Spanish. Another frequent Tarascan criticism of Spanish is that its speakers leave out parts of words. Today the majority of Tarascan speakers are bilingual to some extent, and about a quarter of the population—especially among men and children, and in certain villages—is more fluent in Spanish. Tarascan is replete with Spanish loans, and a great deal of routine conversation can be conducted in either language, the speaker converting with facility between sets of formulae—a sort of potential instant conversion. Spanish language influence has been markedly strong where there has been the greatest exposure to the material culture, political and legal life, and the Catholic ritual of the Mexican nation. Individual Tarascan communities, on the other hand, differ greatly in the degree of this exposure; parts of the Lake Region, all of the Zacapu Valley, and commercial centers are at one extreme; at the other, in a 100 percent Tarascan-speaking hamlet it is said, "Some leave here, but none ever come to stay." Yet there is no necessary connection between geographical marginality and the degree of hispanicization: some towns in the core of the area shifted to Spanish in the last century, while others retain their Tarascan practically intact outside the main perimeter.

Tarascan, despite this interpenetrating bilingualism, was, in 1970, still spoken by about 50,000 peasants, that is, artisans, wife-mothers, fishermen, woodsmen, and small-patch farmers. It was spoken by all or nearly all of the people in about 50 of the 116 towns that are significantly Tarascan in their culture—and are so viewed by their neighbors. In terms of both native opinion and many objective indices, the area falls into three major dialect zones: (1) the Lake Region, (2) the Eleven Pueblos, and (3) the Sierra (with West Sierra as possibly a fourth). At another level, a careful but incomplete dialect survey has established about a dozen specific regions

(Friedrich 1971a). Isolate towns, finally, are recognized in the extreme east (Cuanajo), north (Zipiajo), and west (Pamatácuaro). The towns themselves range from under 100 to over 10,000 in population, but the majority run between 500 and 3,000 (compare West 1948).

According to sensitive speakers, town dialects are recognized after hearing a few words or sentences on the basis of overall intonation (the main clue) and tell-tale words (especially for food and clothes). Also useful for such identification are phonetic segments and grammatical structure; there are, for example, fourteen variants of the past habitual aspect morpheme. The speakers of these dialects do not imitate each other, despite the presence of factors usually associated with such imitation: some pueblos are a few hundred yards (or even a few yards) apart; some neighboring pueblos differ significantly from each other in wealth and power; and the Sierra dialects are felt to be more correct and "legitimate." This is "pueblo dialectology" (as contrasted with the familiar situation of imitation across class lines, or features radiating from a prestige center).

2. DISCOURSE AND STYLE. The differences between villages are transcended by pan-Tarascan styles in discourse that depend on the situation, the status and role of the speakers, and the functions and goals of the act of speech. Out of these many styles, nine can be briefly characterized here.

(1) One striking style is used mainly by women, including adolescent girls, when speaking with each other at a distance—between back yards, or adjoining fields, or even hillsides. One fourteen-year-old, Chucha Aguilar, used to climb a castor oil tree in her yard and converse at great distances: phonetic tension high, every syllable clear, and many final syllables before a pause drawn out clearly. It is called the 'strong throat' style (wiŋá-ča-n, the root for 'strong' plus the suffix for 'throat').

(2) A second style is that of a woman speaking to the child she is nursing, breast feeding, and the like. The tone is soft, the pitch

vertically modulated (as seems to be true for practically all languages).

(3) The third style, of little girls chattering to each other, resembles the mother-child style, at times, but differs in obvious ways—for one thing, it is often an *imitation* of adult conversation.

(4) A fourth style, shared by both sexes, is the practical one where the speaker focuses on a job such as loading pottery on a donkey; the scores of metaphors that are latent in the language for referring to pots and donkeys are in this case left relatively unfelt and unexploited. The boundaries here are loose, however: a given situation or speaker may transform the work-a-day into a fun session. And there are other conversational styles, such as that of unstressful, routine chatting, discussion, and news-swapping.

(5) A fifth style, limited largely to men, involves speaking to animals, whether domestic or wild, or imitating their sounds, which are, of course, partly outside the usual scope of Tarascan phonology; a significant part of a day may be spent using such speech forms by a man working or hunting alone.

(6) A sixth style is that of chatting and joking between men during harvests, drinking, and other group situations. Here there is less stress on the practical and more on playing with the sexual connotations of syllables and words.

(7) Seventh is public speech, used particularly for political debate in the town hall or school room. Limited almost entirely to men, it has the maximum of Spanish words and constructions and of switching between the two languages.

(8) Another style is used for prayers, as at a fiesta, or for pronouncing other fixed and relatively religious texts: it makes use of many Spanish words and even paragraphs, but also many rare and archaic Tarascan elements. Often these texts are memorized, and transmitted by specific persons. The speeches of the matchmaker at a betrothal, for example, or of a performer in the Easter pageant may be sold at a price.

(9) Story telling is practiced principally by tellers before groups at harvests, or in the evening, or during competitions, although parent-to-child and adult-to-adult telling is also important. Stories are unique in the degree to which they include other styles—except, for example, the woman's *wiŋáčan*. And stories are marked linguistically to a unique degree: (a) by introductory formulae, (b) by the artful use of bilingual switching, (c) by a relatively high incidence of long strings of infinitive clauses linked by a copula (this is shared by all narrative and extended report), (d) by the frequency of the past indefinite verbal category (*š-p*) interwoven with the quotative (*ŋa*), sometimes even in the same word, as in the introductory formula *haṛá-š-p-ti-ŋa* 'there once was long ago'; (e) by a high degree of phonetic play, unusual double entendre, and the rhyming of punch lines, as in the story where two thieves are admiring the beautiful purple color of the maize kernels they are stealing, saying, 'It is purple' (*waṛó-ti-s-ti*), only to be pounced on by the landlord who has been listening to them and who shouts, 'And this is an ox goad' (*ka ima garó-ti-s-ti*). Other punch lines have a great deal of internal poetic texture—such as the one concerning the Water Serpent who is a 'very₁-very₂-big-big-one' [*k'ór-méŋk-k'ér-k'ér'má*] (note the five successive stressed syllables and the retention of medial aspiration).

All of the nine discourse styles above can be named by Tarascan words or idioms, but, to my knowledge, only the strong-throat, male joking, prayer, political oratory, and story-telling ones regularly are: explicitness about folk genres is a matter of degree. The story-telling style, ordinary, routine conversation, and paradigmatic interviewing by myself (not a Tarascan style, obviously) are, in any case, the main sources for this sketch.

2.1. SALIENT DIMENSIONS OF MEANING. Let us inspect some salient meanings in the liminal zones between syntactic semantics and cultural semantics, zones that seem interesting from at least three or four points of view: Tarascan; contemporary American; and cross-linguistic and anthropological. The following inventory of such semantic fields and foci is based in part on rigorous descriptions of subsystems (e.g., space categories or local political relations); in part it is frankly, though not purely, impressionistic.

(1) A pervasive classification of objects in terms of shape—long, flat, or round—is observed when counting, and is implicit in several parts of the grammar and in some nonlinguistic patterns.

(2) A deep level of colors that includes black-dark, white-light, red, green, and yellow-golden; and a more superficial level that often involves Spanish loans (e.g., blue, magenta). Both levels have pan-Tarascan associations—for example, red with sex, the body, and infancy, black with non-Tarascan things, and green with beauty.

(3) Extreme sensitivity to details of physical surface, textures, degrees of fineness and coarseness, and whether matter is particulate, continuous, or solid. A relatively differentiated nomenclature for the basic perceptions—sight, touch, hearing, smell; for example, six verbal roots for shades of 'to stink'.

(4) Great, focal attention to maize, the details of its cultivation, the stages of its growth—the initial needle, the stalk, the parts of the plant and the cob, the harvesting process, all the maize products and their preparation and use. The maize plant is often used as a metaphor of the human body.

(5) The body as orienting principle for abstract spatial meanings, and in the object worlds of the home, ceramics, lumbering, etc. Linguistically conditioned sensitivity to positions and conditions of the body (e.g., degrees and varieties of fatness). Corporeal symbolism is not only salient in syntax and lexicon but pervasive morphologically through the thematic suffixes of space.

(6) A critical line between human and animal, and between human-animal and all other, and between verbal (rational) and preverbal (nonrational), is drawn in many parts of the lexicon and grammar, in differing verbal roots, and in uses of the classifier system.

(7) A strong sense for the hidden, domestic, or private, versus the open and public; kinsman, friend, and compadre versus the rest. Typical of the languages of peasant societies, the Tarascan language is rich in terms for suspicions, malicious motives, gossip, witchcraft, vengeance, threats of robbery and conspiracy, seduction or abduction of women. On the other hand, it is also rich in terms for acts and norms of cooperation between friends, relatives, political allies, villagers, and the like: "united or separate?" is the question. There is great semantic elaboration of the details of ritual—individual and communal, calendrical and occasional. Many idioms and sections of the morphology hinge on whether action is alone, or in social groups.

(8) Strong orientation to the physical, concrete, and pragmatic, whether in practical, everyday affairs or in dreams and tales.

(9) Pervasiveness of aspect categories in the grammar.

There are many interconnections between the above categories; for example, the orientation toward the body is reticulated with the predilection for mockery in social control by means of the spatial (usually "body part") suffixes which occur in so many pejorative idioms.

Tarascan, on the other hand, is lacking in such areas as names of stars, complex numbers, and religious emotions, and, grammatically, in certain nuances of tense and cross-linguistically familiar sentence types.

The categories just discussed, particularly the corporeal, public/private, malevolent/harmonious, and individual/social-cooperative, are often accompanied by expressive double entendre, irony, mockery, and the varieties of "Indian humor" (e.g., to laugh at mishap or injury—including to oneself).

2.1.1. PHONETIC-ORTHOGRAPHIC NOTE. This interpretation of Tarascan moves from meaning down through a semantically oriented grammar to a micro-phonetics that is sensitive to sociocultural context (compare Hoijer et al. 1945). Such an arrangement is designed to be relatively interesting to the reader, but also calls for some differences in notation; in particular, in the discussion of semantics, syntax, and most of the morphology, it is the *meanings* (glosses, etc.) which, in general, have to be cited first, followed by the Tarascan *forms*; one exception to this rule is where a form has just been cited and is itself the object of discussion. As we get closer to the "lower" levels, there is a gradual change in the order of citation until in the final, phonological sections the form has to be cited first. This model has the theoretical advantage of suggesting that language is a process both for encoding (mainly from meaning to sound) and decoding (mainly from sound to meaning).

Stress is accompanied by a slight rise in pitch, and is free on nonsuffixal roots; suffixes (with the exceptions indicated) are not stressed. The high retracted or "central back" vowel somewhat resembles the unstressed vowel in the English adverb "just," except that it is retroflexed. The back nasal, $/\eta/$, is generally farther back than the English "*ng*." The units $/kw/$ and $/k'w/$ are something like, respectively, the stop after $/s\text{-}/$ in the English "squint" and the initial in "quick." The flapped $/r/$ resembles the $/t/$ in American English "water," whereas the retroflex $/ṛ/$—produced by curling the tongue tip back—is similar to the retroflex $/r/$'s of the East Indian languages. The letter $/ǰ/$ stands for a sound like the consonants in "judge." Voiceless vowels before a pause are denoted by capital letters, tension by an inverted quotation mark ('). The shishy $/s/$ has not been marked as such where it occurs before the conditioning $/i/$, but elsewhere is denoted by an acute accent $/ś/$. Also, for practical considerations (e.g., the reader's convenience), final unstressed $/i/$ and $/i/$ have been deleted, as they normally are, after $/n/$, $/ś/$, $/š/$, and $/¢/$. Roots and suffixal units, for the same reason, are usually cited without indicating morpheme breaks; for example, the 'head' suffix almost always appears in speech as $/h¢i/$ (except when, for example, the $/h/$ is replaced by $/p/$ in 'suddenly-head'); similarly the link *éŋga* is denoted as such, rather than with the underlying $/én\text{-}ka/$. (For the marginal status of the voiced stops, $/ś/$, and the

labiovelars, see section 6.2 below.) In what follows I have indicated breaks between morphemes with hyphens. All Tarascan forms are italicized without differentiating between structural levels, except when phonemes, for partly heuristic reasons, are set off by slashes. A phonetic notation is enclosed in square brackets [ ]. Dialectal note: in this sketch the forms *-ku* and *-kuṛi* have been used for the nominalizing and individual action suffixes, respectively—except when citing a form found elsewhere and believed not to be used in Cocucho. My reasons for using the Cocucho forms are detailed in Friedrich 1975, Chapter II.

3. SYNTACTIC PROCESS AND STRUCTURE. Basic processes in syntax order symbols linearly. For the clause, the deeper and more intuitive ordering is:

LINK + SUBJECT + MODIFIER + OBJECT + VERB.

Here LINK stands for the copula (*ka*), the subordinating adverbs, and the like; the relative order of VERB and OBJECT is not strongly motivated.

Moving down to a lower level we have the following twelve elements. They not only refer to syntactic functions, but can be converted into actual forms in the terminal words of the linear string:

Copula + Subordinator + Adverb$_1$ + Subject + Enclitics (Adverbial, Pronominal) + Adverb$_2$ + Indirect Object + (Pronominal, or Short) Object + Verbal Auxiliary$_1$ + Main Verb + Verbal Auxiliary$_2$ + Particle.

Obviously, the necessity for such relative ordering varies: the copula-subordinator-subject order is essentially obligatory; the adverb$_2$–(indirect) object order is considerably more flexible; the object-verb rule is weak. Obviously, also, no one clause actually fills out the full potential of this extended formula; for one thing, while a clause may range to over a dozen words in length, the majority have only four to eight words. But the great majority of the protean forms of the actual clause also conform more or less to the order just given, or can be derived from it by simple rules of reordering. Numerous examples

61

of partial realization of this ordering appear in the text below.

Here are some typical and frequent orders and reorderings. Many orders consist of a single word such as a noun subject, or an adverbial phrase set off by pauses, or a full verbal form with seven or eight morphemes. Many near-minimal clauses are limited to LINK plus SUBJECT plus VERB. Many clauses reflect simple but powerful constraints; for example, against more than two adverbs such as 'now' in the adverb$_1$ slot. As one expands the length of the clause there are two general patterns: first, to fill each slot with usually only one and rarely more than two potential members; and, second, not to overload the clause as a whole—in terms of both the number of words and the total information. Major reorderings that prevent overloading are the following:

(1) The word in the adverb$_2$ slot tends, as it gets longer, to be moved to a position after the verb, and this is almost obligatory with an adverbial phrase of several words.

(2) The indirect object may occur after the verb, and there is a set of constructions with first/second person enclitics in which it becomes obligatory to postpose the disambiguating pronominal object or indirect object.

(3) Short objects and, often, pronominal ones are generally preverbal and, in such cases, are fused by sandhi to the following verb, as in *míswámukun* 'to toll mass'. Objects with two or more words, especially long words, tend to be placed after the verb.

These postposings of object and adverb elements, when combined with each other, yield scores of alternate extended formulae: you may find, for example, three successive postposed objects!

(4) The verbal auxiliaries$_1$, which are aspectually inceptive and completive, are in complementary distribution with the verbal auxiliaries$_2$, which are aspectually durative.

(5) Verbal anaphora. When reference has been established in the first clause, the subject, object, and verbal categories are normally left unstated or are only affirmed intermittently in the following concatenations, which may run to a half dozen or more linked clauses; text, social context, and the simple infinitive suffice. For example, 'I went to cut firewood and cut my foot and lots of blood came out', where the infinitive would be used for 'cut' and 'came out'.

Tarascan has a great number of additional, relatively optional rules of syntax, of ways of rendering constructions more or less marked; some are associated with particular styles. Let us look at two examples:

(1) Topicalization of the subject, object, or adverb through preposing before the body of the sentence, as in 'A story, of so-and-so, thus I heard it in my home town . . .' A noun or an adverb may be topicalized through existential verbalization, as in *pawándiku* 'the following day' (from *pawáni* 'tomorrow'), which goes to *pawándikweesti* 'it is the following day'.

(2) Emphasis may be achieved through the many possible commutations of word order within the clause, and this is done, in particular, with noun plus adjective and with auxiliary$_1$ plus verb: 'I to work will go', instead of, 'I will go to work'. Such reordering can become subtly pervasive, as in the spooky Dream Spirit story where almost all of the objects, including short pronominal ones, come after the verb.

Second, the powerful rules of fusing a link with a following subject—or a short object with a following verb—may be broken for emphasis by means of extraposition. For example, 'That's very much stink-stink, the filth' (in other words, 'That's why the filth stunk so much', said, in this case, of a drinking establishment after a fiesta). Here the reduplicated verb, *kiní-kiní-hku-ndi-n*, is followed by the subject, *hin*. Such extraposition is not tied to any one style.

Other major processes in the syntax are dealt with below (some of them in section 4.1.9). Many typologically familiar processes are absent or inconsequential, such as a passive transformation with an overt semantic-agent phrase.

3.1. COORDINATION AND SUBORDINATION:

THE LINKS. The links, as noted, conjoin and subordinate the clauses which they introduce. Coordination is usually simple, and is done mainly with the copula, *ka*; with the adversative 'but', *péru* (and 'yes-but', *hó-peru*); or simply by the paratactic juxtaposition of clauses.

Subordination, the dominant syntactic process, involves complex rules that relate over a dozen subordinators with four moods: the independent and three subjunctives. The features of meaning include time, place, aspect, manner, quantity, probability and possibility, purpose and intention, consequence and cause, evidence and doubt, and direction of implication.

(1) *Pára* ('so that', 'in order that', and the like) subordinates clauses of purpose and result. It calls for a verb in the generic participle (sometimes labeled "infinitive") or, much less often, the imperative: 'Watch out, so you don't fall' (*šé, par nó kwaráḍin*). Two alternate, compound subordinators, *párika* and *páreśka*, meaning 'in order that', take the same verb forms, and the conditional as well. *Pórki*, takes the future; like the others, it is Spanish-derived.

(2) *Éka*, one of the basic subordinators that begin in /e/, means about equally 'if' and 'when' (e.g., it is the translation equivalent of Spanish *si* and *cuando*). Less often it means 'while'. It introduces clauses of result, condition, future state, clauses contrary to fact, and the like. *Éka* as 'when' can refer to a completed action that intersects with the durative time span referred to by the verb in the main clause. 'They met me as I was leaving town' has a dependent clause that consists of 'when/as' (*éka*), first person subject enclitic (*-n*), 'I' (*hi*), 'to come out of the center' (*wé-a-ku-n*), 'to be' (*há-*), past indefinite (*p*), first subjunctive (*ka*). All together: *ékan hi wéakun hápka*. In other cases the reference in the main and subordinate clause can be roughly coterminous, as in 'I saw (her) while she bathed' (*hi shé-š-ka ék-imá hikwá-p-ka*). But the versatile *éka* also often functions to relativize, as in 'The honeycomb that (*éka*) the conifer had on top'. *Éka* takes the first

subjunctive ending (*-ka*), or less often the conditional.

(3) About equally important are *éŋga* 'that' and its half-dozen derivatives, such as *naní-eŋga* 'there where'. These generally serve to introduce completive or complementary clauses with the verb in the first subjunctive mood; for example, '(I've drunk up all) that I earned' (*éŋga-n andá-p-ka*). At other times *éŋga* subordinates a clause with a verb that refers to a duration or state vis-à-vis the completed action referred to by the verb in the main clause: 'There it's all burnt out where I used to live.'

(4) *Emáŋga* can be glossed variously as 'who/he/she', and the like; for example, 'A very little one, who in Spanish (*turí*), is called (*arí-*), *chaparítu*' (*emáŋga túri-himbó arí-h-ka čaparítu*). Although morphologically derivative (*imá* plus *éŋga*), *emáŋga* is coordinate with the main subordinators in frequency and saliency in the semantic field.

(5) *Eśka* means 'when' or 'that'. It appears in several compound subordinators (*kóm-éśk-éŋga*) and takes the independent or sometimes the first subjunctive ending. '(They say) that the mouse is a female' (*éśka kutsí-i-ś-p-ka*).

(6) *Péeka* is at one level a hesitation form, like *áŋku* 'may be'. As a subordinator it introduces a clause, bounded by pauses, that is then followed by a subordinate clause. The mood of the verb in the subordinate clause is, depending on the degree of definiteness, the independent or the first subjunctive. *Péeka* constructions are often preceded by short performative clauses about the evidence, as in, '(I don't know,) I think he bought lots of land': *péeka* 'I think', *kániku* 'much', *ečéri* 'land', *pyá-ka* 'bought'. *Péeka* clauses are common in conversation, almost absent in some other styles.

(7) *Himbóka* 'because (of)' subordinates clauses of explanation, motivation, and the like, and goes with a verb in the second subjunctive, that is, the first/second person *-ka* is used for the third person; for example, the final *-ka* in *himbó-ka akw-ée-ś-ka* 'because it's food'. But sometimes this subordinator is fol-

lowed by the independent mood (for reasons not now clear, but probably emphasis).

(8) The deictic-emphatic particle -*si* is normally suffixed directly to particles such as *andí* 'why', or pronouns, or deictics such as the third person *imá*. But its main instance is after the postposition *himbó* to form an independent causative with a post facto causative meaning that introduces clauses about something that has happened. For example, '(My brothers work,) that's why they harvested a lot' consists, in Tarascan, of 'that's why' (*himbó*), third person plural enclitic (-*ksi*), deictic-emphatic (-*si*), 'a lot' (-*wáni*), plural subject (-*ŋa*), 'harvest' (*koséča*), 'do, make' (*u*), third subjunctive ending (-*h*), third person (-*ti*). All together: *himbóksiś wáŋan koséčúhti*. For subjunctive endings see section 4.1.9.3.

A common kind of subordination has various subordinators, and both verbs in the conditional: for example, 'If-I (*éka-n*) I would/could earn (*andá-pirin-ka*) more, I would/could go (*ní-pirin-ka*) to Mexico'. Either clause can come first, after the subordinator—as is true of many of these constructions. In other such cases the main clause is in the future, the subordinate in the conditional.

Yet another important subordination has *t'wín* ('while' and the like) governing the main clause, with the verb usually in the progressive or habitual aspect, and *éka* governing the dependent clause (or *éka hambéri* 'until').

hučí-i-ti waṛi-i-ti t'win   uṛún
my   wife   meanwhile to-grind

hará-si-n-ti
is (present habitual)

éka   -n   hambéri hí
when (first person enclitic) up to   I

ni-a-nta-   -a-   -ka
arrive-home (future) (person)

My wife is usually grinding corn when I arrive.

64

Many other subordinators have been borrowed from Spanish, such as *ántede* 'before', *ástaka* 'until', and *másdeke* 'moreover'.

The links, including all the subordinators, make up a small, almost closed set. In this they resemble the interrogatives, the various pronominals, and the numbers.

The sketch above has noted the multivocalism of the subordinators, particularly in 'when/if'; concomitantly, their functions overlap to a significant degree.

Six of the eight subordinators above contain the copula *ka* as their final element—all but the borrowed *pára* and the forms in -*si*. *Ka* thus functions as a generic symbol of nexus in syntax. The complex subordinators such as *é-ka* are probably felt as units much of the time, although most of the initial elements are clearly pronominal, and only *pée-* has no independent meaning.

3.2. QUESTIONS AND COMMANDS. Several suprasegmental patterns can mark a question, notably the lengthening of a final vowel, as in *nó-ri waṛá-a?* 'Won't you dance?' Second, a question may be signaled by order, notably by moving the negating particle to initial ·position, as just illustrated. Third, Tarascan has an interrogative particle, *andí*. Fourth, there are several interrogative suffixes: the progressive -*si*, as in *wéka-si-n t'ú t'irén?* 'Do you want to eat?' (This -*si* is homophonic with the deictic-emphatic.) Also, there is the indefinite-dubitative, the suffix -*pi*. The most important question signal is the suffix -*ki*, and it occurs in the large paradigm of interrogatives that correspond to the indicatives: for example, *imá t'irésakí?* 'Is he eating?' The other primary symbol of question is a set of forms that begin in *n-*: *né?* 'who?', *naní?* 'where?', and so forth.

Questions overlap pragmatically with commands, which may be expressed by the generic participle or the bare root, as in *hanó!* or, in the plural, *hanó hé!* 'Come in!' Negative commands are usually formed with the initial particle *á-* plus the deictic-emphatic: *ási hanón!* 'Don't come in!' A command may be made more courteous by adding the second person plural enclitic -*htsi*. For the first

TABLE 4-1. Verbal Roots

	Active	Middle
Free	Class I	Class II
	e.g., *pá-* 'carry, take'; *-ku*, *-ta*, jussive *-ra*	e.g., *p'ukú-* 'ripen'; causative *-ra*
Bound	Class III	Class IV
	e.g., *ȼi-tá-* 'loose'; *-ku*; RD-*ta*	e.g., *hawá-ra-* 'to rise'; RD-*hku*, etc.

RD: reduplication.
See section 4.1.3 for discussion of the suffixes *-ku*, *-ra*, and *-ta*. See section 4.1.2(3) for *-hku*.

person plural hortatory, which is fairly common, the first person plural future is used. Thus, *nirá-* 'to go', is shifted to *niwá-* and the person ending *-ka* is added, followed by the optional pronoun, *hučá* 'we', to yield *niwákač huča!* 'Let's go!'

Perhaps unique to Tarascan is the reproachful mode, formed with *-(r)een* and usually preceded by the question particle *andí*, as in *andí-ni-s maróa-t-een?* 'Why were you serving me?' Such reproaches are usually polite or grateful.

4. WORD STRUCTURE.

4.1. THE VERBAL SYSTEM.
About 700 essentially verbal roots, such as 'to scratch' (*katsí-* and two other forms), function mainly in the verbal morphology. And there are, at the other extreme, roots such as 'leech' that function mainly in the nominal system. But other roots are between these poles, and any nominal root can be verbalized to some extent, just as any verbal root can be nominalized at least in some ways. Many of the 170-odd suffixes are verbal.

For the verb as a whole there are three comprehensive parts: root, theme formative, and conjugational suffix. At a more extended and concrete level there are eleven slots:
Root + Reduplicated Root + (Inner Layer) Voice + (Inner Layer) Adverb₁ + Spatial + Instrumental-Jussive + (Outer Layer) Voice₂ + (Outer Layer) Adverb₂ + First Conjugational (Aspect, etc.) + Second Conjugational (Person) + Enclitics.
In actual output, Tarascans compose and understand words with eight or more morphemes, and such words show up in texts. But few words fill over seven positions, and most fill four to six. Incidentally, the formula for the long verbal word (above) is obviously analogous to that for the clause in section 3 above. This is one aspect of the close relation—here a partial iconicity—between syntax and morphology in Tarascan (and many other American Indian languages).

Let us turn to the verbal theme. The order of presentation below will strictly follow the order of elements in the long verbal word, beginning with classes of roots and continuing through types of motion ("outer layer adverbials"). Conjugational suffixes are then dealt with in *their* proper order. The final enclitics are dealt with later (in section 4.2.2), along with pronouns and deictics.

4.1.1. SIX CLASSES OF VERBAL ROOTS.
The meaning of the class to which a verbal root belongs constitutes a sort of latent anchor to the word and even to the clause. In the discussion that follows, "free" means that the root can take conjugational endings directly, whereas "bound" roots must first take a thematic suffix. "Active" means that the action passes from an actor-agent to(ward) a patient/goal and thus subsumes various transitive, causative, jussive, and instrumental values. "Middle" means that the action reflects back on the subject, or operates reciprocally between subjects, or is immanent in and/or emerges from within the subject; for example, 'to be hard', 'to dance', 'to bud'. Table 4-1 is the grid for the verbal roots.

Most interesting patterns switch the class

status of roots. For example, a free active such as *pá-* 'carry' is switched to the benefactive *pá-ku-n* 'to carry (something) to someone'. A free active such as *t'iré* 'eat' is switched to the jussive *ti'iré-ra-n* 'to order someone to eat'. Other switching of active roots is taken up below. The basic transitivity of bound roots (classes III and IV) can also be switched. Specifically, verbs of the bound class III normally form active themes through the addition of *-ku*, *-ta*, and other transitivizing and causativizing suffixes. But many of these same roots form a minor or alternative theme with *intransitive* value through the addition of different suffixes. A similar switch of status, though less frequent, is possible with many class IV themes; for example, the bound middle *hawá-* 'rise' is switched to the active *hawá-ta-n* 'to wake / get someone up'.

Class V roots refer to shapes and are thematized by spatial suffixes: *iṛá-* 'round', *iṛándu-* 'round at the foot of something', *iṛá-ndu-ta-n* 'to pile round objects at the foot of something'.

Class VI includes the four basic colors ('black', 'white', 'red', 'green') and such basic qualities as 'tasty', 'strong', 'lazy'. These roots are thematized by *-pi* or a spatial; for example, *wiŋá-pi-ti* 'strong', but *wiŋá-ŋaṛi* 'strong-sighted'.

The many other rules, particularly those for co-occurrence of a root class with the spatials or the suffix of individual action (*kuṛi*) cannot be detailed here (but see section 4.1.7).

4.1.2. INITIAL REDUPLICATION. A principal meaning of initial reduplication is repetition, as in *k'waní-k'waní-ta-n* 'to throw up repeatedly'. Another meaning is intensification, as in *meré-meré-hku-n* 'to be very brilliant'. A third is ubiquitous or wide distribution, as in *p'uní-p'uní-hku-n* 'to blow off all over' (as when dusting). These three meanings form part, respectively, of the aspectual, modal, and locative systems. The interaction of reduplication with radical meanings is often idiomatic and creates a host of long words that some Tarascans seem to feel are expressive and poetic.

Formally, single vowel roots and some CV roots such as *pá-* 'carry', are not reduplicated. About seventy roots never occur unreduplicated; for example, *niní-n* 'to ripen'. And about a dozen reduplicate only the first syllable. But in general practically any root can stand either alone or reduplicated. The reduplication may be determined by the class of roots (see the preceding section), or by one of thirty patterns, which fall into the following types:

(1) The roots are followed by a spatial suffix. Two such suffixes with corporeal meanings (the oral and facial) stand out. Reduplicated roots involving smell take a complex suffix, for example, *učú-učú-hku-ndi-n* 'to smell of fish, sex, or carrion'.

(2) The roots may be followed by one of six consonants and the stativizing suffix *-háśɨ* 'class, type of', as in *opó-* 'large, round', but *opó-opó-k-haśɨ* 'swollen' (of the entire body).

(3) The roots are followed by the intransitivizing *-hku*, as in *kwená-* 'lick', but *kwená-kwená-hku-n* 'to lick upward', (as of fire).

(4) The roots plus the *-kuṛi* of individual action yield a reflexive theme, such as *wá* 'strike', but *wá-wá-kuṛi-n* 'to be missing one's teeth, leaves, etc.'

(5) The roots are followed by *-ta* and, often, the reiterative *-nta* to yield a transitive theme, as in *aṛí-* 'say', but *aṛí-aṛí-ta-n* 'to give advice'.

(6) The root is followed by *-¢-ka* or *-¢-pa* or both, *-¢-ka-pa*, as in *yaṛá-yaṛá-¢-ka-pa-n* 'to go about urinating on oneself'. Here, as in many or most of these reduplicates, the *¢* has its lexical (spatial suffix) value of 'bottom'.

(7) Only the first CV is reduplicated (or a larger element up to and including the stressed vowel, and even the following nasal): *šúŋa-pi-ti* 'green' but *šúŋ-šúŋ-á-pi-ti* 'very green'.

There are many other minor, miscellaneous, or unique (limited to one root) reduplications; for example, *tíks-tíks-á-ŋi-n* 'to beat of fright', said only of the heart (*-ŋi* is the cavity / thorax spatial suffix).

4.1.3. INNER LAYER VOICE SUFFIXES (VOICE₁). Voice is, to a large extent, handled

TABLE 4-2. Inner Layer Voice Suffixes

Transitive	Transitive (Environmental)	Jussive
kaká-ku-n 'to break something of another'	*kaká-ta-n* 'to break the soil'	*kaká-ra-n* 'to order someone to break'
kará-ku-n 'to write someone'	*kará-ta-n* 'to clean cotton, etc.'	*kará-ra-n* 'to order someone to write'

by three powerful suffixes that already have been illustrated above: *-ku*, *-ra*, and *-ta*.

The suffix *-ku* may follow a transitive root directly or switch an intransitive class IV root to transitive, or it may focus the action of a verb toward a specific object: *hupí-ku-n* 'to grab *someone*' (versus *hupí-ka-n*, which may have an inanimate object or none at all).

The most complex of the three suffixes is *-ra*. It rarely (if ever?) occurs after a reduplicated root, and rarely after a spatial. It has six, partly overlapping meanings (the first below is the most important):

(1) Middle themes from transitive roots: *maná-ra-n* 'to move by itself'.

(2) Middle themes from intransitive roots: *yuŋú-ra-n* 'to be wavy' (*yuŋú-*, a class IV root).

(3) Causatives: *piší-ra-n* 'to cause to blister'.

(4) Jussives: *hupí-ra-n* 'to order to seize'.

(5) Transitives: *hikwá-ra-n* 'to bathe someone' (*hikwá-*, a class IV root).

(6) Goal-directed transitives: *p'itá-ra-n* 'to aim at a mark' (*p'í-*, *p'-itá-*, both meaning 'pull out').

Various idiomatic themes are also formed with *-ra*, including the politically useful *tepá-ra-kuṛi-n* 'to be arrogant' (from *tepá-* 'fat').

The third suffix, *-ta*, mainly creates causatives and transitives: *k'wí-ta-n* 'to put to sleep', *kará-ta-n* 'to sweep'.

The semantics of these voice suffixes is illustrated lucidly by pairs such as transitive *t'iré-ku-n* 'to eat another's food' versus causative *t'iré-ra-n* 'to feed' and causative *andá-ta-n* 'to earn, pronounce' versus middle *andá-ra-n* 'to climb, rise' and by triplets such as those in Table 4-2.

The underlying meaning of these particular voice suffixes is vague, but definite enough to be called "generic allofactive."

The suffix *-ṛa* (with a retroflex *ṛ*) follows six of the spatial suffixes, the reference of which it changes: *nu* normally means 'groin-buttocks-bottom', but, for example, 'patio' in *iʦí-nu-ṛa-n* 'water is running/standing in the patio'. The *-ṛa* themes are, in any case, usually locative.

4.1.4. THE ADVERBIAL SYSTEM (1): INNER LAYER ADVERBIAL SUFFIXES (ADVERB₁). The adverbials in the first position after a root or radical theme denote the direction or quality of motion. The main members of this small set are *-ŋa* 'upward', *-kwa/-k* 'downward', *-r/-ṛi* 'sudden or total movement', and *-p/-pi* 'sudden, startling, or en passant movement'. These suffixes are extremely productive and are limited in their occurrences only in obvious semantic ways. A typical adverbial use would be *hupí-p-ča-ku-n* 'to suddenly grab someone by the neck'. Sudden, total, and en passant movement are aspect categories that interact with aspect elsewhere in the clause.

4.1.5. SPATIAL SUFFIXES. The roots and the spatials are, at one formal level, largely independent. But in fact they typically interdepend, and their relationship is idiomatic and variegated. At one extreme, for example, a root for 'to cut' co-occurs only with a 'bottom' suffix to yield the theme for 'to castrate': *kapó-nu-n* (*kapó-* probably from the Spanish *capar*). Many roots and themes take only a limited number of spatial suffixes—with varying semantic predictability. At the other extreme, about 200 verbs take *any* of the potentially corporeal suffixes, and about 500 verbs can take at least one spatial.

The suffixes of space are differentiated semantically along several axes, such as relative simplicity. The main sets of suffixes are (1) simple corporeal, such as *-h-ku* 'manual'; (2) simple noncorporeal, such as *-ru* 'road'; (3) fairly complex, such as *-ŋguri* 'midriff, intersection' or *-pa* 'hearth, field, social front'; (4) thirteen semantically quite complex suffixes such as *-mu*, abstractly 'edge-orifice', concretely 'mouth, door, vagina', and so forth. Given this rich polysemy, the total number of potential spatial themes is enormous.

From my analyses of the thematic and spatial systems (e.g., Friedrich 1971c), here are a few examples of the semantics. As noted in section 2, *ča* denotes 'neck, throat'; abstractly it means a narrowing, usually of a longish object or at an intersection:

> *tepó-h-ča-n* 'to be fat-necked'
> *tepó-ča-n* 'to talk with a deep, loud voice'
> *mí-h-ča-ku-n* 'to tighten another's collar'
> *mí-ča-ku-n* 'to recognize by voice'

Note that 'neck' is differentiated from 'throat' by a preceding /h/; the second pair above includes the voice₁ suffix *-ku*.

The suffix *-ndi* denotes the ear, also the side of the neck and inner angle of the shoulder; abstractly, it applies to the inner surfaces of an angle on a vertical axis. Many of the meanings are displayed by the themes on *ambá-* 'good, clean'.

> *ambá-ma-ndi-n* 'to be clear' (especially of the sky at dawn)
> *ambá-ndi-ku-n* 'to prune branches, clean a plow or the ears of a person'
> *ambá-ndi-ta-n* 'to clean a cob' (under the husk)
> *ambá-ndi-ra-n* 'to speak persuasively' (especially in politics). At another level *-ndira* has to be regarded as a unit morpheme.

In addition to forming active themes, the suffixes *-ku* and *-ta* after a spatial suffix have, as some of these examples suggest, the function of shifting the lexical meaning to one of two large sets, as follows: *-ku* shifts the meaning to the body, and to certain sets that are classified with the body, such as pots and trees; *-ta*, on the other hand, switches the meaning to a house and certain other domestic or environmental sets: *hupá-ŋari-ku-n* 'to wash someone's face', versus *hupá-ŋari-ta-n* 'to wash an inside wall'.

Many psychological meanings are generated by the spatial suffixes, notably *-ŋari* 'face/eye/mind' as in *k'amá-ŋari-ku-n* 'to denounce someone', that is, 'to finish off someone's (political) face'. More unusual, comparatively speaking, is the process whereby one of six spatials can have its corporeal reference switched to a genital one by suffixing *-ta*; for example, the neck/throat suffix appears in *yó-h-ča-n* 'long neck', but 'long penis' is denoted by *yó-h-ča-ta-n* (given a context which suggests a genital more than a domestic object). In some sense, then, we find a proportion as follows: genitals: body::house:environment. The spatial suffixes, in sum, are deployed for vessels, plants, psychological and social structures, two sets of body parts, and two sets of environmental parts. They involve much metaphor and metonymy in semantic fields, and contribute greatly to the poetic potential of Tarascan (Friedrich 1969a). Syntactically, they work together with verbal subcategories in the verbal root, with the numeral classifiers, and with aspect—given the implicit categorial interplay between time and space.

4.1.6. Instrumental and jussive.

(1) The unit suffix *-kura* denotes that something is performed by means of something; for example, 'to crumble with something' is *puṛú-kura-n*, whereas 'to crumble in the hand' is *puṛú-h-ku-ṛa-n*.

(2) Any theme in *-ku* may be followed by the jussive *-tara*. Similarly, any of the transitive themes in *-ku* or *-ta* may be followed by *-ta-tara*, which will have either jussive or instrumental values (the choice between either but not both, depending on text or con-

text). Take, for example, *hó-* 'tie' plus *-h-ku* 'manual' plus *-ku* (active) plus *-ta-tara* (jussive or instrumental). This adds up to *hó-h-ku-ku-ta-tara-n*, which means '(to order someone) to tie the hand(s) of someone (with something)'. Similarly, *-ra-tara* can have either causative or instrumental value, as in *kití-ra-tara-n* 'to (make someone) rub (with something)'. These jussive, causative, and instrumental themes are often nominalized to yield the names of tools, body parts, and the like; many of these derived nouns have become idiomatized lexemes.

There are other, less well motivated and far less important thematic suffixes, for example, *-rata*, etc.

4.1.7. OUTER LAYER VOICE (SOCIAL) SUFFIXES (VOICE$_2$).

(a) *-ku/-či*. Aside from the primary, transitivizing value just noted, *-ku* for a third person object and *-či* for a first or second person object form benefactive or malefactive themes in two main ways. First, the free transitive roots of class I may take *-ku/-či* to refer to a second object; for example, 'to carry' is *pá-n*, but 'to carry something to/for someone' is *pá-ku-n*. Since both *-či* and the conjugational ending *-ka* are first/second person, the reference must be disambiguated by a pronoun enclitic:

> *hí-kin* 'I I-to-you' *ašá-či-a-ka* 'I will send (*ašá*) it to you'
>
> *t'ú-rin* 'you you-to-me' *ašá-či-a-ka* 'you will send it to me'

The *-ku/-či* suffix is also common after a transitivizing *-ku* in a class III theme to refer to a second object affected, as in *hupá-ŋaṛi-ku-n* 'to wash another's face', but *hupá-ŋaṛi-ku-ku-n* 'to wash another's face on a third party's behalf'. After a transitivizing *-ta*, however, the *-ku/-či* can only refer to the first personal object, since, as noted, the preceding *-ta* has functioned to switch the reference of the yet earlier preceding spatial to a domestic or environmental object: *hupá-ŋaṛi-ta-ku-n* 'to wash the inner wall of someone's house'.

(b) *-pi/-pera*. A large set of suffixes refer to giving, taking, exchange, and other kinds of reciprocal and/or other-directed action. These suffixes are frequent in ritual and other social activities; for example, 'to harvest for someone else' (but also 'to steal from a harvest'!) is *p'ikú-¢-pi-n*. Here are a few more examples: (1) 'to bet', *andá-pi-ra-n*; (2) 'to assault another on the road', *kwá-ru-k-pi-n*; (3) 'to test one another', *¢'é-h-pera-n*; and (4) 'to accompany', *pá-mbi-ta-n*. As these show, *-pi* and *-pera* are almost always preceded by another element. These elements are *-h*, *-m*, *-ra*, *-ta*, *-¢*, and *-ku*; the two-phoneme endings are contracted to one consonant, as illustrated in the following paradigm:

1.	*-∅*	*-pi*	*-pera*
2.	*-ku*	*-k-pi*	*-k-pera*

An example of such contraction is the form *kwá-ru-k-pi-n* 'to assault another on the road' (from the root for aggressive-defensive action, plus the 'road' spatial suffix, plus *-k-pi*, plus the infinitive ending). The seven initial elements (including zero) combine with *-pi* and *-pera* to yield fourteen suffixes, all of which occur. As for meaning, the *-pera* suffixes usually refer to reciprocal action, as in *warí-pera-n* 'to fight', whereas the *-pi* suffixes usually involve unilateral action toward another, as in *k'atá-pi-n* 'to incarcerate'. Consonant with this, only the *-pi* themes take the *-kuṛi* of individual action—which then shifts the main meaning of the theme to self-interested action. Take two key terms in political discourse: 'to defend another' is *kwá-h-pi-n*, but 'to defend oneself' is *kwá-h-pi-kuṛi-n*. There is, finally, extraordinary idiomaticity and differential productivity to these suffixes; *-¢-pera*, perhaps, has the greatest combinatory power. A good example of a highly idiomatic word with, as would not be unusual, archaic ritual value, is *pá-mbi-ta-n* 'to be helped ritually by assistants at a fiesta'.

(c) *-kuṛi*. The freest of the voice suffixes, *-kuṛi*, can occur anywhere between a root and the motion suffixes. It normally denotes reflexive action, or action that is individual in the sense of being one's own and not with or for another (compare "mediopassive"); for example, *teré-kuri-n* 'to laugh for/by oneself'. Thus *-kuri* often creates an intransitive theme, particularly from class IV (active) roots: 'to break something' is *č'amá-ku-n*, but 'to break' is *č'amá-kuri-n*. Similar reflexive and/or individualizing meanings are often added when *-kuri* follows a spatial suffix, such as *mu* 'mouth': *šačó-mu-kwari-n* 'to take the Host'. This, like many *-kuri* themes, is highly idiomatic. Another example is *pyá-kuri-n* 'to give birth'. The *-kuri* themes often have negative or hostile associations because of the strong value placed on acting in groups; for another political example, the positive root *ȼ'iwé-* 'brave' yields *ȼ'iwé-kuri-n* 'to brag, boast'.

4.1.8. THE ADVERBIAL SYSTEM (2): OUTER LAYER ADVERBIAL SUFFIXES (ADVERB₂).

4.1.8.1. TYPES OF MOTION. The penultimate suffixes in the extended theme denote the quality of motions:

(1) *-p* (general directional, specifically, en route somewhere)
(2) *-m* (en route transiently, intermittently)
(3) *-a* (motion away or round about)
(4) *-u* (motion coming, especially homeward, into a home)
(5) *-ŋgwa* (homeward)

Only the last of these appears alone. Otherwise, either *-p* or *-m* can combine with either *-a* or *-u* to yield four possible suffixes (which for most purposes are units). Both of the resultant *u*-suffixes, *-pu* and *-mu*, can be combined with *-ŋgwa*, as in *p'iré-p'iré-p-u-ŋgwa-n* 'to sing off and on while coming en route homeward'. The only constraints on these suffixes of motion are obvious semantic ones—for example, there are things one cannot do intermittently en route. The meanings of these suffixes are partly aspectual.

4.1.8.2. THE SUFFIX *-nta* 'again and again'

is the most mobile of these final suffixes since it can occur after any verbal root, including some of the bound ones, wherever it is possible semantically; it can occur after any thematic suffix, and is always *last* in the theme (i.e., preconjugational). More abstractly, *-nta* means indefinite extension, mainly in time, as in *eró-pi-nta-n* 'to wait for guests with food' (at a fiesta). By virtue of this meaning, like that of reiteration, *-nta* contributes greatly to the expression, not of progressive, but of habitual and en route aspect. Otherwise, *-nta* switches some intransitive free roots into transitives (and there is some associative link here with the transitivizing *-ta*). Finally, *-nta* creates many transitive themes that are used, in particular, for domestic and industrial activities: 'to write' is *kará-n* but 'to paint' (by a potter) is *kará-nta-n*; 'to make, do' is *ú-n*, but 'to cook' is *ú-nta-n*. Many frequent, idiomatic themes are formed by *-nta*.

4.1.9. CONJUGATION. From an appropriately semantic and clause-based point of view, the underlying meanings in the Tarascan verbal system are handled by many parts of the grammar. Aspect, for example, is handled by initial reduplication (iterative meaning); by the aspectual nuances denoted by the root; by the stative values of postpositions; by the sudden, or intermittent, meanings of some inner theme formatives; in verbal semi-compounds, by the inceptive meanings of first auxiliaries and the durative meanings of second auxiliaries; and, finally, by the many adverbs of aspect—all of which apparatus cooperates with many meanings of the conjugational endings, to which I now turn, beginning with the independent endings in main clauses.

4.1.9.1. THE FUTURE-POTENTIAL MODE, marked by *-a*, refers to intentions, potentials, possibilities, predictions, and beliefs about the future. *Hi huŋgwá-a-ka* 'I will/shall/intend to/hope to/may/think to return (home)'. The future-potential occurs freely and frequently in both main and subordinate clauses. Future durative aspect is indicated periphrastically with auxiliary verbs: *hu-*

ŋgwán háma-a-ka 'I will be coming/on my way home'.

4.1.9.2. ASPECT AND IMMEDIACY. The progressive *ša* implies action here and now, immediately perceived: *indé t'iré-ša-ti* 'he/she is eating'. Action that was completed in the past is signaled by *-s*: *t'iré-s-ti* 'he/she ate, has eaten'. Such action is definite in the sense that it is known through personal experience, good evidence, or reliable report.

The particle *-yá* is frequent after the future, the present progressive, the past definite, and the imperative, and implies definite completion, or feeling and opinion on the part of the speaker: *t'iré-s-t-yá* 'he has (definitely) finished eating'.

Further along on the dimension of definiteness there is action that is distant in time or place, based on hearsay or false report, uncertain, unknown, or in myths and tales. It is signaled by *-p* (*-ś-p* in the past, independent mood), as in a formula that opens stories: 'Once upon a time (it is said) there was' (*mée-ś-p-ti*, derived from the word for 'one', *ma*). This indefinite-removed category, because it often involves distant past completion or duration, is crudely glossed by the Spanish pluperfect.

Action that is continuing over hours, weeks, or more is signaled by the stressed *-šám*, as in *waṛí-šám-ti* 'he/she is/has been in the process of dying'. Such extended continuousness when it is in the past is signaled by the stressed *-šáp*, as in *waṛí-šáp-ti* 'he was in the process of dying'. Semantically overlapping with this past continuous is a second continuous, *-šámeen*, which has the additional or alternative values of inception and/or the idea that the action may be interrupted, intersected, or at least not completed; for example, 'I had begun to bathe and was still bathing (*hikwá-šámeen-ka*) when you came' (i.e., 'when you came and interrupted me'). Or, 'I had begun and/or was chopping wood, when he stole my horse'. In addition to this category of inceptive-interruptable, many inceptive and inchoative values are handled periphrastically, notably with the aspectual auxiliary *nirá-* 'go' for example:

hï nirá-ša-ka   (or *nirá-sïn-ka*
I   am-on-my-way-to   am-going-to

or *nirá-sireen-ka*) *píú-n*
    was-going-to   shuck-corn

Inceptive and completive values of many kinds are expressed through auxiliaries that normally precede the main verb: *imá únda-si-ti ánǰi-kuṛi-n* 'he began (*undasti*) to work.' Other durative and continuous values are attained through periphrastic or semi-compound verbal forms composed with one of two postposed aspectual auxiliaries: *háma-* 'go about, wander' and *haṛá-* 'be'. To take one example: 'to be in the process of bathing oneself' is *hikwá-háma-n* or *hikwán háman*. But these durative forms often are made more complex by also taking *-šám*, the suffix for continuous aspect, as in *ánǰi-kuṛi-háma-šám-ti*, the total aspectual meaning of which is difficult to translate. The alternation between verbal semi-compounds and periphrastic constructions involves all four of the *-ša* forms, as well as the auxiliaries: for example, we have not only the suffixed *t'iré-ša-ti* but also *t'irén śati*. This illustrates part of the continuousness between syntax and morphology; there are other, more complex examples of the alternation of morphologically complex words and, on the other hand, periphrastic constructions.

To conclude with aspect, action that is habitual, customary, or generally true is symbolized by the suffix *-si*, followed by *-n* in the present, and *-reen* in the past: *imá hiní k'wí-sireen-ti* 'he (*imá*) usually slept there (*hiní*)'. The present habitual is common also in pre-verbal, modal auxiliaries such as the 'going to shuck' example above, or in something like 'I want to work', *hí wéka-si-n-ka ánǰi-kuṛi-n*. The presence of /s/, /ś/, or /š/ in all the aspect forms suggests that, at a vague phonetic level, sibilant symbolizes aspect.

4.1.9.3. THE CONDITIONAL AND THE THREE SUBJUNCTIVES. The conditional mode occurs almost entirely in dependent clauses or coordinate clauses where both verbs are in the conditional. It involves a variety of hypothetical, desired, conditional, counterfactual, and contingent categories. It is symbolized by *-pirin* (or *-piin*). Here is an example:

éka -ri t'u hú- -pirin -ka nó
if you come had 1/2 pers. neg.

-ksɨ sɨpá- -či -pirin -di
they steal from-you would-have they

that is, *éka-r t'ú hú-pirin-ka nó-kś sɨpá-či-pirin-di* 'If you had come, they would not have stolen from you'.

The subjunctives occur in subordinate clauses, and there are three paradigms. The first subjunctive endings, as noted in section 3.1, occur after links such as *éka* and *eŋga*. The first subjunctive involves a set of suffixes; for example, in *ti'ré-ka* 'I ate', zero marks the past definite subjunctive. The first subjunctive also entails using only the first/second person ending *-ka* for all persons. This use of *-ka* for all persons is the *only* signal of the second subjunctive; these endings, therefore, differ from the independent endings only in the third person (see Table 4-3). These minimally marked second subjunctives are taken mainly by the subordinator that means 'because' (*himbóka*). The third subjunctive has a complete set of suffixes and uses both the *-ka* and the third person *-ti*; thus it is the only subjunctive that is not signaled, at least in part, by neutralization of person. The third subjunctive endings occur after the deictic *-sɨ* particularly when it is part of the causative-explanatory subordinator *himbósɨ*. The similarities and differences between the independent and the three subjunctive endings merit partial representation, as is done in Table 4-3 (using the third person singular).

4.1.9.4. Two MAJOR SETS OF VERBS. Two morphologically distinctive sets are small but basic, and their members occur frequently.

(1) The present stative verbs take the past ending *-s* in present and generalizing con-

texts, including those where the progressive or habitual would be expected; thus, *hí mɨ́ti-ś-ka* 'I know'. The first subset of present statives includes such basic verbs as 'live', 'be able', 'put', and 'have/put' (*haȼí-*). The second includes scores of properties or states, many belonging to verb classes V or VI, and many forming reduplicated themes: *urá-urá-háši-s-ti* '(It is) white, of the white-light class'. Another typical present stative: *kašú-m-pi-s-ti* '(It is) appropriate'.

(2) The second major set consists of the five strong verbs: *á-* 'eat', *há-* 'be', *hú-* 'come', *ní-* 'go', and *p'í-* 'draw/take out'. Let us look at some conjugations: imperative singular *hú*, future *hu-wá-ka*, progressive *hu-ṛá-ša-ka*, conditional *hú-pirin-ka*, and first subjunctive *hu-ká* (all examples in the first/second person). In brief, the stressed base form occurs before some endings, the future takes an expansion in *-wá* in the singular and in *-ŋá* in the plural, and another expansion in *-rá/-ṛá* occurs everywhere else.

4.1.10. THE ADVERBIAL SYSTEM (3): THE ADVERBS. The adverbial functions of modifying verbal and semiverbal (e.g., adjectival) expressions are, of course, fulfilled in Tarascan by parts of the verbal theme, by the participles, and by the cases and postpositions (see below). Otherwise, there are two kinds of primary adverbs. First, about a dozen adverbial enclitics normally are suffixed to an initial element in the clause (i.e., link, short adverb, or subject). Typical enclitics are *-(h)tu* 'also', *-(h)ku* 'only', *-ŋa* (quotative), and *-čka* (emphatic); many dialects have *-šaru* meaning 'probably'. Let us take one typical instance of such enclitics: 'and' (*ka*), 'he/she' (*imá*), 'also' (*-htu*), quotative (*ŋa*), and third person plural (*-ksɨ*) all together mean 'and they also, it is said'; this comes out phonetically, after sound rules, [*kimáhtUŋś*]. Some of these enclitics, including all those cited, occur after nouns, and some, particularly the emphatic, are common after certain verbal forms.

The second kind of primary adverb consists of about two dozen words that usually occur early in the clause, often after the link

TABLE 4-3. Subjunctives

Meaning	Independent	Subjunctive I	Subjunctive II	Subjunctive III
Progressive Definite	t'iré-ša-ti	t'iré-n haká	ti'iré-ša-ká	t'iré-n hatí
Past Definite	t'iré-s-ti	t'iré-ka	t'iré-ś-ka	t'iré-ti
Past Indefinite	t'iré-ś-p-ti	t'iré-p-ka	t'iré-ś-p-ka	t'iré-p-ti
Present Continuous	t'iré-šám-ti	t'iré-n hámka	t'iré-šám-ka	t'iré-n hám-ti
Past Continuous	t'iré-šáp-ti	t'iré-n háp-ka	t'iré-šáp-ka	t'iré-n háp-ti
Present Habitual	t'iré-sɨ-n-ti	t'iré-h-ka	t'iré-sɨ-n-ka	t'iré-h-ti

or the subject: 'now', 'then', 'here', 'there-near', 'there-far', 'everywhere', 'up to/until', 'straight away' (*má-hku*), 'often' (*méŋku*), 'suddenly' (*ma repéŋku*), 'still', 'a bit', 'thus', emphasis (*tá*), 'more', 'indeed' (*k'óru*), 'good', 'bad', 'many'; note that seven of these contribute aspectual meanings. Clearly, several are morphologically complex; several contain adverbial enclitics. Many function as the subordinators in dependent adverbial clauses—often combined with subordinators: *ék-hambéri*, for example, means '(up) until' and uses the noun for 'boundary', which also functions as a postposition yielding aspect meanings of limit, completion, and the like.

There are several kinds of derived adverbials; for example, the locative participles (see above), or extended phrases built on an adverb, or a noun in the locative; for example, 'in the church yard', *tyóšoo-ekwá-ṛu*. And here is a long adverbial phrase extraposed to postverbal position: *čúrnapan in-játir-yá-merú-sán*, roughly, 'evening, in evening already really a bit'.

4.1.11. PARTICIPLES. The so-called "infinitive" is the most frequent of the forms that are derived from verbal roots but that have about equally verbal and substantival syntactic functions. It may occur alone as a nominal clause, or as an imperative, or as a complement, or in various simple statements where the subject and/or object are understood: '(Someone) doesn't want (something)', *nó wékan*, could be used with any person in myriad contexts. Thus, the "infinitive" is a sort of generic participle.

Infinitives also function in the familiar sort of complementary clause, particularly clauses of result or desired consequence. And the infinitive is almost obligatory after certain subordinators such as *ántede* and *pára*. A political example: '(The leaders didn't) want us to fight', *pár warí-pera-ŋa-n* (here *-ŋa* denotes a plural subject). And as already noted, the infinitive is very frequent as the general unmarked form in successive linked clauses where the actor/agent and other information have been established.

The second set of nominal-verbal forms is the participles proper. These participles are not of the "present tense," as has been assumed. They are aspectual in value and denote action that is *contemporary or concurrent* with that of the verb in the main clause. Of these participles, that in *-parin* occurs mainly with verbs that denote some action (rather than state) by the actor in the main clause. For example, *íś arí-pari-n* 'while speaking thus (he did so-and-so)' (*arí* 'speak'). The form in *-parin* can appear as a separate auxiliary (as can several of the conjugational suffixes—see below). For example: 'And then while we were walking about talking' can be translated as *ka šáš wandó-n¢-kuṛi-n-pári-n huchá*; here the first component consists of the idiomatic *wandó-n¢-kuṛi-n* 'to converse' (*wandó-* 'converse', *-n¢* (social suffix), *-kuṛi* (individual action).

The second main concurrent participle, *-tin*, is common in verbal-nominals that denote a state or at least a protracted condition. They are formed from intransitive and transitive verbs, but in the latter case lose their transitivity: *hó-ta-n* 'to tie (someone)', but *hó-ta-ti-n* 'tied up'. Typically the head noun is bound closely to its participle: *tiṛi-* 'hang', but *garót-tiṛi-hku-ti-n* 'goad-hanging-down'. Perhaps the most frequent and functional of the *-tin* participles are the locatives formed with the verb *ha-* 'be' plus a spatial suffix, which must be stressed, and the suffix *-ku*; for example, *ha-mú-ku-ti-n* 'at the edge of', or *ha-ndú-ku-ti-n* 'at the foot of'. Scores of modifiers are formed this way, and, together with their head, typically postposed to the verb: 'He was taking a stroll, river is-edge'. A far less frequent variant of the concurrent participle is formed with *-rin*; for example, 'being dressed, having clothes (*takúš*) on' is *takúš-huká-ri-n*.

The third set of verbal-nominals is formed from a transitive root plus *-kata* to yield a substantive that refers to the outcome of the action. These *aspectually completive* participles may normally function as adjectives— *pyá-kata* 'bought'—or as nouns; for example, *yawá-* 'harden', 'freeze', *yawa-ṛú-kata* 'adobe', and, verbalized, *yawaṛúkateesti* 'it is adobe'. As to forming these participles, roots vary greatly in their derivational potential. Some do not take *-kata*, or it is awkward. Others can and sometimes do; and in yet other cases it is common and/or idiomatic; for example, the common *ú-kata* (from *ú-* 'do, make') functions mainly as an adjective, including instrumental clauses such as *úkata háhk-himbó* 'handmade'; also *pyákata tumín-himbó* 'bought with money'. Yet further along the line, many *-kata* forms are built on roots, the original meaning of which has been lost, leaving us with an "archaic residue." (The frequent label of "past passive" for these participle forms represents a gratuitous importation of tense and of passivity.)

4.2. THE SUBSTANTIVAL SYSTEM refers to such things as actors, objects, events, and properties. Syntactically, it partly involves the participles, the fifth and sixth classes of verbal roots, the pronouns, and even verbal thematic suffixes. In a narrower sense the substantives include the nominal roots, some

of which are monosyllabic (*ta* 'house'), but the overwhelming majority of which are disyllabic: *wíču* 'dog', *puṛu*, 'squash', and *naná* 'woman'. Simple derived nouns consist of a root plus a nominalizing suffix; most of the latter are made up of one of seven consonants (/p/, /t/, /r/, /n/, /m/, /č/, and /k/) plus one of the three primary vowels: *naná* 'woman', but *naná-ka* 'girl', *čaṛá-* 'red', but *čaṛá-ku* 'infant'. Some of the most frequent of these nominalizers are *-ku* (*-kwa* in almost all towns), and *-ri* and *-ti* (the latter are agentive, and related to the participles in *-rin* and *-tin*). Many syntactic nominals are derived from participial forms; hundreds (or thousands?) of forms in *-kata* have been reclassified as nouns (and in some cases the verbal root has been lost). Complex derived nouns, finally, consist of thematized verbal roots plus a nominalizing suffix; for example, *hó-ŋguṛi-ku* 'sash', which is constituted from *hó-* 'to tie' plus *ŋguṛi* 'intersection' plus *-ku*. In this extremely productive derivational morphology any verbal root can, in principle, be thematized and nominalized, but there is, in practice, great variation in productivity, and there is much idiomaticity. A large set of verbal roots is, in any case, far more productive than are the nominal roots—particularly the names of plants and animals. Nouns, otherwise, are the set that takes declensional endings.

There are two classes of nouns: (1) persons and animals (with subsets), and (2) other.

There are seven cases. The *nominative*, with zero ending, is used for the agent of an active form and the subject-locus of an intransitive middle or stative verb: 'The woodpecker (*¢oré-ki*) saw', *¢oré-ki šé-s-ti*.

The *genitive* suffix *-ri* is limited to class (1); for example, *¢íkatee-r-k 'wirípita* 'chicken-of meat'. The genitive is often deleted in such modifier-modified orderings, yielding a compound.

The *objective* suffix *-ni* is used for both direct and indirect objects, but consistently only with nouns that refer to people and animals (plus a miscellany that includes 'drinking bout', 'dream', and 'book'). The objective case may be used to emphasize objects in other categories but, if so, in verb-object order and then with a following pause: '(I found) a/the stone' (*ȼakápu-n*). The objective is normally deleted within a tightly bound clause, particularly when preverbal.

The *positional* case, characterized by the suffix *-ṛu*, has mainly locative value: *paráŋgu-ṛu* 'on/by the hearth'. It is hardly ever used with persons or animals but is very common with nouns that disambiguate the spatial reference of verbs: the part of the body *where* one is sick. Its locative value has contributed a number of basic adverbials—'in the mountain, ravine, river, water-hole, garden'—that are petrified to the point of themselves sometimes taking the locative: *kawáṛu-ṛu* 'in the ravine'. This *-ṛu* is also a basic derivational suffix and occurs in many place names, such as Pátzcuaro. A second locative, *-oo* is limited to the words for church and parish, and personal names and third person kin terms when these refer to a home: *hwán-oo* 'at Juan's house'. Third, we have the place-of-origin postposition, *-anápu*, which is common with names of towns: *Kukúč-anápu-ee-ča* 'people from Cocucho'.

The *comitative* case is used most often with persons and animals—'I went with her'—but is also taken by certain other categories that one may be acting on, including inanimates. The form varies greatly by dialect, and depends notably on various pragmatic factors. At one extreme, a postposition takes primary stress and is set off by juncture: *hiŋgún* 'with'. At the other extreme we find an unstressed, closely bound suffix, as in *kuṛínd-iŋgun* 'with bread'.

The *instrumental* is, in general, used with nouns that do not refer to persons and animals to denote a means or an instrument. Thus it sometimes overlaps with the comitative: *ȼakáp-hiŋgún* 'with a stone', versus *ȼakáp-himbó* 'by means of a stone'. And it overlaps with the positional, as in *irét-himbó* 'at/from the village'. It is standard in expressions of time (*eránd-himbó* 'at dawn'), and manner (*turí-himbó* 'in Spanish'), and cause (*wíč-himbó* 'because of the dog'); space precludes giving fuller context for these uses. In addition to extreme multivocalism, the instrumental varies in form as much as the comitative: from an *-(i)mbo* suffix to the fully stressed *himbó*; the latter when combined with the deictic as *himbóś* is one of the main subordinators in the syntactic system.

A seventh case, the *vocative*, could be posited, as in *táta pitáa* 'Mr. Pita', but this seems to be the same emphatic lengthening as we find in the imperative.

There are three degrees of number: singular, plural, and mass. The plural ending *-ča* is taken most regularly by persons and animals plus a miscellaneous set that includes 'house', 'pot', 'pistol', and 'honeycomb'. Other categories, including inanimates, are pluralized when the particulate or distributive meaning is to be emphasized, but this is hard to predict and very sensitive to social context.

In sum, the declensional endings have to be seen ranging from the regular genitive ending to the variously qualified objective and locative, to the relatively postpositional comitative and instrumental, to the vocative.

4.2.1. NAMES AND KIN TERMS. First names are almost always converted to nicknames, mostly disyllabic: *Feliciano* yields *Felí*. But some are poly- or monosyllabic: *Ramón* yields *Mon*.

The paradigms for kinship include, in many cases, special terms for address, and first, second, and third person reference. The third person ending *-mba* (e.g., *pirémba* 'his/her sister') has, like some declensional endings, a postpositional alternate that is used for compadres, friends (e.g., *amik-hémba*), and the like—it is a morphological symbol for a set of culturally defined primary ties.

4.2.2. PERSON AND NUMBER: PRONOUN, ENCLITIC, DEICTIC. The pronouns trichotomize into the subject pronouns (*hi* 'I', *t'ú* 'you', etc.), the object pronouns (*híndin* 'me', etc.), and the possessives (*hučíiti* 'my', etc.).

For the so-called third person, Tarascan employs deictics, which fall into a four-way series in terms of proximity and immediacy: 'this-here' (first person's view), 'this-here' (second person's view), 'this/that' (perceptible), and 'that' (out of the perceptible field, indefinite—and hence common to stories, dictation forms, and the like). The deictics are inflected for person and case and, provided the context warrants it, may be pluralized: *-imá* 'that' gives *im-ée-ča-n* 'them'. The deictics cross-reference degrees of definiteness in the verb. They are semi-enclitics, practically always fused with the copula or the subordinator: *éŋg-imá* 'that one . . .' or *éŋg-indé* 'this one . . .'.

The major syntactic functions of the pronominal enclitics are two: first, to link anaphorically, both within and between clauses; second, to disambiguate the conjugational endings with respect to person (the conjugational ending *-ka* is first/second person). They also disambiguate number, outstandingly in the third person, where the enclitic *-ksi* is added to the singular *-ti*.

The subject enclitics typically are suffixed to the first word in the clause after the copula. This is usually a subordinator: *himbóka-kś* 'because they'; *nó-kś* 'not they'. Or a subject enclitic may follow the subordinator, as in *éka-n hí ni-wá-ka* 'if I go'. A final example, using the word *č'aná-ri* 'player', is *č'aná-ri-i-ča-kś háma-si-n-ti* 'the players usually go about' (here the enclitic *-kś* could also follow the verb).

The omission of the second person singular enclitic, *-ri*, implies an order, discourtesy, or emphasis, whereas use of the relatively optional second person *plural* enclitic implies politeness. The first person plural plus the pronoun conveys the inclusive plural meaning: *hučá ni-wá-ka-č* 'We (I and you [sg. or pl.]) shall go'. On the other hand, combining the same first person plural pronoun with the first person *singular enclitic* yields the *exclusive* plural. The third person plural enclitic *-ksi* is the freest in distribution and the most apt to be repeated within the clause. One reason for such repetition is formal, since the enclitic is attracted primarily to the initial link in the clause, but also to its verb, and it may also occur elsewhere. The third person plural enclitic may be repeated for emphasis or stylistic effect; it is repeated in three positions within one clause in one of the stories in my texts.

There is a second, minor set of subject enclitics that may be attached to an accusative form: *-imá-n-ti* 'him-you (sg.)', *-imá-n-č* 'him-we', etc.

The subject-object enclitics have multiple reference. For example, a first person singular action on a second person singular is symbolized by *-kin*: 'I will pay you' is *hí-kin mayá-mu-a-ka* 'I-you pay-will'. Or, turning to the plural, one of the enclitics, *-hҫin*, denotes a first person acted on by a second or third person such that either the subject or the object or both are plural; for example, 'you (-all) will pay me (us)' would be *t'ú-hҫin* (or *čá-hҫin*) *mayá-mu-a-ka*. There is another enclitic for second person objects. The ambiguities of number in the case of such enclitics are most often handled by a postposed object pronoun, when necessary. The subject-object enclitics, although units syntactically, are also fully segmentable morphologically: *-kin* consists of *-ki-n*, and so forth.

The enclitics and the pronouns, last of all, collaborate with two sets of verbal thematic suffixes. First, there are the social suffixes such as the reciprocal *-pera*, and there are the two object suffixes: *-či* (first or second person), and *-ku* (third person) (all described above). Let us take just one example of such cross-referencing.

'You never wrote to me' consists of 'you-to me' (*t'ú-rin*), 'not ever' (*nó meŋku*), 'write-to me-past definite-you' (*kará-či-ś-ka*), 'to me' (*híndi-n*). After sound rules this comes out, phonetically in rapid speech, as [*t'Urinó-méŋk-karáčiśkA*].

In the second place, the Sierra dialects in particular denote a plural subject or a plural object by incorporating the respective suffix *-ŋa* or *-a* into the body of the verb (in the last part of the theme, just before the repetitive suffix *-nta*). The plural suffix *-ŋa* can also be added to other, nonverbal elements, such as adverbs. These two suffixes do not occur in the same verb. A simple example of their placement would be the generic participle of the verb for 'to work (plural subject)' *ánǰikuṛiŋan*. A more complex example is 'where she had covered the pots with something', which consists of 'where' (*naní*), 'that' (*eŋga*), 'cover' (*ó-*), 'right angle' (*-hča*), instrumental (*-kura*), plural object (*-a*), past definite dependent (*-ka*), 'pot' (*poṛéči*), plural-objective (*-i-ča-n*)—which after sound rules comes out [*naníiŋga óhčakuraakA poṛéčiičan*].

4.2.3. COUNTING. The number 1, *ma*, is also the first ingredient in many verbs for joining together, sticking together, or working together. It also occurs in quantifiers, and in adverbs such as *má-r-ku* 'together' (i.e., 'one-only', as against *tá-mu* 'apart'). The numbers 3–6 end in *-mu*; e.g., *t'á-mu* 'four'. The numbers ½, 1–6, 10, 20, and 'two twenties' are generally known and used. Rarely used are 7–9, 11–19, and from 21 on, since these are cumbersome products and, after 20, figured in multiples of 20: 57 is 'two twenties plus ten plus five plus two'. Tarascanized Spanish words are the norm for these numbers, and for all calculations in the hundreds and up (although counting and adding with Tarascan numbers above 6 is an in-group game for, inter alia, demonstrating fluency). Collectives are formed with the numbers 2–6 and 10, usually from the social suffix *-peran*, as in *t'á-peran* 'foursome'; collectives are practically obligatory when describing small-group activities. The same six numbers also form derivatives in *-puru* or *-poru* (which contains a derivative of the locative *-ṛu*); these are used for locative expressions, especially about land; for example, *t'á-puru* '(in) four places'. Finally, "objects" are counted by the obligatory formula Number plus Classifier plus Object(s). The objects must be sorted out as long, flat, or round, that is, one-, two-, or three-dimensional: 'two long-tree(s)' is [*¢imán ičák-aŋátapU*]. Such classifiers are used for people only in special contexts, with marked results, as in 'women, three round-ones'.

5. MORPHEME STRUCTURE. Any vowel, stressed or not, can occur between consonants, or at the end of morphemes—except that /*e*/ and /*o*/ do not occur in a suffix in the dialects being focused on here (the exceptional locative suffix *-oo* has been discussed in section 4.2). Let us illustrate with /*i*/: *ík-sta-* 'angry', *hupí* 'grab!', *púki* 'mountain lion', *apá-si-ku* 'oak gall', *wíču* 'dog', *píú-n* 'to shuck corn'. Any vowel, except for /*i*/ can occur in glide diphthongs or clusters. The glides combine with all but homorganic vowels (barring some Spanish-derived exceptions): for example, *yeré-* 'cross-eyed', *ayá-* 'advise', *wé-* 'emerge', and *iwá-* 'pus'. The six main clusters usually combine a stressed high with a low central vowel: for example, *šaṛia* 'swim/float'. Long vowels are lexical in the case of the two dozen roots with double /*a*/ or /*e*/: *háa-kuṛi-* 'astounded', *apée-nda* 'little cob', and so forth. Morphological lengthening may involve up to three successive vowels; for example, 'pile up/round object' *umbá-* plus plural object *-a-* plus the spatial 'field' *-a-* plus *-ni* yields *umbá-a-a-ta-ni* 'to pile up round objects in a field', which reduces phonetically to [*Umbá:tan*].

The consonants that can occur after a pause are the twelve stops, the four spirants, and the nasals /*m*/ and /*n*/. Of the spirants, /*h*/ occurs only word initially and before certain stops, /*š*/ occurs only before vowels, /*ś*/ mainly before /*i*/, and /*s*/ before any vowel and four of the consonants. The sonant /*ṛ*/ and the sonant /*ŋ*/, as a definite underlying segment, occur only in intervocalic position. The lateral /*l*/ occurs only in Spanish-derived words such as *azúli* 'blue', and the same holds for the trilled /*r̃*/ except for a few odd words like 'the cat's meow', *r̃aú-r̃aú-mi-n*.

Initial consonant clusters are of two kinds. The first consists of /*s*/ or one of the non-labialized stops followed by /*w*/ as in *p'wá-n* 'to sprinkle'. /*Sw*/ and /*kw*/ also occur medially. The second kind of cluster is illustrated by *tpéri* 'fallow land', *¢tún* 'blackberry', and *¢kwá-n* 'to be blotchy', and it can be summarized by a rule: /*t*/, /*¢*/, or /*č*/ before /*p*/; /*¢*/ or /*č*/ before /*k*/ or /*kw*/. Eight clusters of this sort occur initially in at least twenty-seven roots. These clusters are phonetically tense, complex, and unstable, with dialectal and individual reduction, or intrusive vowels (*tukúmbu* from *tkúmbu* 'fir-spruce').

Medially within morphemes (or opaque lexemes) the clustering of consonants is mainly nasal plus homorganic stop, as in *hembé* 'to burn'. These clusters occur in the following order of frequency: (1) labials, (2) centrals, (3) dorso-velars, the latter illustrated by *tiŋgwá* 'roadrunner'. The remaining miscellany of clusters includes many with /s/ or /š/, such as *áš-pi-n* 'to taste good'.

Medial clusters around the boundaries between morphemes within a word are much more common and can be illustrated by *hós-ku* 'star'. The status of *h*-stop sequences, incidentally, is ambiguous; by one analysis they are units and phonetically pre-aspirates; by the present one they are clusters: *hahki* 'hand' consists of *hah-* and *-ki*, not *ha-* and *-hki*. The total chart of intermorpheme clusters shows that /p/, /t/, /k/, /h/, and /m/ and /n/ are relatively free, since each may be followed by one of four or more consonants.

The foregoing rules and tendencies define the canonical forms, as shown in Table 4-4. Most roots are disyllabic, stress-final. Most suffixes are *CV*, although some have an inseparable nasal (*-ndi*, *-pi-ndi*), whereas others have a separable laryngeal (e.g., *-h-ku*, *-p-ku*), and some are disyllabic: *-ŋaṛi* 'face/eye/mind'.

5.1. VOCALIC SYMBOLISM occurs in suffixes, as when a form in *-a* denotes 'going' or 'en route', whereas the other suffix, in *-u* denotes 'coming', particularly 'coming back home'; for example, *-pa* 'en route going' versus *-pu* 'en route coming home'. In three important suffixes the *-a* form denotes a transitive, whereas the *-i* form is nontransitive or specifically locative: *-ma* 'at, into water' versus *-mi* 'in the water'. Also, there are about sixty minimal pairs or even triplets of roots differing in a final, stressed *-a* versus an *-o*. Here the *-a* usually has an allofactive voice meaning whereas the *-o* is middle voice. In ten cases the *-a*/*-o* contrast involves action

directed outward versus action directed inward or within: *p'amá-* 'to wrap—for example, a tamal' versus *p'amó-* 'to feel, to feel sorry for'. Lexical length in roots and long vowels that reflect two contiguous morphemes with the same shape have already been discussed. Finally, as also noted in section 3.2, long vowels occur in interrogatives, vocatives, and imperatives: *wiṛí-i* 'run!'. Emphatic lengthening is common: *hóo* or *hóoo* 'yes!' whereas *hó-hó or *hó-hó-hó is not only wrong but funny.

5.2. HOMOPHONY. Almost all the potential of phonemes plus the rules for their combination is actually realized, often multiply so. For example, from /¢/ plus *V*: *¢í-* 'pretty', 'life', and four other meanings; *¢é-* 'soft', 'a kind of worm'; *¢á-* 'shine', 'crack', 'lizard'; *¢ó-* 'smell bad', 'bright'; *¢ú-* 'sneeze'. Many *CV*'s have four to six meanings: *ku*, for example, means, in various themes, 'grunt', 'meet', 'cut off', 'small', and 'female/moon', as well as its seven meanings as a suffix. The nonoccurrence of a *CV* most probably reflects the northern dialects I worked with; for example, *šo-* and *č'u-* turned up in the Lake dialects as 'row' and 'drive'. Homophony is also luxuriant in the suffixes, where any simple stop or nasal or flap or /š/ can be followed by any primary vowel, as in: *p-* 'suddenly', 'plaza', 'hearth', 'field'; *pi-* (class marker, action toward/with, animate); *pa-* 'en route', 'suddenly'; *pu-* 'en route coming'. In terms of lexical roots, the numbers of meanings (in parentheses) include: /pi/ (6), /pe/ (1), /pa/ (3), /po/ (2), /pu/ (1). All of this homophony works, in part, because in the same slot in a theme a suffix usually means one and the same thing; different meanings normally occur in different slots.

6. FEATURE AND PHONEME. The segmental phonemes are laid out on the paradigm in Tables 4–5 and 4–6. I prefer this paradigm with its twenty-two concrete features to the twelve binary, universalistic features of my 1971 analysis (Friedrich 1971b) (granted that some of these are useful for stating rules): vocalic, consonantal, peripheral/central, back/front, tense/lax, high/non-high, continuant,

78

TABLE 4-4. Canonical Forms

Basic		Geminate		Clusters	
V	ú- 'do', 'make'	CVV	káa- 'have', 'care for'	CCV	¢kí- 'pinch'
CV	čú- 'chase'			CVCCV	henǰé- 'tremble'
VCV	i¢í- 'water'	CVCVV	sïráa- 'smoke', 'vapor'	CVCVV	pelée- 'bold'
CVCV	kará- 'write'	CVVCCV	téeksa- 'stumble'	VCCV	umbá- 'pile round objects'

TABLE 4-5. Segmental Phonemes: Consonants

	Labial	Dental	Alveolar Affricated	Alveopalatal	Dorsal	Labiovelar	Laryngeal
Stop:							
Simple	p	t	¢	č	k	kw	
Tense	p'	t'	¢'	č'	k'	k'w	
Voiced	b	d			g		
Nasal	m	n			ŋ		
Glide	w			y			
Flap, trill		r, r̃					
Retroflex			ṛ				
Lateral		l					
Spirant	s	ś	š				h

nasal, strident, voiced, retroflex, and lateral. The pros and cons of the two sets cannot, in any case, be entertained here.

6.1. SANDHI RULES. Although Tarascan is primarily an agglutinative language in which suffixes are tacked on without alteration, there are also important changes in the sound shape of morphemes in construction (all of them already illustrated above).

(1) After a main stress there is an alternation of unstressed and secondarily stressed syllables within a word; this rule is blocked under a number of conditions.

(2) A final unstressed vowel is devoiced before a pause: [wíčU] 'dog'.

(3) A final unstressed /i/ or /ï/ is normally deleted between /n/, /s/, /š/, or /¢/ and an open juncture or a pause.

(4) The final vowel in a root or a theme is normally dropped before conjugational endings: wéka-ṣï-n-ti becomes [wékṣïndI]. There

TABLE 4-6. Segmental Phonemes: Vowels

	Front	Central	Back
High	i	ï	u
Mid	e		o
Low		a	

are other, less regular reductions and losses of unstressed vowels.

(5) Tense stops, which never occur in suffixes, are de-aspirated if they become medial, as in reduplication: č'aná-ni 'to play', but [č'anáčanán].

(6) Before the plural -ča, the genitive -ri, and the existential verbalizing -s, the final vowels /i/, /é/, and /ï/ are geminated, whereas /ee/ is added to any other vowel (with deletion of a final /a/); for example, tíndi-i-ča

79

'flies', *aṛó-ee-ča* 'maize stalks', and *šakw-ée-ča* 'edible greens' (also 'female genital hair', jokingly).

(7) The ending *-ni*, whether in the participle or the objective case, is frequently deleted—for example, from the object fused with its following verb, or from a main verb fused with its aspect auxiliary, as in [*č'aná-háman*], 'to go about playing'.

(8) The copula is normally fused with the following subordinator and/or short adverb and/or subject, as is the second adverb or object with the following verb.

Under certain discourse conditions all the words in a clause may lose their final vowels and terminal *CV* elements and get fused into one continuous unit.

Finally, although a case is in print (Friedrich 1975: Ch. vii) for partial ordering, it is simpler to treat these rules as reciprocally unordered, to say that they apply as they are called for during articulation (which may include simultaneous application, as in the case of stop-nasal assimilation).

6.2. PHONOLOGICAL PROBLEMS.

(1) A nasal assimilates to the position of a following stop, and a stop is voiced after a nasal. This automatic rule generates many /ŋ/ segments in the morphology; for example, /ŋ/ before the first/second ending *-ka*, but /n/ before the third person *-ti*. The back nasal /ŋ/ however, may also be an independent segment between vowels within a morpheme or a lexeme, as in *aŋá-* 'upright'. The status of /ŋ/ within many lexemes seems to be intermediate between these extremes. In some towns, finally (including San José), /ŋ/ has merged with /n/.

Aside from voicing after nasals (a pre-Spanish rule), voiced stops occur almost exclusively in words of Spanish origin, and even here, in monolinguals, they tend to be devoiced when initial, and /b/ merges with /w/ or is interpreted as /p/. The voiced stops, like /ŋ/ therefore, are phonologically interstitial between phonemes and phoneme alternates.

Otherwise, stop-nasal assimilation does not occur across internal open juncture, nor under nine specific morpholexical conditions—such as in the reiterative suffix, *-nta* or after the stressed continuous suffix, *-šám*.

(2) The labiovelars. The glide, /w/, like /y/, patterns like a consonant in its distribution and contrasts with the vowel /u/; for example, *pwá-* 'wheat smut' versus *púá-* 'to conform' (especially in a political sense). Otherwise, *pw-* initiates one other root, and *p'w-*, *tw-*, *t'w-*, and *hw-* initiate one to three each, all these roots being onomatopoetic or extremely rare, and the position of /Cw-/ is limited to root-initial before /a/ or /i/. Turning to the labiovelars, the glide element in *kw* and *k'w* is articulated closely with its stop, and contrasts with *kú-* and *k'ú-*: *kúchi* 'pig', *k'úni* (a species of oak). Moreover, the labiovelars pattern like unit consonants and are frequent (initiating forty and sixty base roots, and occurring in some suffixes). I have concluded that the status of the labiovelars, while interstitial between cluster and unit, is close enough to the latter to be treated as such in the system, whereas all the other /Cw/'s are clusters.

(3) Perhaps the most interesting problem is posed by the retroflex /ṣ/, which ranges in sound from a near /s/ to a shishy /š/ to an extreme retroflex with a slight whistle effect (incidentally, /s/ also varies markedly, being replaced by /h/ in some dialects, whereas in others we find something that sounds like /s/ and /h/ produced simultaneously). In many Sierra dialects, in any case, there is a strong rule (with a few, infrequent exceptions): /ṣ/ occurs before /i/, /p/, and certain suffixes in /ka/, and /s/ never does. In other dialects /ṣ/ has been replaced by /s/ (with various degrees of such merger reflected individually). In still other dialects /ṣ/ is an allophone of /š/ (as it was in the sixteenth century). In any of these cases, only two sibilants, /s/ and /š/, need be posited. This is congruous with two other pairs of front and back alveolar obstruents (/¢/ and /č/, /¢'/ and /č'/). It has served practical purposes, such as the (superb) translation of the Bible (Lethrop and Lethrop 1960). On the other hand, the arguments in favor of treating /ṣ/ as an independent phoneme include: (1) definite contrasts

exist in many dialects, including some northern ones (words such as *hís-ka-n* 'hide' with /s/ before suffixal /k/); (2) the feature of retroflexion has to be posited for the lateral /r̥/ and the central vowel /i/. Thus, /ś/ is a marginal phoneme.

(4) The liquids. The trilled /r̃/ is fairly regular in the speech of full bilinguals; /r̃/ contrasts with /r/. But the trill merges with /r/ in the speech of many monolinguals. The lateral /l/ overlaps phonetically with the marked /l/-color of the retroflex lateral /r̥/, and the two phonemes merge fully in the speech of many children, some adults, and the dialects of two towns. The retroflex /r̥/ contrasts clearly with the flapped /r/ (e.g., in at least seventeen minimal pairs in medial position: *koró-* 'crawl' versus *koṛó-* 'make a noise'). On the other hand, there is considerable dialectal and diachronic alternation between /r/ and /r̥/ in certain suffixes.

6.3. PHONETICS. General phonetic rules hold for two or more phonemes.

The main consonantal rules cannot be detailed here but were partly noted above, or involve the phonetic character of certain distinctive features.

For vowels the important rules are: differential nasalization next to nasals; differential height in differentially stressed final position; for both high and mid vowels, relatively higher variants occur under stress or next to peripheral consonants; after the central stops the low and mid-low variants of the peripheral vowels occur—for example, [tUmín] 'money', and [t'U] 'you'. For great detail on Tarascan phonetics, see Friedrich 1975:76–158, 171–223.

Unique phonetic rules hold for one phoneme only. Perhaps the most interesting of the unique vocalic rules concerns /e/. The phoneme /e/ is realized as a low-mid [ɛ] in a stressed nonfinal position but as a mid-mid [E] in unstressed position, and as a high-mid [e] in stressed final position or whenever lengthened.

This phoneme also illustrates the variation whereby the low-mid [ɛ] variant follows an aspirated stop, whereas the mid-mid variant

FIGURE 4-1. Vowel Phones

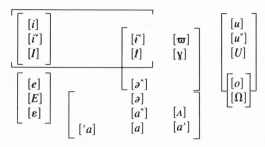

[E] or even the high-mid [e] follows a simple stop. This rule works consistently only for some idiolects (and perhaps dialects), and even there it works with high frequency only after the six central stops /t/, /t'/, /¢/, /¢'/, /č/, and /č'/:

[t'ɛtÉkwa] 'anus' [tÉkwa] '(something) sweet'
[¢'ɛ́mun] 'to taste' [¢Ekán] 'to hew'

In the idiolects in question the pattern also works beyond random with peripheral consonants:

[p'ɛ́maRin] 'to belch' (of humans) [pÉEran] 'to bring'
[k'ɛ́n] 'to grow' [kÉni] 'fiesta official'

The approximately two dozen rules result in an output of twenty-two vowel phones (Figure 4–1). The morpholexically conditioned intersection between /u/ and /o/ and /i/ and /i/ is denoted by overlapping brackets.

The most interesting unique rules for consonants involve the laryngeal, which is lightly co-occluded with the laryngeal or palatal area, is related to aspiration in special ways, and varies with [s] before *-ti* or *-tu* in practically all dialects but with enormous differences in frequency. The Tarascan laryngeal has been given six clearly different (if sometimes very similar) definitions by as many field phoneticians: John Attinasi, Mary Foster, Paul Friedrich, Charles Hockett, Norman McQuown, and Morris Swadesh (Friedrich 1975:84–86).

Let us turn to the aspiration of the tense (i.e., initial) affricates; for example, *ȼimán* 'two' versus *ȼ'ítu* 'bird'. The degree and the quality of this aspiration varies greatly and provides one of the many cases where microphonetics symbolizes individual differences. In one San José–Ocumichu extended family, for example, the grandfather and daughter-in-law—the least careful in general—totally lacked affricate aspiration; the grandfather's second wife, from one of the Eleven Pueblos, had it sporadically. The household head aspirated his affricates before /a/, and otherwise signaled the contrast through the tension of the affricates themselves. And tension was the only way that aspiration was signaled by his son. Both men perceived and described the presence of aspiration as a matter of 'strength' (*sánderu wiŋápiti*). The household head's wife (from Ocumichu) was extremely shy and resisted requests for the repetition of words, but, when discreetly overheard, did seem to aspirate the affricates—very softly. The recently engaged fourteen-year-old daughter, Chucha Aguilar, whom we met above conversing in the 'strong-throat' (*wiŋáčan*) style, always aspirated the affricates in the clear and audible way that is characteristic of the women of the Sierra Tarasca.

5. A Sketch of San Luis Potosí Huastec

NORMAN A. McQUOWN

0. PREFACE. The Huastec people (and the Huastec language) occupied and continue to occupy sizable portions of eastern San Luis Potosí and northern Veracruz. Speakers of modern Huastec probably number, at the present time, upward of fifty thousand. Both the sketch of classical and modern San Luis Potosí Huastec presented here and the fuller presentation of the data available in McQuown (1982) are based on previously collected (and, in some cases, published, or, minimally, partially edited) materials: Tapia Zenteno (1727; 1767), Andrade (1946; 1975),

Redd (1975), McQuown (1976a; 1976b; 1980), and R. S. Larsen (1955). Other sources on Huastec, some of which provided additional data, are Aschmann (1962), Guiteras Holmes (1948), K. Larsen (1949), R. S. Larsen (1971; 1972), R. S. Larsen and Pike (1949), and Lorenzana (1896). Although Manuel J. Andrade gathered a fair quantity of materials on the Huastec of the Mexican state of Veracruz (and Juan de la Cruz published the earliest known classical Huastec document, his *Doctrina christiana . . .* [1571]), these and other Veracruz Huastec materials are not included here. I trust they will be the object of another study.

The presentation here (and in the fuller grammar) represents the dialects of Tampamolón (Tapia Zenteno) and of Aquismón, Pequetzén, San Antonio, Tamaletón, Tampamolón, Tancanhuitz, and Tancoltzi (Andrade and McQuown), all in the Mexican state of San Luis Potosí.

1. INTRODUCTORY NOTES.

1.1. SOURCES OF DATA. The sources, both of non-elicited (Andrade 1946; 1975) and of elicited (all other) field-recorded materials are identified in McQuown (1980; 1982). The order of presentation of the present sketch follows that of the former source to facilitate access to further exemplification of the grammatical materials presented here. All texts were checked in the field in 1947, retranscribed and retranslated in 1948, and are now available in microfilm or hard copy (Andrade 1975). Magnetic tape copies of Andrade's original aluminum disc recordings are available from the University of Chicago Language Laboratory.

1.2. ABBREVIATIONS. The following abbreviations are used:

Cl: Classical
Hu: Huastec
Mn: Modern
Nt: Nahuat
Ntl.: Nahuatl
Sp: Spanish
To: Totonac
Zap: Zapotec
Zo: Zoque

Superscript ^{i} and ^{f} indicate informal and formal pronominal prefixes, respectively. Superscript numerals identify the order of morphological elements. Subscript numerals are used to differentiate homonyms, except in section 4.3.2.2, where they distinguish strong ($?_1$ h_1) and weak ($?_2$ h_2) phonemes. Subscript $_p$ (plural) distinguishes for example homonymic 'you sg.' and 'us'. A prefixed asterisk (*) indicates a reconstructed or unattested form.

2. PHONETICS. Some of the details of Huastec phonetics are presented in McQuown (1980:1–25). I shall not repeat them here.

3. PHONEMICS. The Huastec phonemic system may be seen in Table 5-1.

Since Huastec stress in Huastec words (and in fully adapted loan words from Spanish) is completely predictable in terms of sequences of long and short vowels, and in terms of the distance from open junctures, it is not marked here. The rules governing this automaticity may be found in McQuown (1980), together with the discussion and marking of intonation patterns (and paralinguistic phenomena other than nasalization).

The consonants in row (1) are voiceless, fortis, and, before vowels, unaspirated. Before other consonants, however, they may be lightly released. Those in row (2), with the exception of /b/, are lightly glottalized in native Huastec items. Both native Huastec /b/ and the consonants in row (2) in Spanish loans in Huastec are initially (i.e., after open junctures and after nasals) voiced stops; medially (i.e., in close juncture) voiced fricatives, and finally (i.e., before open junctures) a voiceless fricative (/b/ only). Those of row (3) are voiceless fricatives (/θ/ is interdental and /h/ is only lightly aspirated). The voiced fricatives of row (4) are lacking, both in modern Huastec and in modern Spanish (except allophonically), although they were present, in part, in Classical Spanish. Those of row (5) are nasals. Those of row (6) are semiconsonants (voiceless in final position, i.e., before open junctures). Native Huastec /l/ of row (7) is partially voiceless in final position (i.e., before open junctures). Those of row (8) are taps, and those of row (9) are trills.

The consonants in column (1), in native Huastec forms, are bilabial, in column (2) dental, in column (3) apico-alveolar, in column (4) apico-palatal, in column (5) midpalatal, in column (6) mid-palatal labialized, and in column (7) glottal. In Spanish loans in Huastec, the consonants in column (1) are bilabial labialized, in column (2) labiodental, in column (3) labiodental labialized, in column (4) dental, in column (5) dental labialized, in column (6) front palatal, in column (7) mid-palatal, in column (8) mid-palatal labialized, and in column (9) glottal labialized. Most of these consonants in Spanish loans, of course, are not fully integrated into the native Huastec system, and remain marginal.

The vowels are, in quality, much as in Spanish. In quantity, the first set is quite short, the second long and relatively steady. All vowels may be nasalized in a limited number of onomatopoetic forms.

The junctures, as used in this sketch, are indicators of morphological and syntactic boundaries (although they do, of course, have their phonetic characteristics, manifested in the surrounding segments [McQuown 1980]).

4. MORPHOPHONEMIC ALTERNATION.

4.1. CONTRACTION. Some longer Huastec forms have shorter variants: #tikin₅≠ne?θančihi¢# 'take it away from me, already!': #tikin₅≠ne·nči·¢# 'id.' Especially prone to loss (with subsequent contraction) in such contexts are Huastec /?/ and /h/.

4.2. NASALIZATION. Some Huastec forms are conventionally nasalized: ?ĩhĩhĩ·l 'neigh (of a horse)', mõ·?'mute', yõ·y 'mosquito' (Cl).

4.3. CONSONANT VARIATION.

4.3.1. CONSONANT ADDITION.

4.3.1.1. /n/-INSERTION. In verb-stems with root-medial (or stem-medial) long vowels, or root-final consonants /t t' ¢ ¢' č č'/, or stem-medial consonant clusters, Huastec /n/ is inserted between a stem-final vowel (deleting final /? w y/) and indirective /č/:

TABLE 5-1. Huastec Phonemes

Consonants

	(1)	(2)	(3)	(4)	(5)	(6)	(7)		(1)	(2)	(3)	(4)	(5)	(6)	(7)	(8)	(9)
	Native Huastec								*Spanish Loans in Huastec*								
(1)	p	t	¢	č	k	kʷ	ʔ	(1)	pʷ								
(2)	b	t'	¢'	č'	k'	k'ʷ		(2)	bʷ			d			g	gʷ	
(3)		θ	s	š			h	(3)		f	fʷ				x	xʷ	hʷ
(4)								(4)									
(5)	m	n						(5)	mʷ				nʷ	ñ			
(6)	w			y				(6)									
(7)		l						(7)					lʷ				
(8)		r						(8)					rʷ				
(9)								(9)				r̃	r̃ʷ				
	(1)	(2)	(3)	(4)	(5)	(6)	(7)		(1)	(2)	(3)	(4)	(5)	(6)	(7)	(8)	(9)

Vowels

Short

i				u
	e		o	
		a		

Long

i·				u·
	e·		o·	
		a·		

Nasalized

ĩ				ũ						ĩ·				ũ·
	ẽ		õ								ẽ·		õ·	
		ã										ã·		

Junctures

# open	≠ semi-open	- hyphen	[no marking=] close

ʔa¢'e·θa(ʔ) 'wet it' : ʔa¢'e·θanč 'wet it for him'

pašk'u(w) 'boil it' : pašk'unč 'boil it for him'

k'ʷeto(y) 'sweep it' : k'ʷetonč 'sweep it for him'

4.3.1.2. /in/-INSERTION. In verb-stems with root-final consonant, /ʔ/, Huastec /in/ is inserted between the /ʔ/ and indirective /č/:

k'a·ʔ 'burn' : k'a·ʔinč 'burn for (desire) it'

4.3.2. CONSONANT LOSS.

4.3.2.1. REDUCTION OF GEMINATES. Huastec geminate consonants may optionally reduce to a single consonant:

ʔehattala·b : ʔehatala·b 'life'

k'ʷahȧt≠ti… : kʷaha(t≠)ti… 'be…ing'

4.3.2.2. LOSS OF /ʔ/ AND /h/. Huastec /ʔ/ and Huastec /h/ have similar patterns of loss.

Each has both a strong (/$ʔ_1$/ /h_1/) and a weak (/$ʔ_2$/ /h_2/) variety. The strong varieties (/$ʔ_1$/ /h_1/) are retained, both in initial /#…/ (1) and in final /…#/ (2) positions in the utterance. Medially /$ʔ_1$/ may, however, be lost in word-final /…≠/ position (3).

Stem-final Huastec /$ʔ_1$/ may be lost before suffix-initial consonant (4), and, in some phrases, before words beginning with /$ʔ_1$/ (5).

Word-internally, Huastec /$ʔ_1$/, in the sequence /k'oʔ/, may be lost before a suffix-initial vowel /…V/, with subsequent changes in the preceding consonant (/k'o/ becomes /k'ʷ/) (6).

Word-internally, Huastec /$ʔ_2$/ is optionally lost, between vowels /…V($ʔ_2$)V…/ (7), and, in some cases, in a longer sequence, in which it is preceded by a vowel and followed by a consonant /...V($^{?}_{2}$)C/ (8).

Phrase-medially, word-initial Huastec /$^{?}_{2}$/ (/...≠($^{?}_{2}$).../ is *always* lost (9).

Huastec stem-final /h_1/ may be lost in an extreme case, where there is fusion of other elements in a complex sentence (10).

Huastec stem-final /h_1/ is *not* lost before a consonant initial (/...h_1C.../) in a following suffix (11).

Huastec word-final /h_2/ is, likewise, *not* lost before a vowel (resulting from loss of word-initial /$^{?}_1$/) initial (/...h_2≠V.../) in a following word (12).

Huastec stem-final /h_2/, however, is *always* lost before a consonant initial in a following element (13), and is optionally lost (/...V(h_2)V.../) (with ensuing fusion of the resulting cluster) before a vowel initial in such an element (14).

Huastec word-medial /h_2/, finally, is likewise optionally lost (with or without fusion of the resulting vowel cluster) (15).

Examples: (1) #$^{?}$an≠$^{?}$ek^{w}et# 'the chachalaca(s)'; (2) #šowe·$^{?}$# 'now'; (3) #kin$_2$≠θay (a$^{?}$≠)in$_3$≠k'ubak# 'let him raise his hand!'; (4) #tana·($^{?}$)k'i(h)≠... 'right there ...' but: #šo·$^{?}$k'i(h)≠... 'right now'; (4) *pakθa$^{?}$ + čik : #pakθačik# 'thick things'; (5) #šowe·$^{?}$≠ $^{?}$ohni$^{?}$# : #šo$^{?}$o·ni$^{?}$# 'now, yes!'; (6) #pik'o$^{?}$# 'dog'; #pi·k'^{w}al# '(one's) dog'; (7) #$^{?}$alwa-$^{?}$i¢# : #$^{?}$alwa·¢# 'good, already!'; (8) * #tikin$_5$≠či$^{?}$θančih# 'bring it to me!' : #tikin$_5$≠ či·nč(ih≠$^{?}$)u$_4$≠kita·l# 'bring me my load!'; (9) #k'al(≠$^{?}$)an≠ma¢e·t# 'with the machete'; (10) #šowe·$^{?}$≠$^{?}$ohni$^{?}$# : #šo$^{?}$o·ni$^{?}$# 'now, yes!'; (11) #bih# 'name' : #bihčik# 'names'; (12) ≠hu·n≠($^{?}$)i$_6$≠$^{?}$o·rah≠($^{?}$)an≠$^{?}$akal# 'at one o'clock in the morning'; (13) #$^{?}$in$_1$≠ $^{?}$o·wme·θa·(h)≠ma≠... 'I have slowed down until ...'; (13) *la·huh + čik : #la·hučik# 'tens'; (14) #$^{?}$in$_2$≠$^{?}$o·lčihi¢# : #$^{?}$in$_2$≠$^{?}$o·lči·¢# 'he already apprised him'; (14) * #$^{?}$abal≠ka≠ tiša·k'nančihat# : #$^{?}$abal≠ka≠tiša·k'nanča·t# 'so that it may be taken away from him'; (15) #tehe·$^{?}$# 'here' : #te·($^{?}$)≠... 'here ...'; *mahul + lab : #mawlab# 'paint'.

4.3.2.3. LOSS OF /n/. Word-internally, before suffix-initial /m/ or /w/, stem-final /n/ may be lost:

* *hilk'on + mač* : *hilk'omač* 'left-overs'

* *k'ambin + wa·l-eh* : *k'ambiwa·leh* 'person deceived'

4.3.2.4. LOSS OF /w/ AND /y/. Word-internally, between vowels (/...V(w/y)V.../), Huastec /w/ (1) and Huastec /y/ (2) may be lost (with subsequent fusion of preceding and following vowels):

* *$^{?}$ehtow + a·mal* : *$^{?}$ehto·mal* '(to) have been able'

* *nuhuw + a·mal* : *nuhu·mal* '(to) have sold it'

* #kit≠¢'akiyi¢# : #kit≠¢'aki·¢# 'arise, already!'

* Ø$_3$≠taleyi¢# : #Ø$_3$≠tali·¢# 'it ended, already'

4.3.2.5. LOSS OF /l/. Word(1)- or phrase(2)-medially, Huastec /l/ may be lost (with subsequent fusion of preceding and following vowels):

* #kit≠belali¢# : #kit≠bela·¢# 'walk, already!'

* #kit≠koyoli¢# : #kit≠koyo·¢# 'rest, already!'

#pe·l≠($^{?}$)in$_1$≠Ø≠$^{?}$inik# : #pe·n≠Ø≠$^{?}$inik# 'I (am) (a) man'

Stem-final Huastec /l/ may be lost before a suffix-initial consonant:

* *¢ipil + čik* : *¢ipičik* 'small ones'

4.3.3. CONSONANT METATHESIS. In Huastec sequences of vowel plus /$^{?}$/ or /h/ plus vowels /o/ or /u/ (1) plus consonant, the second vowel is converted into /w/ and metathesizes with the /$^{?}$/ or /h/ to form the sequence /Vw$^{?}$C/ (or /VwhC/), and, if the second vowel is /i/ (2), it is converted into /y/ and metathesizes with the /$^{?}$/ or /h/ to form the sequence /Vy$^{?}$C/ (or /VyhC/).

Examples: *ni$^{?}$o(y) + č + ih : niw$^{?}$čih '(to) dirty it for him'; (1) *ya$^{?}$ul + a¢ : yaw$^{?}$la·¢ 'sickness'; *t'a$^{?}$i(y) + p + iy : #$^{?}$in$_2$≠t'ay$^{?}$-piy# 'he sowed it quickly'; *¢'a$^{?}$i(y) + č + ih : #maš≠ki$_2$≠¢'ay$^{?}$čih# 'if we bought it for him'; *k'a$^{?}$il + a¢ : #Ø$_3$≠k'ay$^{?}$la·¢# 'water was carried'; *bahu(w) + č + ih : #tu$_6$≠ bawhčih# '(in that) I extended it to you';

*?ahi(y) + č + ih : #?in₂ ≠ ?ayhčih# 'he read it for him'; *pahi(y) + čik + iy : #?im₂ ≠ payhčikiy# 'he sharpened many things'.

4.3.4. CONSONANT SUBSTITUTION.

4.3.4.1. ASSIMILATION. Some cases of substitution of Huastec consonants, one for another may be characterized as *assimilation*:

/C/ : /C'/   pič(a?) 'snap it' : pič'(k'an) 'snap'

/?/ : /y/   *haha·? + ik'ih : #haha·yk'ih# 'that (is), indeed, it!'

/n/ : /m/   *k'an + b : k'amb 'cause to fall in love'

4.3.4.2. DISSIMILATION. Others may be characterized as *dissimilation*:

/¢/ : /š/   holči·¢ + čik : #ka₁ ≠ holči·ščik ≠ patal# 'you (pl.) pour it all on him, already!'

/¢'/ : /š/   ši¢ 'blood' : šiš-te? 'sangre-gado (tree)'

/č/ : /š/   *?uč + ne·nek : #Q₃ ≠ ?uš-ne·nek# 'it has been said to him'

4.3.4.3. REPHONEMICIZATION. Others may be characterized as products of *rephonemicization*.

/k'ʷ/ : /k'/   *t'ik'ʷ + on : t'ik'on 'jump about'

/k'ʷ/ : /?/   yak'ʷ (a?) 'grasp it' : ya?(ub) 'fistful'

4.3.4.4. SURVIVALS. Some cases of apparent substitution of /C'/ for /C/ may constitute *survivals* of an earlier active process of semantic derivation:

/¢/ : /¢'/   ¢a?uw 'mash it' : ¢'a?uw 'chew it'

/k/ : /k'/   kakay 'burnt-smelling' : k'ak'al 'heat'

/k/ : /k'/   ≠Q₃ ≠ kaleh ≠ 'he went out' : ≠Q₃ ≠ k'aleh ≠ 'he went away'

4.3.4.5. SURVIVALS. Some cases of apparent substitution of /č/ for /¢/ or of /č'/ for /¢'/ may likewise constitute *survivals* of another earlier active process of semantic derivation:

/¢/ : /č/   ¢il 'bald (hairless)' : čil 'bare (branchless)'

/¢'/ : /č'/   ¢'i¢' 'cheep' : č'i·č' 'screech'

4.3.4.6. CROSS-OVER. Some such cases of semantic derivational survivals may consti-

tute instances of *cross-over* along the two dimensions /¢/ : /¢'/ (glottalization) and /¢/ : /č/ (palatalization):

/¢'/ : /č/   ¢'a?(ublek) 'cheek' : ča?(u·l) 'cheeky'

/¢'/ : /č/   ?a¢' 'get wet' : ?ač 'bathe'

4.3.4.7. LABIALIZATION. Some cases of Huastec consonant substitution, however, may constitute instances of *labialization* and/or *semi-consonantization*:

/h/ : /w/   mah(uy) 'paint it' : maw(čal) 'paint it for him'

/m/ : /w/   ¢am(ay) 'cool' : ¢aw(θa·l) 'cool it'

4.3.4.8. DELABIALIZATION. Some cases of Huastec consonant substitution, finally, may constitute, before rounded vowels /o/ and /u/, instances of *delabialization* of basically labialized consonants:

/k'ʷ/ : /k'/   pi·k'ʷ(al) '(one's) dog' : pik'(o?) 'dog'

/k'ʷ/ : /k'/   ≠Q₃ ≠ pak'ʷ(čin)≠ 'it was washed for him' : pak'(ul) 'washer-woman'

4.4. VOWEL VARIATION.

4.4.1. VOWEL FUSION. Huastec like vowels may fuse into a single long vowel:

/i·/   *¢'i·w¢'i· + i·l : #Q₃ ≠ ¢'i·w¢'i·l# 'it cheeps'

/e·/   *?ẽ·h?ẽ· + e·l : #Q₃ ≠ ?ẽ·h?ẽ·l# 'he moans'

4.4.2. VOWEL FUSION AND LENGTHENING. Huastec sequences of /V₁?V₂/ (1), /V₁hV₂/ (2), /V₁wV₂/ (3), /V₁yV₂/ (4), and /V₁lV₂/ (5), after losing the intervocalic consonant, may fuse the two vowels, resulting in a /V₁·/ (except for /e/ plus /i/, which results in /i·/).

Examples: (1) #?alwa?i¢ : #?alwa·¢# 'good, already!'; (1) hita?ak : hita·k 'whoever (it) was'; ¢u?u·mal : ¢u·mal '(to) have seen it'; (2) #?in₂ ≠ ?o·lčihi¢# : #?in₂ ≠ ?o·lči·¢# 'he apprised him of it, already'; (2) #Q₃ ≠ waklehi¢# : #Q₃ ≠ wakle·¢# 'it got late, already'; (2) #Q₁ₚ ≠ wanahi¢# : #Q₁ₚ ≠ wana·¢# 'let's go, already!' (3) *¢u?uwa·mal : ¢u?u·mal '(to) have seen it'; (4) #kit ≠ ¢'akiyi¢# : #kit ≠ ¢'aki·¢# 'get up, already!' (4) #kit ≠ taleyi¢# :

#kit-≠tali·¢# 'wind up, already!'; (5) #kit≠
belali¢# : #kit≠bela·¢# 'walk, already!'; (5)
#kit≠koyoli¢# : #kit≠koyo·¢# 'rest, already!'

Longer sequences of /V₁ʔCV₂/, after losing
both the /ʔ/ and the other consonant, may
fuse the two vowels, sometimes with the
quality of /V₁/ (1), sometimes with that of /V₂/
(2).

Examples: (1) neʔθančih : ne·nčih '(to) take
it away from him'; (2) čiʔθančih : ča·nčih '(to)
bring it for him'.

4.4.3. Vowel lengthening. Some short
vowels may be replaced by the corresponding long vowels, in processes of phonologically and/or morphologically conditioned
variation, with distinct semantic results,
both lexical and grammatical:

/i/ : /i·/　yahčik 'painful' : yahči·k(na·l)
'makes him suffer it' (causative)

/i/ : /i·/　pik'(oʔ) 'dog' : pi·k'ʷ(al) '(one's)
dog' (possessed form)

/i/ : /i·/　¢ipil(iʔ) 'small' : ¢ipi·l-t'uhub
'small stone' (dependentizing)

/e/ : /e·/　k'ʷet(oy) 'sweep it' : k'ʷe·t
'broom' (noun formative)

/e/ : /e·/　k'ʷet(oy) 'sweep it' : k'ʷe·t(ol)
'sweeps' (intransitivizing)

/e/ : /e·/　¢'at'en(čih) 'stick to him' :
#ʔin₂≠¢'at'e·n(čal)# 'he follows him
closely' (augmentative)

/a/ : /a·/　¢ap(ik) 'strong' : ¢a·p(la·b)
'strength' (noun formative)

/a/ : /a·/　ʔa¢' 'get wet' : ʔa·¢' 'wet' (adjective formative)

/a/ : /a·/　hay(k'iʔ) 'when?' : ha·y 'how
much?' (particle formative)

/o/ : /o·/　ʔok 'skull' : ʔo·k 'head' (noun
derivative)

/o/ : /o·/　bišom 'dancing' : bišo·m(a·b)
'dancer' (noun formative)

/u/ : /u·/　kuhuw 'tasty' : #ʔin₃≠ku-
hu·w# 'its taste' (possessed form)

/u/ : /u·/　nuh(uwal) 'sells it' : nu·h(ul)
'sells; seller' (intransitivizing)

4.4.4. Vowel loss. Huastec word-medial
short vowels between single consonants may
be lost (1); in certain derivatives the loss is
obligatory (2).

Examples: (1) #ʔu₃≠kaniya·mal# 'I have

called him' : #ʔu₃≠kanya·mal# 'id.'; (1)
*#ʔu₃≠č'učubiyal# 'I kissed her' : #ʔu₃≠
č'učbiyal# 'id.'; (2) hi·k'ib 'fear' hi·k'b(eh)
'fearful'; (2) #tam≠ti≠θ₃≠šeʔe¢in≠(ʔ)a₃≠
diyo·s≠… 'when God walked …' šeʔ¢in(ta-
la·b) 'conduct'; (2) ʔišak 'breath' : ʔišk'(al)
'breathes'.

4.4.5. Vowel shortening. In certain
derivative uses of Huastec forms which
contain a long vowel, the long vowel is
shortened:

/i·/ : /i/　k'i·θ 'thorn' : k'iθ-ʔu·t' 'por-
cupine'

/i·/ : /i/　mi·m 'mother' : mim-leʔ 'stepmother'

/e·/ : /e/　pe·m 'rubber' : pem(a·l)
'(one's) buttocks'

/e·/ : /e/　le·y 'lightning' : ley(oyo·l)
'brilliant'

/a·/ : /a/　la·huh 'ten' : lahu(h)hu·n
'eleven'

/a·/ : /a/　ma·l 'swelling' : mal(ul)
'large toad'

/o·/ : /o/　θo·t 'rattle' : θot(oθ) 'rattler'

/o·/ : /o/　ho·l 'hole' : hol(tayʔ) 'pot-
ash'

/u·/ : /u/　θu·m 'worm' : θum(aθ)
'wormy'

/u·/ : /u/　pu·lik 'large' : pulik(¢'e·n)
'Large Mountain'

4.4.6. Vowel substitution. A survival of
old *vowel-ablaut* seems to occur in Huastec,
a variety in which lower (back) vowels in base
forms are replaced by higher (front) vowels in
derivatives:

/e/ : /i/　#ʔin₂≠t'ek'(a·l)# 'he shafts
it' : t'ič'(ok'la·b) 'shaft, arrow'

/a/ : /i/　ʔat'(aš) 'bad' : ʔit'(iš) 'an-
noyance'

/a·/ : /i/　θa·m 'nose' : #ʔin₂≠θim-
(iyal)# 'he blows (his nose)'

/u/ : /i/　ʔuš(um) 'woman' : ʔiš
'female-…'

/e·/ : /i·/　pe·l(na·l) 'separates it' : pi·l
'separate'

/a·/ : /e/　bekla·k '(one's) bone' : beklek
'bone'

/o·/ : /e·/　ʔo·m 'sows corn' : ʔe·m 'corn
plant'

/a·/ : /o/   ma·m 'grandfather' :
  mom(ob) 'grandson'
/o/ : /u/   ʔoh 'fragrant avocado' : ʔuh
  'avocado'
/o·/ : /u/   šo·ȼ'(anal) 'wrinkles up' :
  šuȼ'(el) 'wrinkles'

4.4.7. VOWEL INSERTION. In roots with
final consonants /t t' ȼ ȼ' č č'/, an echo vowel
(V₁) is inserted before a following suffix-initial
consonant:

  *pit'(iy) 'smooth it' : pit'i(me·θaʔ)
  'smoothed it'

4.4.8. /Vn/-INSERTION. In verb roots (or
stems) with final /ʔ/, final dental, or final consonant cluster, the sequence /Vn/ (or, in
some cases, optionally, /V/ alone) is inserted
before a following suffix-initial /č/ (such as in
-č indirective or in -čik repetitive); the /V/ is
that of the stem-formative:

  kʷiʔ(iy) 'shot it' : kʷiʔi(čikiy) 'shot it
    repeatedly'
  mat(iy) 'lent it' : matin(č-ih) 'lent it to him'
  puȼ(iy) 'plucked it' : puȼi(čikiy) 'plucked it
    repeatedly'
  taʔp(aʔ) 'guarded it' : #tikin₅≠taʔpan-
    (čih)# 'guard it for me!'
  beletn(aʔ) 'took care of him' : beletnan-
    (čikiy) 'took care of him repeatedly'
  bi·našn(aʔ) 'bestowed it' : bi·našnan(čikiy)
    'bestowed it repeatedly'
  wenk'(ow) 'turned it
    around' : wenk'o(čikiy) 'turned it around
    repeatedly'

4.5. VOWEL HARMONY. Although there
seems to be some limitation in the variety of
vowels in subsequent syllables, as one passes
from prior to subsequent, in a succession of
syllables, examples seem to be lacking, quali-
tatively, only for sequences of /i/, /e/, and /o/,
followed by /u/. In subsequent syllables, then,
only /u/ does not occur after /i/, /e/, or /o/.

4.6. PHONOLOGY OF LOAN WORDS.

4.6.1. A SAMPLING OF HUASTEC LOAN
  WORDS.
pik'oʔ 'dog' : Cl Zap biʔkùʔ
pi·taʔ 'chicken' : (?)
pen(a·l) 'gathering up' : Cl Ntl peʔpena
pelo·tah 'ball' : Mn Sp pelóta (Mn Hu
  paθa·l≠pelo·tah)

pe·gruh 'Peter' : Sp pédro
pe·šuh '(pound) weight' : Cl Sp péso
(ȼ'u·ȼ'-)pa·p '(woman's) uncle' : (?)
pa·tuš 'duck(s)' : Cl Sp pátos
pa·kaš 'cow(s)' : Cl Sp bákas
pa·ynuh 'kerchief' : Cl Sp páño
pa·leʔ 'priest' : Cl Sp pádre
pula·tuh 'plate' : Cl Sp pláto
timaʔ 'cup' : Cl Zo *tima (?) (Mn Zo ȼima)
tiyo·pan 'church' : Cl Ntl teo·pan(λi)
  'temple'
tena·m '(stone-fenced) ranch' : Cl Ntl
  tena·m(iλ)
te·paʔ '(ancient) fire-bearer', 'conqueror' :
  Cl Ntl tepe·(wa·ni)
tarapi·ȼ 'sugar-press' : Cl Sp trapíče
ta·t 'mat' : Nt (pe)ta·t (?)
ta·tah 'poppa' : Nt ta·tah
tumi·n '(one) "bit"' : Cl Sp tomín
ȼiȼalo·n 'cracklings' : Cl Sp čičařón
kine·yaʔ '(Guinea) banana' : Cl Sp ginéa
ke·šuh 'cheese' : Cl Sp késo
kaȼi·n 'brains' : To kaȼi·n(i[h])
kanȼi·l(a·b) 'belt', 'bandage' : Cl Sp (?)
kalani·yo(h)(≠pat'a·l) 'chain' : Cl Sp
  kadeníλa
koto·n(la·b) 'blouse' : Cl Sp kotón
košta·l '(gunny-)sack' : Cl Sp kostál
kole·kiyoh 'school' : Mn Sp koléxio
ko·čeh 'automobile' : Mn Sp kóče (Mn Hu
  belθa·l≠ko·čeh)
kuȼi·l 'knife' : Cl Sp kučíλo
kuȼila·n(≠košol) 'fighting(-cock)' : Cl Sp
  kučiλán(o) (?)
kuθine·l '(a) cook' : Cl Sp koθinér(o)
kuθi·nuh 'kitchen' : Cl Sp koθína
kuma·leh   'co-female-parent-in-spirit' : Cl
  Sp komádre
kumpa·leh   'co-male-parent-in-spirit' : Cl
  Sp kompádre
kum(payʔlo·m) 'god-father' : Cl Sp kom(-...)
kʷayaʔ 'twin(s)' : Cl Ntl ko·a·ʔ (?)
kʷe·ntah 'account' (Sp cuidado) : Sp kuénta
ʔelbe·naš 'mint (plant)' : Cl Sp yèřbas
  buénas
ʔanȼana·ʔ 'thus' : Cl Sp ànsiná
ʔanȼe·ʔ 'thus' : Cl Sp ansí
ʔalmuθa·l(a·b) 'lunch' : Cl Sp almořθář
ʔa·šuš 'garlic' : Cl Sp ážos

ʔa·muh 'master' (Sp *patrón*) : Cl Sp *ámo*
bi·noh 'liquor' : Mn Sp *bíno*
bi·nuh 'liquor' : Cl Sp *bíno*
bale·yaʔ 'watermelon' : Cl Sp (?)
θimalo·n 'wild' : Cl Sp *θimaᷓón*
ši·laʔ 'saddle' : Cl Sp *síʎa*
šabu·n 'soap' : Cl Sp *žabón*
šumpele·l 'hat' : Cl Sp *sombrér(o)*
ha·ȼah 'axe' : Cl Sp *háča*
miȼuʔ 'cat' : Cl Ntl *mis(to·n)*
me·šah 'table' : Cl Sp *mésa*
maȼe·t 'machete' : Cl Sp *mačét(e)*
maš 'whether' : Cl Sp *màs* ... (?)
mã·šuh 'tame' : Cl Sp *mánso*
moȼoʔ 'maimed' (Sp *manco*) : Cl Sp *móčo*
na·nah 'momma' : Nt *na·nah*
weh(eʔ) 'ancient' : Nt *weh(ika)* 'long time'
limo·šnah 'alms' : Cl Sp *limósna*
lana·š 'orange(s)' : Cl Sp *(na)ránžas*
la·buš 'nail(s)' : Cl Sp *klábos*

(*Sources*: Andrews 1975; Aschmann 1975; Harrison and Harrison 1948; Key and Key 1953; Molina 1571; Pickett 1959.)

4.6.2. Phonological shifts in Huastec loan words. The phonological source systems (and their phonetic ranges) involved are those of sixteenth-century Spanish (before 1555), Classical Nahuatl (Andrews 1975:3–12), (modern) "Mejicano" (Key and Key 1953:iv–v), modern Mexican Spanish, and other possible source languages such as Totonac (McQuown 1974), Zapotec (Pickett 1969), and Zoque (Wonderly 1951).

The phonological recipient systems are those of Classical Huastec (Tapia Zenteno 1727; 1767), and slightly divergent varieties of modern Huastec of San Luis Potosí (Tapia Zenteno 1767; McQuown 1980; R. Larsen 1955) and of Veracruz (Cruz 1571; Andrade 1946). Modern San Luis Potosí Huastec has /ȼ/ where modern Veracruz Huastec (like earlier Classical Huastec?) has /č/.

Details of these systems are presented in McQuown (1982), as is a full listing of the phonological shifts involved in passing from source systems to recipient systems.

5. Morphology. I shall begin the presentation of Huastec morphology with a discussion of morpheme shapes and the reduplica-

tional alteration of such shapes, two aspects which cross-cut its full range.

5.1. Morpheme shapes.

5.1.1. /C/. Some derivational morphemes have this shape:

/p/ 'quickly' : ȼ'ayʔ-p-iy 'bought it quickly'
/č/ (indirective) : ȼ'ayʔ-č-ih 'bought it for him'
/k/ (stem-formative) : ȼ'iʔ-k-in 'began'

5.1.2. /CV/. A few preposed particles have this shape:

/ti/ (preposition) : 'among', 'at', 'for', 'from', 'in', 'to'
/ka/ (subordinating conjunction) : '(so) that ...'
/ʔi₂/ (pronominal subject of transitives) : 'we'
/ma/ (concessive conjunction; preposition) : 'as far as', 'even', 'until', 'up to'

5.1.3. /CVC/; /CV·C/.

5.1.3.1. /CVC/. Many roots and some suffixes have the shape /CVC/: tip '(small) tick', pop(aʔ) 'scrubbed it', ȼ'up(iθ) 'pointed', pet 'turtle', t'ot 'turkey-buzzard', nut' 'tar', čuč 'coyote', θakʷ 'soapstone', ȼ'iʔ 'anus', teʔ 'tree', teh 'implicitly', tam 'when', paw 'smoke', -čik (plural), -maʔ 'prone to ...', -waʔ 'full of ...', -leʔ 'step-...', -lab (non-possessed entity).

5.1.3.2. /CV·C/. Some roots and some suffixes have the shape /CV·C/ : pa·p '(woman's) father', ʔi·t 'new', ʔu·t' 'opossum', ʔi·ȼ' 'moon', 'month', le·ȼ' 'ulcer', ʔa·č 'grandmother', ȼ'u·č 'a quarter' (measure), wa·k 'cowbird', ȼo·k 'shotgun', 'rifle', k'a·k 'hot', θek'ʷ '(kind of) lizard', pa·k'ʷ '(one's) nest', ti·ʔ 'scare(-crow)', ȼe·ʔ 'four', ʔo·ʔ 'small frog', t'u·ʔ 'naked baby', ʔi·b 'no', ʔe·b 'sky', ʔa·b 'rain', θu·b(ayal) 'whistles at him', k'i·θ 'thorn', kʷa·θ 'cow's-tongue (vine)', ʔe·š 'small palm basket', ʔo·š 'three', ku·š 'back', ti·h 'in truth', ʔa·h 'hunts', ȼo·h 'lion', yu·h(uyal) 'mixes them (corn with beans)', t'i·m 'frog', θe·m 'harvest-mite', ʔa·m 'spider', to·m 'grass', ču·m, 'point', te·n 'plum', ya·n 'lots of...', ko·n(ol) 'requests' (: kon(oyal) 'asks for it'), hu·n 'one', ka·w 'speaks', 'word', ʔo·w 'far', pe·l 'it is', ʔa·l 'inside', ʔo·l 'prays', -me·h (intransitivizing).

5.1.3.3. /CVS$^{\textipa{P}}$/; /CV·S$^{\textipa{P}}$/. Some few roots have these shapes, involving the semi-vowels (S), /w/ and /y/: tiw$^{\textipa{P}}$ 'thither' (: tiwa$^{\textipa{P}}$), ¢iw$^{\textipa{P}}$ 'chayote (vine and fruit)' (: *¢i$^{\textipa{P}}$iw), ha·w$^{\textipa{P}}$ 'straw' (: *ha·$^{\textipa{P}}$uw), tay$^{\textipa{P}}$ 'lime' (: *ta$^{\textipa{P}}$iy), may$^{\textipa{P}}$ 'limestone' (: *ma$^{\textipa{P}}$iy), way$^{\textipa{P}}$ 'cob of corn' (: *wa$^{\textipa{P}}$iy).

5.1.4. /CVCV/. A single root has this shape: tala 'finish …-ing' (: tala$^{\textipa{P}}$ 'finished').

5.1.5. /CV·CVC/; /CVCV·C/. A very few roots have these shapes: ta·tah 'poppa', bele·w 'nine'.

5.1.6. /CV·CCVC/. Consonant clusters of this type occur only in roots borrowed from Spanish: k^{w}e·ntah 'accounting, care'.

5.1.7. /VC/; /V·C/. Numerous suffixes have these shapes: -i¢ 'already'; -i¢ (derivational suffix) : θan-i¢ 'ant'; -oy (verbal thematic suffix); -i·θ (transitivizing suffix); -i·b 'derivational suffix) : $^{\textipa{P}}$ol-i·b 'testicles'; -a·h (passivizing completive suffix).

5.2. REDUPLICATION. There are a number of types of reduplication in Huastec, for roots of all kinds. Its semantic function seems to be augmentative, both energetically and temporally.

5.2.1. /V$_1$C$_2$(C$_3$)/ (SUFFIXED TO THE ROOT). This is the commonest type of root-reduplication, both verbal (1) and nominal (2); some of these reduplications contain a vowel different from that of the root (/iC$_2$/, /oC$_2$/, /uC$_2$/).

Examples: (1) ¢alp(ay) 'thought about it' : ¢alpap(ay) 'thought on it well'; (1) ¢u$^{\textipa{P}}$(uw) 'saw it' : ¢u$^{\textipa{P}}$u$^{\textipa{P}}$(uy) 'glimpsed it'; wip(ol) 'turning' : wipop(o·l) 'twirling'; (1) k'uč(iy) 'scrubbed it' : k'učič(i·l) 'thrashed'; (2) ket(eθ) 'seated' : ketet(eθ) 'well-seated'; (2) yaš(u$^{\textipa{P}}$) 'green' : yašuš(u·l) 'very green'.

5.2.2. /C$_1$oC$_2$/ (SUFFIXED TO THE ROOT). This type, consisting of total-root reduplication and replacement of the root-vowel, is not common:

*pit' : pit'pot' 'blue lizard'.

5.2.3. /C$_1$/ (SUFFIXED TO THE ROOT). This type is not common:

θal(¢'a¢'aθ) 'pallid' : θalθ(am) 'quite tender'
*k'oč : k'očk'(ol) 'setting hen'
*kuš : kušk(um) 'small gray owl'

5.2.4. /C$_1$V$_1$w$^{\textipa{P}}$/; /C$_1$V$_1$y$^{\textipa{P}}$/ (PREFIXED TO THE ROOT). These onomatopoetic types are preposed:

*č'i·h : č'iw$^{\textipa{P}}$č'i·h 'sound of the "flit" gun'
*wahu·$^{\textipa{P}}$: way$^{\textipa{P}}$wahu·$^{\textipa{P}}$ 'hoots', 'howls'

5.2.5. /C$_1$V$_1$y/ (PREFIXED TO THE ROOT). This type, likewise preposed, is rare:

*θam : θayθam 'roach'

5.3. PLURALIZATION. Huastec verb roots and/or stems may be pluralized, by adding the suffix -čik, preceded by /θ/ (1), or by adaptations of stem-final formatives, consisting of stem-formative vowel alone (2) (/V[$^{\textipa{P}}$]/, /V[h]/, /V[w]/, /V[y]/), or by such stem-formative vowels in combination with /n/ (3).

Examples: (1) mu$^{\textipa{P}}$(uw) 'broke it up' : mu$^{\textipa{P}}$čik 'break it up repeatedly'; (1) *k^{w}ah(a$^{\textipa{P}}$) 'struck it' : k^{w}ahčik 'strike it repeatedly'; (2) *šap-k(a$^{\textipa{P}}$) 'inserted it' : šapkačik 'insert it repeatedly'; (2) pak'^{w}l(eh) 'was washed' : pak'^{w}lečik 'be washed repeatedly'; (2) wenk'(ow) 'turned it around' : wenk'očik 'turn it around repeatedly'; (2) pu¢(iy) 'plucked it' : pu¢ičik 'pluck them repeatedly'; (3) beletn(a$^{\textipa{P}}$) 'took care of it' : beletnančik 'take care of it repeatedly'.

6. VERB MORPHOSYNTAX. This section will cover both *verb morphology* (processes which take place between potentially open junctures, on either side of the verb complex) and a limited *verb-phrase syntax* (processes that include the particle or particles that are preposed to this core [postposed particles are enclitic, that is, are preceded by close junctures, in the same way that suffixes are, and are, on occasion, interspersed with these latter]).

6.0. ORDER OF PREPOSED ELEMENTS. Elements *preposed* to the verb-complex appear in the following order:

(0) (Negative) adverbial particles
(1) Subordinating (conjunctional) particles
(2) Adverbial particles
(3) ([Object-] subject) pronominal particles
(4) Adverbial particles

These numerals are superposed over the relevant elements in the examples to follow.

Examples: (0) #$\overset{0}{\textipa{P}}$i·b≠$\overset{1}{t}$ikin$_5$≠k^w$\overset{3}{i}$$^{\textipa{P}}$iy#$^{\textipa{P}}$ata-tal# 'don't shoot me, brother!' ≠$\overset{0}{wa}$·y≠$\overset{1}{ku}$$_3$≠ $^{\textipa{P}}$u¢'a$^{\textipa{P}}$≠ 'in truth did I drink it'; (1) #$\overset{}{tin}_2$≠

93

ʔalwaʔ≠t'oke·θaʔ≠ 'in that he cleaned it well'; *≠kit≠k'al(eh)≠tikin₅≠tolmiy#* 'so that you go in order that you may help me'; *#tokatkʷaʔ≠(ʔ)i₁≠ k'ʷahat≠* 'just, they say, he is'; *#wala·m≠(ʔ)i₂≠t'o·hončih)≠* 'perhaps we worked at it'; (3) *≠ši≠θ₃≠wa·yi¢≠t'aha·l ≠ti≠ʔušum#* 'who, in truth, already, acted like a woman'; (4) *#yab≠ki₃≠hayk'iʔ≠k'a-ni·θa·l≠* 'we do not ever appreciate her'; *#ʔi·b≠ka₁≠ʔa₂≠ʔiči·č≠le·ʔnaʔ≠* 'not that in your heart you desire her' (Cl); *#ʔit≠leh≠ ¢ekenek#* 'you've tired a lot'; *#ʔantik'al≠ki₂ ≠ʔalk'iθ≠¢'ehwališnaʔ≠* 'and with that, that we for nothing perform charity on it'.

6.1. POSITIONS WITHIN THE VERB-STEM COMPLEX. Positions *within* the verb-stem complex are the following:

(1) (Root and/or) stem
(2) Status markers
(3) Status changers
(4) Indirectives
(5) Stem formatives
(6) Voice changers
(7) Aspect markers
(8) Terminals
(9) Anterior modal marker
(10) Plural marker
(11) Adverbial clitics

These numerals are superposed to the relevant elements in the examples; see section 6.4(9)ff.

Positions (10) and (11) are interchangeable, as are Positions (9) and (10), and (9) and (11).

6.2. VERB ROOT (AND STEM) TYPES.

6.2.1. INHERENTLY NEUTRAL-STATUSED (ZERO ARGUMENT). These are either intransitive (1), or transitive (2), in their derivatives, in accordance with the particular non—semantically derivative status marker, with which, in order to be used, they are necessarily linked.

(1) *k'ib(eh)* 'be lost' : *#kum≠θ₃≠neʔe¢ ≠ku₁≠k'ibehi¢#* 'since it is going to be lost, already'
(2) *k'ib(aʔ)* 'lose it' : *#ta·ʔ≠(ʔ)in₂≠k'i-baʔi¢≠* 'there he lost it, already'

6.2.2. INHERENTLY INTRANSITIVE (ONE ARGUMENT):

-*θ* 'be' : *#pe·l≠(ʔ)it≠θ≠ʔešo·bčiš#* 'you (are) (a) teacher'
paʔ(iy) 'descend' : *#θ₃≠paʔiy≠(ʔ)an≠ t'ot#* 'the turkey-buzzard descended'

6.2.3. INHERENTLY TRANSITIVE (TWO ARGUMENTS):

hol(ow) 'empty it out': *#yab≠(ʔ)in₂≠holo-wal≠(ʔ)in₃≠ʔat'aška·w#* 'he doesn't empty out his bad words'

6.2.4. TRANSITIVES WITH INHERENT OBJECT (THREE ARGUMENTS): An externally expressed object is necessarily a *second* object, either indirect (1), or direct (2), if it is the indirect object which is inherent:

(1) *tawn(aʔ)* 'say it to someone': *#ʔin₂≠ta-wna·l≠(ʔ)in₃≠tomki·l#* 'he says to his spouse'
(2) *piθ(aʔ)* 'bestow it on him': *#θ₁≠neʔe¢ ≠ku₃≠piθaʔ≠(ʔ)i₆≠t'ohla·b#* 'I'm going to give him some work'

6.3. COMPOUND VERB STEMS.

6.3.1. VERB WITH VERB:

talaʔ 'end it' + *ʔo¢(i¢)* 'enter' : *tala(ʔ) ʔo¢* 'enter all-the-way' : *#ta·mkʷa(ʔ≠ ʔa)n≠ʔolom≠θ₃≠talaʔo¢eneki¢kʷaʔ≠* 'when, they say, the pig had entered all-the-way, already, they say ...'

(See section 4.3.2.1.)

6.3.2. NOUN WITH VERB:

¢ab 'two', 'twice', 'again' + *wat'b(aʔ)* 'ferry it across' : *¢abwat'baʔ* 'ferry it across again' : *#tikin₅≠¢abwat'baʔ≠ʔabal≠-tu₄≠ku·š#* 'in order that you might again ferry me back across'

6.3.3. VERB WITH NOUN:

pe·n 'pick up' + *limo·snah* 'alms' : *pe·nlimo·snah* 'gather alms' : *#θ₃≠šeʔ-eš≠ti≠θ₃≠penlimo·snah≠(ʔ)u₄≠ mi·m#*

'she goes about gathering alms, my mother'

6.4. DERIVED VERB STEMS. In positions (1) through (10) in the verb complex occur the derived verb stems, some more purely derivational, some more purely inflectional.

In position (1) occur the verb *bases*, simplex (roots), and compound (or complex) (stems), as well as those recycled complex stems which are reintroduced into the base position, to be in turn subjected to further derivation and inflection.

In position (11) occur the adverbial *clitics*, found with the other major form-classes, the nominals, and the particles, as well.

Positions (1) through (8) constitute the core of the verb complex (exhibiting the *terminals* of position [8]); position (9) adds the *anterior-modal* marker to this core, position (10) further adds the *plural* marker, and this expanded core (without [9]) is particularly susceptible to recycling through the base position.

It is not surprising, then, that positions (9) and (10), as well as positions (9) and (11), are interchangeable, as are (10) and (11), as the focus shifts from restricted core—(1) through (8)—to anterior-modally marked core—(1) through (9)—to plurally marked core—(1) through (10) without (9).

Examples: (1) *roots* (intransitive): *ʔah(at)* 'sing', *¢em(e¢)* 'die', *ʔač(in)* 'bathe', *paʔ(iy)* 'descend', *hik'(ey)* 'be afraid', *bač(uy)* 'wilt', *ʔa·θ(il)* 'run', *kal(el)* 'exit', *¢'ih(al)* 'excrete', *koy(ol)* 'rest', *yaʔ(ul)* 'be sick', *¢'ak(i·l)* 'rise', *hob(el)* 'bloat', *ʔa·ʔ(a·l)* 'murmur', *ʔo·ʔ(o·l)* 'sing', *¢ah(u·l)* 'get cold'; *roots* (transitive): *ʔik(iʔ)* 'cart it', *pal(aʔ)*, 'hang it', *loʔ(ow)* 'pierce it', *mut'(uw)* 'close them (eyes)', *t'uč(iy)* 'stuff it', *t'en(ey)* 'play it (instrument)', *ʔib(ay)* 'barbecue it', *kon(oy)* 'ask it', *pah(uy)* 'smoke it'; *stems* (intransitive): *ka·w-θ-(in)* 'speak', *ʔoh(o)b-θ-(al)* 'cough', *waʔ-a¢-(in)* 'be born', *wayʔ-wah-u·ʔ-(in)* 'howl', *kul-b-(e·h)* 'be happy', *¢al(a)p-aθ-m(e·h)* 'become sad'; *stems* (transitive): *k'ap-θ-(al)* 'eat it', *ʔok'(o)š-θ-(iy)* 'lead it', *k'aθ-a·t-n-(aʔ)* 'make it proud', *pok'-o·n-(aʔ)* 'break it up', *tam-¢'-(uw)* 'bring them together', *ʔu¢-k-(ey)* 'curl it', *wen-k'-(ow)* 'transform it', *θib-k'-(oy)* 'interrupt it', *ʔik'-l-(ay)* 'ventilate it'.

Examples of the derivations and inflections in positions (2) through (8) are found in McQuown (1982). They will merely be outlined here.

(2) *Status markers*.
Desubstantive:

Neutral	-θ
	-b -m
Intransitive	-Vn -Vl
	-ʔ
	-V·ʔ (augmentative)
Transitive	-θ
	-V·y (augmentative)
	-θ -n -l

Deverbative:

Neutral	-Vt	-Vb -Vn
	-V·t -V·k' -V·b -V·n -V·w -V·y	
	(augmentative)	
	-p (celeritive)	
	-t -¢ -¢' -k -k' -kʷ -k'ʷ -ʔ	
	-b	
	-m -n	
	-l	
Intransitive	-θ	
	-V¢ -Vm -Vl	
	-V·ʔ -V·l (augmentative)	
Transitive	-θ	
	-(V)· (augmentative)	

(3) *Status changers*.
Transitivizing:

	-Vθ	
Augmentative	-V·θ	-θ
	-¢ -¢' -k -k'	
	-b	
	-n	
	-l	

Intransitivizing:

	-(CV)·(C)
Augmentative	-V·ʔ
Ingressive	-e·h
Ingressive	-Vš (reciprocal)
Augmentative	-V·š (reciprocal)
	-Vn
	-Vl
Augmentative	-V·l

(4) *Indirectives*.

| Singular | -Vnč | -č |
| Plural | -Vnčinč -čVnč -činč -čič |

(5) *Stem-formatives*.
Neutral with respect to marking:
-θ

—

-iʔ -Vy

Intransitive-marking:

-at -V¢ -ik
-Vn
-(n)V(·)nek   (perfect 1)
-V·m(aθ)   (perfect 2)
-V·m(eh)   (perfect 2)

Transitive-marking:
-aʔ -Vw
-V·m(al)   (perfect)

(6) *Voice changers*.

Anti-passivizing:
-Vm -V·m

Passivizing:
-ah -a·h   (completive 1)
-Vč   (completive 2)
-at -a·t   (completive 3)
-Vn   (completive 4)
   -a·b   (incompletive)
-eh   (perfect)

(7) *Aspect markers*.

Intransitive completive:
-Ø   imperative; subjunctive; indicative;
   indicative perfect; indicative perfect passive
—   imperative; subjunctive; indicative
-V·¢   subjunctive; indicative

Intransitive incompletive:
-Ø   indicative (fused); indicative passive
—   indicative
-Vl   indicative
-aθ   indicative perfect

Transitive completive:
-Ø   imperative; subjunctive; indicative;
   indicative perfect
—   imperative; subjunctive; indicative
-(ih)   indirective; subjunctive; indicative

Transitive incompletive:
—   indicative
-Vl   indicative
-al   indicative perfect

(8) *Terminals*.

With intransitives (completives):
-Ø   imperative; subjunctive; indicative;
   indicative passive; indicative perfect; indicative perfect passive
-eh   imperative; subjunctive; indicative
-ah   imperative

With intransitives (incompletives):
-Ø   indicative; indicative passive; indicative perfect

With transitives (completives):
-Ø   subjunctive; indicative; indicative
   perfect
-ih   indirective; imperative; subjunctive;
   indicative
-ah   subjunctive; indicative
-oh   imperative

With transitives (incompletives):
-Ø   indicative; indicative perfect

(9) *Anterior-modal marker* -ak *(hy-pothetical)*.

Preceded by *maš* 'if': *conditional* (1).
With the incompletive: *imperfect* (2).
With the perfect: *pluperfect* (3).

Examples: (1) *či²-Ø-θ-Ø-a(ʔ)·m-Ø-al-Ø-ak 'might have brought it' : #maš≠nan≠(ʔ)uₓ≠či²θa·malak≠patal≠(ʔ)an≠ʔanam# 'if I had brought all the soil'; (2) *ʔeš-om-Ø-Ø--Ø-Ø-Ø-ak 'might go along' : #ʔinₓ≠ʔešo-mak≠tinₓ≠t'ohnal# 'I was going along working'; (3) *t'ah-Ø-Ø-č-iya·m-Ø-al-Ø-ak-i¢ 'might have done it for him, already' : #ʔuₓt'ahčiya·malaki¢# 'I would have done it for him' (Cl).

(10) *Plural marker* -čik (of any agent, any recipient, or any combination).

Examples: *wal-k-Ø-anč-Ø-Ø-Ø-i(h-i)·¢-čik 'they freed him, already' (see sections 4.4.8, 4.3.2.2, 4.4.2, 4.3.4.2) : #tamanaʔ≠tinₓwal-kančı·sčik≠ti≠Øₓ≠ʔa·θil# 'then they freed him for running'; *ye(h)-Ø-e·θ-Ø-a(ʔ)Ø-Ø-Ø-Ø-čik 'raised them' (see sections 4.3.2.2, 4.4.1) : ≠ (ʔ)an ≠ ʔolom ≠ ʔaš ≠ (ʔ)iₓ ≠ ye·-θa(ʔ)čik≠ 'the pigs which we raised'.

Such plural forms may be taken as units of repetitive action, and may be recycled, as verb-stems (see section 5.3), through the derivational processes involved in positions (2) through (7).

(11) *Adverbial clitics*. There are four sets (the members of set 1 are mutually exclusive); they occur in the following relative order within position (11): [1] -i¢ (-iš) 'already'; -eh 'still, yet'; [2] -(i)k'ih (-(i)k'eh) 'indeed'; [3] -kʷaʔ 'it is said, they say'; and [4] -anaʔ 'in fact'.

Examples:
[1] *ʔeš-o·b-(a)1-Ø-Ø-Ø-a·¢-Ø-Ø-Ø-i¢ 'stud-ied, already' (see section 4.4.4) : #maš≠kuₓ ≠ ʔešo·bla·¢i¢# 'if we studied, already';

*ȼoʔ-o·b-Ø-Ø-Ø-Ø-Ø-Ø-Ø-iȼ -čik 'know it, already' (see section 4.3.4.2) : #komoh≠(ʔ)a₁ ≠ȼoʔo·biščik≠šaša·ʔ# 'as you (pl.) know it, already, you'; *k'al-Ø-Ø-Ø-Ø-Ø-Ø-eh-Ø-Ø-eh 'go still' (see section 4.3.2.2[13]) : #Ø₁ₚ≠ neʔeȼ≠ku₁≠k'alehe(h)≠niši≠k'eʔatčik# 'they are going to go, still, these others'.

[2] *tal-Ø-Ø-Ø-e(y-Ø-a)·l-Ø-Ø-Ø-k'ih 'is finishing, indeed' (see sections 4.3.2.4, 4.4.2) : ≠ Ø₃ ≠ taley ≠ (ʔ)an ≠ tumi·n#Ø₃ ≠tale·l-k'ih# 'the money ran out; it was, indeed, running out'.

[3] *k'al-Ø-Ø-Ø-Ø-Ø-Ø-e(h-Ø-Ø-i)ȼ-k'aʔ 'went away, already [1], they say [3]' (see sections 4.3.2.2[15], 4.4.2) : #ʔani(h)≠Ø₃≠k'ale·ȼkʷ aʔ≠ 'and he went away, already, they say ...'.

[4] *neʔ-eȼ-Ø-Ø-Ø-Ø-Ø-Ø-Ø-ana 'will go, in fact' : #kala·m≠ši≠ȼabk'iʔ#Ø₁ ≠neʔeȼana ≠ku₃ ≠ ʔa·tanči(h)≠ ʔaše·ʔ# 'tomorrow or day-after-tomorrow, I'm going, in fact, to earn this for them'.

6.5. SUPPLETIVE VERBAL ASPECTUAL AND MODAL MARKING.

Three verbs have suppletive forms for different aspects and modes: 'go' (1), 'come' (2), and 'be' (3).

Examples:

(1) *win*, *wan*, and *k'al* : (intransitive completive imperative) : *win-Ø-Ø-Ø-iʔ-Ø-Ø-Ø 'go away' : #winiʔ# 'go away!'; *wan-Ø-Ø-Ø-Ø-Ø-Ø-ah '(we) may go' : #wanah# 'let's go!'; (intransitive completive subjunctive) : *k'al-Ø-Ø-Ø-Ø-Ø-Ø-eh 'may go' : #pero(h)≠kit≠leh≠ k'aleh# 'but may you surely go away!'; (intransitive completive indicative) : *k'al-Ø-Ø-Ø-Ø-Ø-Ø-eh 'went away' : #huʔt≠(ʔ)it≠k'a-leh# 'where did you go?'; (intransitive completive indicative perfect 1) : *k'al-Ø-Ø-Ø-(Ø)(e)nek-Ø-Ø-Ø 'having gone' (see section 4.4.4) : #Ø₃ ≠k'alnek≠ ʔa·l≠ȼ'oho·l# 'he had gone to the grass(land)'; (intransitive incompletive indicative) : *k'al-Ø-Ø-Ø-Ø-Ø-el-Ø 'goes' : #tamanaʔ≠(ʔ)u₂≠k'aleliš≠ti≠ ʔa·l ≠(ʔ)i₃≠k'ima·ʔ# 'then we're going, already, to our house'. (2) *či·č*, *ta·l*, and *čeʔ* : (intransitive completive imperative) : *či·č-Ø-Ø-Ø-Ø-Ø-Ø-Ø# 'come' : #Ø₂ ≠či·š≠te·ʔ 'come here!' (see section 4.3.4.2); (intransitive completive subjunctive) : *či·č-Ø-Ø-Ø-Ø-Ø-Ø-Ø 'may come' : #huʔta·m ≠ taka ≠ Ø₃ ≠ či·č ≠ (ʔ)an ≠

ȼ'ehwalištala·b# 'whence may come misfortune'; (intransitive completive indicative) : *či·č-Ø-Ø-Ø-Ø-Ø-Ø-Ø 'came' : ≠ komo(h) ≠ Ø₃ ≠ či·č≠(ʔ)an≠we·wȼištala·b≠ 'as the revolution came ...'; (intransitive completive indicative perfect 1) : *čeʔ-Ø-Ø-Ø-(Ø)(e)nek-Ø-Ø-Ø 'having come' (see section 4.4.4) : #ʔin₁ ≠ čeʔnek≠ku₃ ≠nuhuw≠ 'I've come to sell it'; (intransitive incompletive indicative) : *ta-(h-a)·l : *ta·l-Ø-Ø-Ø-Ø-Ø-Ø 'comes' : #Ø₃ ≠ ta·l≠ti≠berakru·s# 'he comes from Veracruz'. (3) *kʷačik*, *pe·l≠Ø₃≠Ø*, and *Ø* : (intransitive completive imperative-subjunctive) : *kʷa-čik-Ø-Ø-Ø-Ø-Ø-Ø 'may be' : #ʔanȼan≠Ø₃ ≠ kʷačik# 'let it be!'; (intransitive completive indicative) : *kʷačik-Ø-Ø-Ø-Ø-Ø-Ø 'was, were' : ≠ti≠bo·ʔ≠Ø₃ ≠kʷačik≠(ʔ)a₃ ≠ ma·yoh≠ 'the fifth, it was, of May'; (intransitive incompletive indicative) : *kʷačik-Ø-Ø-Ø-Ø-Ø-Ø-Ø 'am, is, are' : ≠tata·ʔ≠Ø₂ ≠kʷačik ≠Ø≠(ʔ)it≠t'ohnal≠ 'you are (the one who) works'; *pe·l≠Ø₁ ≠Ø : #nana·ʔ#pe·l≠(ʔ)in₁ ≠Ø≠ maye·so(h) ≠ ti ≠ tampe·moč# 'I am (a) teacher from Tampemoch'; *pe·l≠Ø₂≠Ø : #pe·l≠(ʔ)it≠Ø≠ ʔešo·bčiš# 'you are (a) teacher'; *pe·l≠Ø₃≠Ø : #pe·l≠(ʔ)i₁ ≠ ʔešo·bčiš# 'he is (a) teacher'; ≠komo(h)≠ pe·leh≠Ø₃ ≠Ø≠(ʔ)u₄ ≠ ʔat-te·nek≠ 'since they are, still, my fellow-Huastecs'; #waw≠pe·l≠ (ʔ)u₂ ≠Ø≠ ʔešo·bčiš# 'we are teachers'; #pe·l≠Ø₃ ≠Ø≠ ʔab≠(ʔ)in₂ ≠t'ila·l≠ 'it is because he remembers it'; #pe·lak≠Ø₃ ≠Ø ≠(ʔ)i₆ ≠le·ȼah≠ 'it was (some) milk'; #ʔim₃ ≠bih#Ø₃ ≠Ø#pe·gruh# 'his name (is) Peter'; #ʔančik≠Ø₃ₚ ≠Ø#ʔim₃ ≠pakθa·ʔ# 'those they (are) their sizes'; #nana·ʔiȼ≠Ø₁ ≠Ø# 'I, already (am)!'

6.6. VERB STEM-TYPES.

Verb roots, as we have seen, form stems of a great many different types, differentiated by their variation in their completive and incompletive aspects, and in their perfects, as illustrated in the following list:

(1) (Intransitive incompletive defective) -at *k'ʷah : k'ʷahat 'be there'

(2) (Transitive incompletive defective) -al *kʷaʔ : kʷaʔal 'possess it'

97

(3) (Intransitive completive / incompletive / perfect) -∅/-—/-e·nek
  *waʔ-a¢ : waʔ(a)¢in/waʔa¢/waʔ-¢ine·nek 'exist'

(4) (Intransitive completive / incompletive / perfect) -∅/-el/-e·nek
  *ton-eh-in : tonehin/tonel/tonehine·-nek 'stroll'

(5) (Intransitive completive / incompletive / perfect) -∅/-e·l/-e·nek
  *wik'-in : wik'in/wik'(i)ne·l/wik'(i)-ne·nek 'wind'

(6) (Intransitive completive / incompletive/ perfect) -∅/-al/-e·nek
  *t'ik'-on : t'ik'on/t'ik'ʷnal/t'ik'ʷne·nek 'jump'

(7) (Intransitive completive / incompletive/ perfect) -∅/-al/-i·maθ
  *ʔač-in : ʔačin/ʔač(i)nal/ʔači·maθ 'bathe'

(8) (Intransitive completive / incompletive / perfect) -∅/-el/-nek
  *ʔul-i¢ : ʔuli¢/ʔulel/ʔulnek 'get here'

(9) (Intransitive completive / incompletive / perfect) -∅/-el/-enek
  *ʔo¢-i¢ : ʔo¢i¢/ʔo¢el/ʔo¢enek 'enter'

(10) (Intransitive completive / incompletive / perfect) -∅/-al/-a·maθ
  *way-i¢ : wayi¢/wayal/*wayla·maθ 'sleep'

(11) (Intransitive completive / incompletive / perfect) -∅/-el/-enek
  *¢em-e¢ : ¢eme¢/¢emel/¢emenek 'die'

(12) (Intransitive completive / incompletive / perfect) -a·¢/-—/-a·maθ
  *wač(i)b-il : wačbila·¢/wačbil/wač-bila·maθ 'dream'

(13) (Intransitive completive / incompletive / perfect) -o·¢/-—/-o·maθ
  *koy-ol : koyo(l-i)·¢/koyol/koyo(l-a·)·maθ 'rest'

(14) (Transitive completive / incompletive / perfect) -∅/-t-al/-i·mal
  *ʔik'-ʔ : ʔik'iʔ/ʔik'tal/ʔik'i·mal 'bring it'

(15) (Transitive completive / incompletive / perfect) -∅/-al/-a·mal

(16) (Transitive completive / incompletive / perfect) -∅/-—/-a·mal
  *¢oʔo·b-n-aʔ : ¢oʔo·bnaʔ/¢oʔo·b/¢oʔo·bna·mal 'know it'

(17) (Transitive completive / incompletive / perfect) -∅/-a·l/-a·mal
  *piθ-aʔ : piθaʔ/piθa·l/piθa·mal 'give it to him'

(18) (Transitive completive / incompletive / perfect) -∅/-al/-a·mal
  *ʔal-č-(ih) : ʔalčih/ʔalčal/ʔalča·mal 'hunt it for him'

(19) (Intransitive completive / incompletive / perfect) -∅/-el/-nek
  *k'al-(eh) : k'aleh/k'alel/k'alnek 'go'

(20) (Intransitive completive / incompletive / perfect) -∅/-el/-enek
  *¢ek-(eh) : ¢ekeh/¢ekel/¢ekenek 'tire'

(21) (Intransitive completive / incompletive / perfect) -∅/-e·l/-enek
  *ʔeč'-(eh) : ʔeč'eh/ʔeč'e·l/ʔeč'enek 'waver'

(22) (Intransitive completive / incompletive / perfect) -∅/-e·l/-ene·nek
  *wak-l-(eh) : wakleh/wakle·l/wak-lene·nek 'get late'

(23) (Intransitive completive / incompletive / perfect) -∅/-e·l/-e·nek
  *niw-iw-i·l-b-e·h : niwiwi·lbe·h/niwi-wi·lbe·l/niwiwi·lbe·nek 'smell good'

(24) (Transitive completive / incompletive / perfect) -∅/-al/-a·mal
  *ʔeh-čik-(ah) : ʔehčikah/ʔehčikal/ʔehčika·mal 'survey it'

(25) (Transitive completive / incompletive / perfect) -∅/-al/-V·mal
  *pok'-ow : pok'ow/pok'owal/pok'o-(wa)·mal 'split it'

(26) (Transitive completive / incompletive / perfect) -∅/-t-al/-V·mal
  *¢uʔ-uw : ¢uʔuw/¢uʔtal/¢uʔu(wa)·mal 'see it'

(27) (Intransitive completive / incompletive / perfect) -∅/-i·l/-inek
  *paʔ-iy : paʔiy/paʔi·l/paʔinek 'descend'

(28) (Intransitive completive / incompletive / perfect) -∅/ -e·l / -enek

kub-iy : *kubiy / kube·l / kubenek* 'stand up'

(29) (Transitive completive / incompletive / perfect) -∅/ -al / -a·mal

nuh-čik-iy : *nuhčikiy / nuhčikal / nuh-čika·mal* 'sell it repeatedly'

(30) (Intransitive completive / incompletive / perfect) -∅/ -el / -nek

pay-ey : *payey / payel / paynek* 'get seasoned'

(31) (Intransitive completive / incompletive / perfect) -∅/ -e·l / -nek

tal-ey : *taley / tale·l / talnek* 'finish'

(32) (Intransitive completive / incompletive / perfect) -∅/ -el / -enek

ʔut-ey : *ʔutey / ʔutel / ʔutenek* 'come near'

(33) (Intransitive completive / incompletive / perfect) -∅/ -e·l / -e·nek

lem-em-ey : *lememey / lememe·l / lememe·nek* 'flutter'

7. NOUN MORPHOSYNTAX. This section will cover both the *noun morphology* (processes which take place between potentially open junctures, on either side of the core of the noun complex) and a limited *noun-phrase syntax* (processes that include the particle or particles that are preposed to this core [postposed particles are enclitic, that is, are preceded by close junctures, in the same way that suffixes are, and are, on occasion, interspersed with these latter]).

7.0. ORDER OF PREPOSED ELEMENTS. Elements *preposed* to the noun-complex appear in the following order:

(1) Subordinating (prepositional) particles
(2) Adverbial (adjectival) particles
(3) Adjectival (adverbial) particles
(4) Deictic particles
(5) Adverbial (adjectival) particles
(6) Adjectival (adverbial) particles
(7) Possessor pronominal particles
(8) Adverbial (adjectival) particles
(9) Adjectival (adverbial) particles
(10) Collective / deferential particles
(11) Adverbial (adjectival) particles
(12) Adjectival (adverbial) particles

These numerals are superposed over the relevant elements in the examples to follow.

It seems that the relative order (1), (4), (7), (10) is constant, but that the adverbial and adjectival elements (in *that* relative order) may occur, interspersed, after each of these.

Examples: (1) ≠tin₃ ≠leh ≠čukul# 'in his very belly'; ≠ʔa·l ≠hu·n ≠(ʔ)i₆ ≠karoh# 'into a car'; (2) ≠leh ≠putat≠ 'just everything'; (3) ≠wala·m ≠patal ≠(ʔ)a₃ ≠ʔi·č' # 'perhaps the whole (deferenced) month'; (4) ₂niši ≠ši ≠leh ≠ ʔolom# 'that very pig'; (5) #leh ≠tekeθ ≠k'ihiθ ≠ š ≠ ... 'very highly amusing that ...'; (6) ≠ti ≠pi·l ≠(ʔ)i₆ ≠kʷe·nča·la·b# 'in separate wards'; (7) ≠k'al ≠patal ≠(ʔ)u₈ ≠kulbe·tal# 'with all my liking'; (8) ≠leh ≠yantam ≠(ʔ)i₆ ≠tamub# 'a very great deal of years'; (9) ≠k'al ≠hu·n ≠(ʔ)i₆ ≠kʷito·l≠ 'with one boy'; (10) ≠k'al ≠(ʔ)i₆ ≠k'ih# 'with some time'; ≠k'al ≠(ʔ)an ≠koy# 'with a certain rabbit'; ≠ti ≠bu·k ≠(ʔ)a₃ ≠ʔi·č' # 'in seven (deferenced) months'; (11) #wa(la)·m ≠leh ≠ ʔalwa ʔ≠ 'perhaps very good...'; (12) ≠k'al ≠(ʔ)i₆ ≠leh ≠ ʔušumla·b# 'with some of those very Ladino women'.

7.1. POSITIONS WITHIN THE NOUN-STEM COMPLEX. Positions *within* the noun-stem complex are the following:

(1) (Root and / or) stem
(2) Deriving elements
(3) Possessed form markers
(4) Anterior (modal) marker
(5) Plural marker
(6) Ad-verbial clitics

These numerals are superposed over the relevant elements in the examples in section 7.4.

Positions (5) and (6) are interchangeable, as are positions (4) and (5), and (4) and (6).

7.2. NOUN ROOT (AND STEM) TYPES.

7.2.1. INHERENTLY NEUTRAL. These are invariable with respect to possession:

ʔaleh 'cultivated plot' : ≠k'al ≠(ʔ)an ≠ ʔal-eh# 'with a certain cultivated plot' (non-possessed) : #niši ≠nan ≠(ʔ)u₄ ≠ ʔaleh# 'that plot of *mine*' (possessed)

7.2.2. INHERENTLY NON-POSSESSED:

θahuw 'morning' : #hu·n ≠(ʔ)i₆ ≠θahuw# 'one morning'

99

7.2.3. INHERENTLY POSSESSED:

ba·ʔ 'self' : *≠ka₁ ≠k'aθatnaʔčik≠ta₂ ≠ba·ʔ≠*
'that you (pl.) may elevate yourselves'

7.3. COMPOUND NOUN-STEMS.

7.3.1. (SUBSTANTIVE) NOUN WITH NOUN:
ʔik' 'wind' + *teʔ* 'tree' : *ʔik'-teʔ* 'cedar'

7.3.2. (ATTRIBUTIVE) NOUN WITH NOUN:
kʷete·m 'alone' + *ʔinik* 'man' : *kʷete·m-ʔinik*
'bachelor'

7.4. DERIVED NOUN-STEMS. In positions
(1) through (3) in the noun complex occur the
derived noun-stems, some more purely derivational, some more purely inflectional.

In position (1) in the noun complex occur
the noun *bases*, simplex (roots) and compound (or complex)(stems); as well as those
recycled complex stems which are introduced
into the base (1) position, to be in turn subjected to further derivation and inflection.

In position (6) occur the ad-verbial *clitics*,
found with the other major form-classes, the
verbals, and the particles, as well.

Positions (1) through (3) constitute the core
of the noun complex; position (4) adds the
anterior-modal marker to this core, position
(5) further adds the *plural* marker, and this
expanded core—without position (4)—is particularly susceptible to recycling through the
base position.

It is not surprising, then, that positions (4)
and (5), as well as positions (4) and (6) are
interchangeable, as are positions (5) and (6),
as the focus shifts from restricted core—(1)
through (3)—to anterior-modally marked
core—(1) through (4)—to plurally marked
core—(1) through (5) without (4).

Examples:

(1) *Roots*: *paw* 'smoke', *tayʔ* 'lime', *t'i·w*
'hawk', 'eaglet', *t'ot* 'turkey-buzzard', *¢a·m*
'ice', *¢'ak* 'flea', *čuč* 'coyote', *koy* 'rabbit', *k'ih*
'time', *ʔa·b* 'rain', *ʔa·moh* 'master', *ʔe·b*
'heaven', *ʔi¢* 'chili-pepper', *ʔo·t* 'star', *ʔu¢*
'louse', *bi·l* 'fragile', *bale·yaʔ* 'watermelon',
θa·m 'nose', *ši·ʔ* 'hair', *ši·laʔ* 'saddle', *ha·wʔ*
'straw', *he·l* 'dew', *ho·h* 'crane', *hom* 'in-
cense', *ma·y* 'tobacco', *mõ·ʔ* 'mute', *na·ʔ*
'there', *nut* 'pitch', *we·w* 'tail', *wi¢* 'flower',
ya·n 'much', *yo·y* 'mosquito', *le·y* 'lightning',
lo·k' 'corn-fungus'; *stems*: *pik'-oʔ* 'dog', *pi·k'-*

ib 'forehead', *po¢'-o¢'* 'cactus-fruit', *pu·l-ik*
'large', *tiw-aʔ* 'thither', *te·n-ek* 'Huastec', *toʔ-
ol* 'fish', *tol-ow* 'dense', *t'ah-ab* 'on purpose',
t'in-o·m 'brown sugar', *t'oθ⁼oy* 'mange', *t'uy-
ik'* 'wax', *¢ip-il-iʔ* 'small', *¢ap-ik* 'strong', *¢al-
ap* 'thought', *¢ol-at* 'loose', *¢'ah-ib* 'mortar',
¢'eh-et 'thigh', *¢'i¢-in* 'bird', *¢'um-e¢'* 'spark',
čiθ-an 'virgin', *čun-un* 'humming-bird', *č'ak'-
ay* 'tasteless', *č'uč-ub* 'finger', *kam-ab* 'tooth',
kol-ol 'cockroach', *kuk-uʔ* 'dove', *k'im-a·ʔ*
'home', *k'el-ab* 'row', *k'ay-u·m* 'slow', *k'ok'-o¢*
'sweet corn', *k'ut'-ub* 'fish-hook', *kʷeč-oč-o·l*
'round', *kʷay-aʔ* 'twin', *kʷit-o·l* 'boy', *k'ʷe¢-
eʔ* 'lame', *k'ʷiš-iš* 'powder', *k'ʷan-ik* 'wave',
ʔi¢'-am 'horn', *ʔel-ab* 'better', *ʔeθ-em* 'rac-
coon', *ʔat'-em* 'salt', *ʔok-ow* 'hive', *ʔoθ-o·w*
'iguana', *ʔun-up* 'ceiba', *ʔu¢-un* 'papaya', *ʔuθ-
uʔ* 'monkey', *bič-ow* 'city', *beš-eʔ* 'ground-
hog', *θit'-om* 'curer', *θik-ab* 'sieve', *θaʔ-ub*
'lung', *θuh-al* 'foam', *šim-i·l* 'unkempt',
šek-l-ek 'leaf', *šaš-a·ʔ* 'you', *šol-ok* 'snot',
šu¢-un 'ear', *hik-at* 'quick', *hep-aθ* 'split',
hah-n-ek 'fly', *hoh-ob* 'corn-husk', *huč-ub* 'bel-
lows', *mil-iʔ* 'dotted', *me¢-me¢* 'cartilage',
mol-ow 'damp', *muʔ-b-ač* 'crumb', *muθ-m-uč*
'Pleiades', *niw-aʔ* 'there (nearby)', *not'-o·l*
'choleric', *nuh-um* 'worms', *way-a·m* 'dream',
wil-il 'cradle', *weh-eʔ* 'ancient', *wa¢-ib*
'brush', *ya·h-ab* 'trigger', *yeh-e·m* 'tallness',
yun-eʔ 'curve', *lin-i·l* 'stubby', *le·t'-eh* 'mis-
erable', *lap-an* 'attic', *lol-iy* 'slippery', *lup-e·m*
'depth'.

Examples of the derivations and inflections in positions (2) through (6) are found in
McQuown (1982). They are merely outlined
here.

(2) *Deriving elements*. See Tables 5-2 and
5-3.

(3) *Possessed-form markers*:

-∅   *(CV[C]CV)·(C)*
      (CV[C]CV)a·(C)

-il
      (CV[C]CV)·(C)-il

-i·l

-al
      (CV)·([C]VC)-al
      (CV[C]CV)·(C)·al

-a·l *(CV[C]CV)(·)(C)-a·l*

-o·l *(CV[C]CV)(·)(C)-o·l*

100

TABLE 5-2. Deriving Elements: Deverbative

-∅				(CV)·(C)				—	
-iC	-i·C	-eC	-e·C	-aC	-a·C	-oC	-o·C	-uC	-u·C
				-ap	-a·p			-up	
		-et	-e·t	-at					
-i¢				-a¢		-o¢	-o·¢	-u¢	-u·¢
-ič				-ač	-a·č			-uč	
-ik									
-ik'		-ek'				-ok'		-uk'	-u·k'
-ik'ʷ									
-iʔ		-eʔ	-e·ʔ	-aʔ		-oʔ		-uʔ	
-ib	-i·b	-eb	-e·b	-ab	-a·b	-ob	-o·b	-ub	-u·b
-iθ		-eθ		-aθ	-a·θ	-oθ		-uθ	
-iš	-i·š			-aš	-a·š	-oš		-uš	
-ih	-i·h	-eh	-e·h	-ah	-a·h			-uh	
-im	-i·m	-em	-e·m	-am	-a·m	-om	-o·m	-um	-u·m
-in	-i·n	-en	-e·n	-an	-a·n		-o·n		-u·n
-iw						-ow		-uw	
-iy				-ay		-oy	-o·y		
-il	-i·l	-el	-e·l	-al	-a·l	-ol	-o·l	-ul	-u·l
		-t		-t-eh	-t-al	-t-a·l			
		-č		-č-ik	-č-al				
		-b		-b-iʔ	-b-il	-b-eh	-b-e·l		
		-m		-m-ač	-m-uč	-m-aʔ			
		-n		-n-e·l					
		-w		-w-al	-w-a·l-eh				
		-l		-l-iθ	-l-ab	-l-a·b	-l-om		

-u·l   (CV[C]CV)(·)(C)-u·l
-l-i·l

(4) *Anterior-modal marker -ak* (hypothetical) : (preceded by *maš* 'if': *conditional* [1]); (with the incompletive: *imperfect* [2]).

Examples:

(1) * #maš≠niš≠Ø$_3$≠Ø≠ʔalwaʔ-ʔinik-ak# 'if that (were) (a) good man'.

(2) #hant'oh≠(ʔ)in$_3$≠ʔe·y≠Ø$_3$≠Ø≠tam≠ʔa·nima·l-ak# 'what kind of an animal (was) it?'; #Ø$_3$≠Ø≠hitaʔ-ak# 'who (was) it?'; #niš≠Ø$_3$≠Ø≠ʔalwaʔ-ʔinik-ak# 'that (was) (a) good man'; ≠Ø$_3$≠k'ʷahat≠hu·n≠Ø≠Ø$_3$≠Ø≠niš≠(ʔ)u$_4$≠ʔešla·l-ak# 'there was one (who was of) these friends of mine'.

(5) *Plural marker -čik:*

(1) plurality of *animate* objects (Cl and Mn).

(2) plurality (or collectivity) of qualities.

Examples: (1) *bičow* 'town' : #bičow-čik# 'citizens!'; *ʔi¢ak'* 'nephew' : #patal≠(ʔ)u$_4$≠ʔi¢ak'-čik# 'all my nephews'; (2) *nakθaʔ* 'long' : *nakθa(ʔ)-čik* 'long (ones)' (see section 4.3.2.2) : #ʔin$_2$≠k'ʷaʔal≠(ʔ)in$_3$≠kamab≠Ø≠Ø$_3$≠Ø≠leh≠nakθa(ʔ)čik# 'he has (his) teeth (which are) very long (ones)'; *¢ipil-...* 'small' : *¢ipi(l)-čik* 'small (ones)' : ≠š≠k'eʔat≠¢ipičik# 'those other small ones'.

(6) *Ad-verbial clitics.* There are four sets (the members of set 1 are mutually exclusive); they occur in the following relative order within position (6): [1] *-i¢* (*-iš*) 'already', *-eh* 'still, yet'; [2] *-(i)k'ih* (*-[i]k'eh*) 'indeed'; [3] *-k'ʷaʔ* 'it is said, they say'; [4] *-anaʔ* 'in fact'.

101

TABLE 5-3. Deriving Elements: Desubstantive

			([CV(C)]CV)·(C)						
-iC	-i·C	-eC	-e·C	-aC	-a·C	-oC	-o·C	-uC	-u·C
				-ap				-up	
		-et		-at		-ot			
-i¢				-a¢	-a·¢			-u¢	
		-e¢'	-e·¢'	-a¢'		-o¢'		-u¢'	
-ič	-i·č					-oč		-uč	
-ik		-ek		-ak				-uk	
-ik'		-ek'		-ak'				-uk'	
-ik'ʷ				-ak'ʷ					
-i?	-i·?	-e?	-e·?	-a?	-a·?	-o?		-u?	
-ib	-i·b			-ab	-a·b	-ob	-o·b	-ub	-u·b
-iθ	-i·θ	-eθ		-aθ	-a·θ	-oθ		-uθ	
-iš	-i·š			-aš		-oš		-uš	
		-eh		-ah	-a·h	-oh		-uh	
-im	-i·m	-em	-e·m	-am	-a·m	-on	-o·n	-un	
			-e·w	-aw		-ow	-o·w	-uw	
-iy		-ey		-ay		-oy		-uy	
-il	-i·l	-el	-e·l	-al	-a·l	-ol	-o·l	-ul	-u·l
		-t	-t-at	-t-a·h	-t-a·m	-t-el	-t-al		
		-t'	-t'-in	-t'-oθ	-t'-oh				
		-č	-č-ik	-č-il	-č-i·l	-č-al			
		-b	-b-i?	-b-eh	-b-e·l				
		-m	-m-a?						
		-n	-n-i?	-n-ab					
		-w	-w-a?						
		-l	-l-ek	-l-e?	-l-eb	-l-ab	-l-a·b		
			-l-am	-l-om	-l-o·m				

Examples:

[1] *?utat* 'near' : *?utat-i¢* [1] [2] [6[1]] 'near, already' : #*?ani(h)* ≠ *tam*≠*ti* ≠ Q₃ ≠ Q ≠ *?utati¢* ≠ 'and when (they were) near, already'; *haha·?* 'he' : *haha·?-i¢* [1] [2] [6[1]] 'he, already' : #Q₃ ≠Q≠*haha·?iščik*# 'they (are) the ones, already' (see section 4.3.4.2); *kʷito·l* 'boy' : *kʷito·l-eh* [6[1]] '(a) boy, still' : #*tam*≠*tin*₁ ≠Q≠*kʷito·leh*# '(then) when I (was) a boy, still'; *t'ele?* 'baby' : *t'eley-eh* [6[1]] '(a) baby, still' (see section 4.3.4.1) : #*t'i?om*#*ha·¢*≠Q₃ ≠Q≠(*?)i*₆ ≠*t'eleyeh*# '(a) fawn, that, already, (is) one of the babies, still'; *¢ipi(l)-...* 'small' : *¢ipil-eh* [6[1]] 'small, still' : #*komo(h)*≠Q₃ ≠Q≠*¢ipi(l)čikeh*# 'since they (are) small ones, still'.

[2] *wali·m* 'many' : *wali·m-k'ih* [1] [2] [6[2]] 'many, indeed' : #*komo(h)*≠*yab*≠Q₃ ≠Q≠*wali·mk'ih*≠ (*?)i*₆ ≠*?i¢'a·mal*# 'since there (are) not many, indeed, of the deer'; *hay-eh* 'that, still; also, too' ; *hayeh-i¢-ik'eh* [1] [2] [6[2]] 'too, already, indeed' (*hay-eh* recycled as *hay-eh*) : *haye·¢ik'eh* 'id.' (see sections 4.3.2.2, 4.4.2, and 4.4.7) : #Q₃ ≠Q≠*haye·¢ik'e(h)*≠Q≠*tokot*≠(*?)in*₂ ≠*tolmiy*≠ 'it (is) also, already, indeed, (that) he just helped him'.

[3] Cl, Mn *?eh-at* [1] [2] 'alive' : *?ehat-ak* [1] [2] [4] 'were alive' : *?ehatak-kʷa?* [6[3]] 'were alive, they say' : ≠*maš*≠Q₃ ≠Q≠ *?ehatakkʷa?*≠(*?)u*₄ ≠*mi·m*# 'if perhaps she were alive, they say, my mother'.

[4] *yab-k'ih* [1] [2] [6[2]] 'not, indeed' : *yabk'i(h-a)-*

naʔ ^{6[4]} 'not, indeed, in fact' (see section
4.3.2.2[14]) : #yabk'inaʔ≠ka₁≠ʔuluw≠ 'not,
indeed, in fact, may you say it'.

7.5. TERMS OF ADDRESS AND REFERENCE (KIN AND OTHER).

7.5.1. TERMS OF ADDRESS (VOCATIVES).

7.5.1.1. e·ʔ (Cl):

ʔa(h)a·t(i)k-e·ʔ 'O Lord!'

payʔlo·m-e·ʔ 'O Father!' : #tat≠(ʔ)u₄≠
payʔlo·me·ʔ# 'O Thou (who art) my
Father!'

7.5.1.2. (NO SUFFIX) (Cl):

(Women) pap 'Father!'

(Women) pa·p 'Father!' (from a distance)

(Men) pa·p 'Father!'

7.5.2. TERMS OF REFERENCE (OR ADDRESS).

7.5.2.1. MEN's:

payʔlo·m 'father', 'poppa', 'sir' (Cl, Mn)

mi·m 'mother', 'momma', 'ma'am' (Cl, Mn)

ma·m 'grandfather' (Cl, Mn)

ʔa·č 'grandmother' (Cl, Mn)

ʔatik 'son', 'daughter' (Cl)

¢akam 'child' : #ʔin₃≠¢aka·mil# 'his son'
(Mn)

k'očim-ʔatik 'older child' (Cl)

¢'u·¢'-ʔatik 'younger child' (Cl)

momob 'grandchild' (Cl, Mn)

¢abil-momob 'great-grandchild' (Cl)

ʔat-mi·m 'older brother' (Cl); 'brother-in-
law' (Mn)

ʔata·tal 'younger brother' (Cl); 'first cousin'
(Mn)

ʔiša·m 'sister', 'sister-in-law' (Mn)

ʔat-mu·l 'sister-in-law' (Cl, Mn)

ba·y 'brother-in-law' (Cl); ba·yil (Mn)

ʔi¢ak' 'sister's child' (Cl, Mn)

¢anu·b 'aunt' (Cl, Mn)

ʔi¢a·n 'uncle' (Cl, Mn)

yelam-payʔlo·m 'father's older brother' (Cl)

¢'u·¢'-payʔlo·m 'father's younger brother'
(Cl)

haʔu·b 'brother' (Cl); 'relative' (Cl); 'friend'
(Mn); #ʔu₄≠haʔu·b# 'my relative' (Cl);
kʷete·m-haʔu·b 'near relative' (Cl)

mimleʔ 'stepmother' (Cl, Mn)

payʔlo·mleʔ 'stepfather' (Cl); tatleʔ 'id.'
(Mn)

ʔat-mimleʔ 'older stepbrother' (Cl)

ʔat-ʔatleʔ 'younger stepbrother' (Cl)

ʔiša·mleʔ 'stepsister' (Cl)

ʔi¢ak'leʔ 'stepsister's child' (Cl)

kʷitotleʔ 'stepson' (Mn)

¢'ik'a·čleʔ 'stepdaughter' (Mn)

ʔi·šal 'wife' (Cl, Mn)

tomol 'spouse' (Cl, Mn)

#piθo·b≠k'al≠(ʔ)a₃≠diyo·s# 'bestowed by
God' (Cl)

ʔiya·m 'father-in-law' (Cl, Mn); ʔi·yeh ʔi·yah
'id.' (Mn)

ʔušum-ʔiya·m 'mother-in-law' (Cl, Mn)

ʔa¢i·h 'parent-in-law: the male parent of
his son- or daughter-in-law' (Cl)

ʔušum-ʔa¢i·h 'parent-in-law: the female
parent of his son- or daughter-in-law' (Cl)

ʔatleʔ 'brother(s)-in-law' (Cl)

ʔiya·m 'son-in-law' (Cl, Mn)

ʔalʔi·b 'daughter-in-law' (Cl, Mn)

ʔat-ʔiya·m 'brother-in-law' (Cl)

ʔišliθ 'married (man)' (Cl)

tomkiθ 'married (man)' (Cl)

ta·tah 'father', 'poppa' (Mn)

na·nah 'mother', 'momma' (Mn)

ʔebčal 'brother'; ʔinik-ʔebčal 'id.' (Mn)

ʔušum-ʔebčal 'sister' (Mn)

ʔok'oš-ʔata·tal 'older brother' (Mn)

pot'lab 'younger brother' (Mn)

#ta·yil≠¢akam# 'younger child' (Mn)

ʔaha·tik 'Lord' (Mn)

kumpa·leh 'co-(ritual) father' (Mn)

kuma·leh 'co-(ritual) mother' (Mn)

kumpayʔlo·m 'boy's godfather' (Mn)

kumpalmi·m 'boy's godmother' (Mn)

*kumpal-ʔatik '(man's) godchild' (Mn)

ba·yila·b 'brother-in-law' (Mn)

ʔa¢i·hla·b 'co-parent-in-law' (Mn)

haʔu·bla·b 'relationship', 'genealogy' (Cl)

7.5.2.2. WOMEN's:

pap 'father', 'poppa', 'sir' (Cl)

mi·m 'mother', 'momma', 'ma'am' (Cl)

ma·m 'grandfather' (Cl)

ʔa·č 'grandmother' (Cl)

t'a·m 'son', 'daughter' (Cl, Mn)

¢akam 'child'; #ʔin₃≠¢aka·mil# 'her child'
(Mn)

k'očim-t'a·m 'older child' (Cl)

¢'u·¢'-t'a·m 'younger child' (Cl)

ʔiyib 'grandchild' (Cl)

* ¢abil-ʔiyib 'great-grandchild' (Cl)

ba·y 'older sister' (ba·yil) (Cl)

ʔakab 'younger sister' (Cl)

šiba·m 'brother' (Cl); 'brother-in-law' (Mn)

ʔat-mu·l 'brother-in-law' (Cl)

hawan 'sister-in-law' (Cl, Mn)

ʔiyak' 'brother's child' (Cl)

¢anu·b 'aunt' (Cl, Mn); ¢'u·¢'-mi·m 'id.' (Mn)

¢'u·¢'-pap 'uncle' (Mn)

yelam-pap 'father's older brother' (Cl)

¢'u·¢'-pap 'father's younger brother' (Cl)

ʔebčal 'father's brother's child' (Cl); 'sibling' (Mn)

ha·ʔu·b 'father's brother's child' (Cl); 'relative' (Mn); kʷete·m-ha·ʔu·b 'near relative' (Cl)

* mimleʔ 'stepmother' (Cl)

papleʔ 'stepfather' (Cl)

* ʔat-mimleʔ 'older stepsister' (Cl)

* ʔakableʔ 'younger stepsister' (Cl)

* šiba·mleʔ 'stepbrother' (Cl)

* ʔiyak'leʔ 'stepbrother's child' (Cl)

* kʷitotleʔ 'stepson' (Cl)

* ¢'ik'a·čleʔ 'stepdaughter' (Cl)

ʔilaw 'husband' (Cl); ʔilow 'id.' (Mn)

tomol 'spouse' (Cl, Mn)

#piθo·b≠k'al≠(ʔ)a₃≠diyo·s# 'bestowed by God' (Cl)

ʔalʔi·b 'father-in-law' (Cl)

ʔušum-ʔalʔi·b 'mother-in-law' (Cl)

* ʔa¢i·h 'parent-in-law: the female parent of her son- or daughter-in-law' (Cl)

* ʔinik-ʔa¢i·h 'parent-in-law: the male parent of her son- or daughter-in-law' (Cl)

ʔat-ʔalʔi·b 'sister(s)-in-law' (Cl)

ʔiya·m 'son-in-law' (Cl, Mn)

* ʔušum-ʔiya·m 'daughter-in-law' (Cl)

ʔat-ʔalʔi·b 'sister-in-law' (Cl)

ʔilwaθ 'married (woman)' (Cl)

tomkiθ 'married (woman)' (Cl)

ta·tah 'father, poppa' (Mn)

na·nah 'mother, momma' (Mn)

ʔebčal 'sister' (Cl, Mn); ʔušum-ʔebčal 'id.' (Mn)

ʔinik-ʔebčal 'brother' (Mn)

* ʔok'oš-šiba·m 'older brother' (Cl)

* pot'lab 'younger brother' (Mn)

* #ta·yil≠t'a·m# 'younger child' (Mn)

ʔaha·tik 'Lord' (Mn)

kumpa·leh 'co-(ritual) father' (Mn)

kuma·leh 'co-(ritual) mother' (Mn)

kumpalpa·p 'girl's godfather' (Mn)

kumpalmi·m 'girl's godmother' (Mn)

kumpalt'a·m '(woman's) godchild' (Mn)

ba·yila·b 'sister-in-law' (Mn)

ʔa¢i·hla·b 'co-parent-in-law' (Mn)

haʔu·bla·b 'relationship', 'genealogy' (Cl)

7.5.3. PLURALS.

7.5.3.1. SIMPLE:

(Man speaking) #ʔu₄≠ʔatik-čik# 'my children' (Cl)

kʷito·l-čik 'young men' (Sp mancebos) (Cl)

¢'ik'a·-čik 'young ladies' (Sp doncellas) (Cl)

7.5.3.2. REDUPLICATED:

* čik-kʷito·l 'small boy' : čičik-kʷito·l 'small boys' (Sp niños) (Cl); (čičik [Cl; Veracruz dialect?]) (note ¢ip-il-i·n 'small'?) (Mn)

¢'ik'a·č 'girl' : ¢'i-¢'ik'a·č 'small girls' (Sp niñas) (Cl)

7.5.3.3. COLLECTIVE:

(Man speaking) ʔatiklo·m 'children' : #ʔatiklo·mčik# 'children!' (Cl)

ko·ʔošlo·m 'guardians' : ko·ʔošlo·mčik# 'guardians!' (Cl)

7.6 PRONOMINALS.

7.6.1. INDEPENDENT PERSONAL PRONOUNS:

(1 sg.)

nana·ʔ 'I' (Cl, Mn)

nan 'I' (Cl)

na·ʔ 'I' (Cl)

ne·h 'I' (Mn)

neh 'I' (Mn)

ʔin₁ 'I' (Mn)

(2 sg. informal)

tata·ʔ 'thou; you' (Cl, Mn)

tat 'thou; you' (Mn)

ta·ʔ 'thou; you' (Cl)

te·h 'thou; you' (Mn)

* teh 'thou; you'

ʔaʔ 'thou; you' (Mn)

(2 sg. formal)

šaša·ʔ 'you' (Cl, Mn)

*šaš 'you'

*ša·ʔ 'you'

    (3 sg.)

haha·ʔ 'he (she, it)' (Cl, Mn)

hah 'he (she, it)' (Mn)

ha·ʔ 'he (she, it)' (Cl)

baba·ʔ 'he (she, it)' (Cl)

    (1 pl.)

wawa·ʔ 'we' (Cl, Mn)

waw 'we' (Mn)

*wa·ʔ 'we'

*ʔu ʔ 'we'

    (2 pl. informal)

tata·ʔčik 'you (pl.)' (Mn)

tatčik 'you (pl.)' (Mn)

ta·ʔčik 'you (pl.)' (Cl)

    (2 pl. formal)

šaša·ʔčik 'you (pl.)' (Mn)

šaša·ʔ 'you (pl.)' (Cl, Mn)

*šaščik 'you (pl.)'

šaš 'you (pl.)' (Mn)

*ša·ʔčik 'you (pl.)'

*ša·ʔ 'you (pl.)'

    (3 pl.)

haha·ʔčik 'they' (Cl, Mn)

hahčik 'they' (Mn)

*ha·ʔčik 'they'

baba·ʔ(čik) 'they' (Cl)

7.6.2. DEMONSTRATIVE(-RELATIVE) PRONOUNS (ADJECTIVES).

7.6.2.1. NEAR DISTANT:

ʔaše·ʔ 'this (here)', 'that (there)' (Cl, Mn)

ʔeše·ʔ 'this (here)', 'that (there)' (Cl)

ʔaše·ʔ≠ši 'this (here)', 'that (there)' (Mn)

ʔaše·ʔčik 'these (here)', 'those (there)' (Mn)

ʔaši 'this (that)', 'which' (Mn)

ʔaš '(the one) who(m)', '(the one) which' (Mn)

ši '(the one) who(m)', '(the one) which' (Mn)

š '(the one) who(m)', '(the one) which' (Mn)

ʔana·ʔ 'this', 'that', (Cl)

ʔan(i[h]) 'who(m)', 'which' (Cl, Mn)

7.6.2.2. FAR DISTANT:

naše·ʔ 'that (yonder)' (Cl)

neše·ʔ 'that (yonder)' (Cl)

niše·ʔ 'that (yonder)' (Mn)

niše·ʔ≠ši 'that (yonder)' (Mn)

niši 'that (yonder)' (Mn)

niši≠ši 'that (yonder)' (Mn)

niš 'that (yonder)' (Mn)

*niščik 'those (yonder)'

niščik≠ši 'those (yonder)' (Mn)

maša ʔ 'which(ever)' (Cl)

7.6.3. 'ALTER':

k'e ʔat (separate), 'other', 'another', 'the other …' (Cl, Mn)

k'e ʔatčik 'others', 'the others …'

hek'at (opposite), 'the other side'

pi·l (apart), 'other'

ʔotroh '(an)other'

7.6.4. 'ALTERUM':

hu·nak 'another (thing)' (Mn)

ʔana·ʔhu·n 'another (thing)' (Cl)

7.6.5. DISTRIBUTIVE:

hunčik 'each one', 'one by one' (Cl, Mn)

ka·da(h)≠hu·n 'each' (Mn)

talčik 'several', 'some …' (Mn)

7.6.6. INTERROGATIVE(-RELATIVE) PRONOUNS (ADJECTIVES).

7.6.6.1. THING:

hat' 'what' (*ha ʔ-t-…) (Cl)

hat'am 'what' (Cl)

hat'amt'oh 'what' (Cl)

hat'wa ʔ 'somewhat' (Mn)

hant'oh 'what', 'that which', 'something', 'anything' (Mn)

hant'o(h)≠tam 'what kind of (a thing)' (Mn)

hančih 'what', 'that which' (Mn)

haw([a]ʔ) 'what', '(that) which' (Mn)

*hawa ʔčik 'what ones', '(those) which'

hawa ʔ≠…≠tam 'what kind of', '(the kind[s]) which' (Mn)

šat'a ʔ 'which (thing)', 'something', 'anything' (*[ʔa]š[i≠h]at'a ʔʔ)

šat'am 'which (thing)', 'something', 'anything'

šat'amt'oh 'which (thing)', 'something', 'anything'

šat'awaθ 'some', 'any'

7.6.6.2. PERSON:

hit 'what (which) person', 'who(m)', 'the one which', 'the one who(m)' (Mn)

hita ʔ 'who(m)', 'the one who(m)', 'someone' (Mn)

hita ʔ≠tam 'what kind of a (person)' (Mn)

hitam 'who(m)' (Cl, Mn)

hitam≠ta·mi? 'what kind of a (person)' (Cl)

hitama? 'who(m)' (Cl)

hitamt'oh 'who(m)' (Cl)

šita? '(some)one who(m)' (Cl) (*[?a]š[i≠ h]ita? ?) (Cl)

šitam 'who(m)' 'some', 'any' (Cl)

šitama? 'who(m)' (Cl)

šitamt'oh 'who(m)', 'some(one)', 'any(one)' (Cl)

7.6.7. NEGATIVE PRONOUNS (ADJECTIVES).

7.6.7.1. THING:

ša·nt'oh 'it's not anything', 'there's nothing there', 'it's not there' (= *yab≠ša·nt'oh?) (*yab≠š[i≠ha]·nt'oh?) (Mn)

nihant'oh 'nothing', 'anything' (Mn)

nihawa? 'no thing', 'no one', 'none', 'not anyone' (Mn)

yab(a?)(k'i[h]≠ha)ha·? 'not, indeed, that!' (Mn)

yaba?≠hant'oh 'not anything', 'nothing!' (Mn)

yaba?≠hawa? 'not anything which . . .' (Mn)

yab≠hant'oh 'nothing', 'anything' (Mn)

7.6.7.2. PERSON:

?i·ba·¢≠šita? 'not, already, anyone!' (Cl)

?i·b≠šitama? 'no one', 'not anyone' (Cl)

nihita? 'no person', 'no one' (Mn)

yabk'i(h)≠hita? 'not, indeed, anyone', 'it's no one!' (Mn)

yab≠hit 'no one', 'not anyone' (Mn)

yab≠hita? 'no person', 'no one', 'not anyone' (Mn)

yaba?≠hita? 'not anyone', 'no one!' (Mn)

7.6.8. DEPENDENT PERSONAL PRONOMINAL (PRO-ADJECTIVAL) PARTICLES.

7.6.8.0. HUASTEC INDEX ([MORPHO]-PHONOLOGICALLY ORDERED).

Classical	Glosses	Modern
?i-		
?i[t!]-	'he (she, it)'	?i₁-
ya₂-	'(him ...) we'	?i₂-[...-čik]
ya₃-	'our'	?i₃-
[t]ati₀₃-	'(you ...) he'	[t]i₄-
*[t]i₄-	'you (who are) ... his'	[t]i₄-
[t]ati₅-	'(you ...) I'	[t]u₆-
?i₆-	'some ...'	?i₆-
?it-		
?it-	'thou', 'you'	?it-
?it-...-čik	'ye', 'you'	?it-...-čik
?iš-		
* ?iš-	'you (sg.) (formal)'	* ?iš-
?iš-	'you (pl.) (formal)'	* ?iš-
?in-		
?in₁-	'I'	?in₁-
?in₂-	'(him ...) he'	?in₂-
* [t]in₂-	'he (who is) ... his'	* [t]in₂-
?in₃-	'his (her, its)'	?in₃-
[t]anin₂-	'me (... he)'	[t]in₄-
* [t]in₄-	'I (who am) ... his'	[t]in₄-
[t]ana₁-	'me (... you)'	[t]in₅-

Classical	Glosses	Modern
*$[t]in_5$-	'I (who am) ... your'	$[t]in_5$-
*$[t]ani_2$-	'me (... we)'	*$[t]in_6$-
$ʔa$-		
$ʔa_1$-	'(him ...) you'	$ʔa_1$-
*$[t]a_1$-	'he (who is) ... your'	*$[t]a_1$-
$ʔa_1$-...-čik	'you (pl.)'	$ʔa_1$-...-čik
$ʔa_2$-	'your'	$ʔa_2$-
$ʔa_3$-	'the deferenced'	$ʔa_3$-
$ʔat$-		
$[t]atu_3$-	'(you ...) I'	$[t]atu_3$-
		$[t]utu_3$-
		$[t]u_6$-
$[t]ati_{ø1}$-	'(you ...) I'	$[t]u_6$-
*$[t]ati(n_2)$- : $tati_{ø3}$-	'(you ...) he'	$[t]iti_{ø3}$-
		$[t]i_4$-
$[t]atiya_7$-	'(you ...) we'	$[t]u_7$-
$[t]ati_2$-	'(you ...) we'	$[t]u_7$-
$ʔaš$-		
*$[t]ašu_3$-	'(you [pl.] ...) I'	$[t]u_6$-...-čik
$[t]ašu_4$-	'you (pl.) (who are) ... my'	$[t]u_6$-...-čik
*$[t]aši_{ø1}$-	'(you [pl.] ...) I'	$[t]u_6$-...-čik
$[t]aš(i)$-	'(in that) you (pl.)'	*$[t]iš$-
*$[t]aši(n_2)$- : $taši_{ø3}$-	'(you [pl.] ...) he'	$[t]i_4$...-čik
*$[t]ašiya_7$-	'(you [pl.] ...) we'	$[t]u_7$-...-čik
$[t]aši_2$-	'(you [pl.] ...) we'	$[t]u_7$-...-čik
$ʔan$-		
$[t]anin_2$-	'(me ...) he'	$[t]in_4$-
$[t]ana_1$-	'(me ...) you'	$[t]in_5$-
*$[t]in_5$-	'I (who am) ...your'	$[t]in_5$-
*$[t]ani_2$-	'(me ...) we'	*$[t]in_6$-
$ʔan(a·ʔ)$-		
$ʔana_1$-	'(that which [it] ...) you'	
$ʔana·ʔ...(ʔ)a_1$	'(that which [it] ...) you'	
$ʔaw$-		
$[t]aw(a)$-	'(in that) we'	$[t]u_2$-
$[t]uw(a)$-	'(in that) we'	$[t]u_2$-
*$[t]awu_3$-	'(us ...) I'	*$[t]u_8$-
*$[t]awa_1$-	'(us ...) you'	*$[t]u_9$-
*$[t]awi(n_2)$- : *$tawi_{ø3}$-	'(us ...) he'	$[t]u_{10}$-

107

Classical	Glosses	Modern
ʔu-		
ʔu[t!]-	'he (she, it)'	ʔu$_1$-
wa$_2$-	'we'	ʔu$_2$-
ʔu$_3$-	'(him …) I'	ʔu$_3$-
*[t]u$_3$-	'he (who is) …my'	*[t]u$_3$-
ʔu$_4$-	'my'	ʔu$_4$-
*(ʔ)u$_5$-	'you (object)'	*(ʔ)u$_5$-
*(ʔ)u$_{5p}$	'us (object)'	*(ʔ)u$_{5p}$
[t]atu$_3$-	'(you …) I'	[t]u$_6$-
*[t]u$_6$-	'you (who are) …my'	[t]u$_6$-
[t]ati$_2$-	'(you …) we'	[t]u$_7$-
[t]aši$_2$-	'(you [pl.] …) we'	[t]u$_7$-
*[t]…(ʔ)u$_{5p}$-…(ʔ)u$_3$-	'(us …) I'	*[t]u$_8$-
*[t]…(ʔ)u$_{5p}$-…(ʔ)a$_1$- : [t]u$_9$-	'(us …) you'	[t]u$_9$-
*[t]u$_9$-	'we (who are) …your'	[t]u$_9$-
[t]…[ʔu$_{5p}$]…ya$_4$-	'(us …) you'	[t]u$_9$-
*[t]…(ʔ)u$_{5p}$…(ʔ)i(n$_2$)-	'(us …) he'	[t]u$_{10}$-
*[t]u$_{10}$-	'we (who are) …his'	[t]u$_{10}$-
wa-		
wa$_1$-	'he (she, it)'	ʔu$_1$-
wa$_2$-	'we'	ʔu$_2$-
wa$_3$-	'(us …) we'	ʔi$_2$-
wa$_4$-	'our'	ʔi$_3$-
ya-		
ya$_1$-[*[t]ya$_1$:]	'(in that) he (she, it)'	[t]i$_1$-
[k]ya$_1$	'(so that) he (she, it)'	ka$_{03}$-
ya$_2$-	'(him …) we'	ʔi$_2$-
ya$_3$-	'our'	ʔi$_3$-
ya$_4$-	'(him …) you (pl.)'	ʔa$_1$-…-čik
ya$_6$-	'(us …) you (pl.)'	[t]u$_9$-
[t]atiya$_7$-	'(you …) we'	[t]u$_7$-
∅-		
∅$_1$-	'I'	∅$_1$-
∅$_2$-	'you'	∅$_2$-
∅$_3$-	'he (she, it)'	∅$_3$-
∅$_4$-	'him (her, it)'	∅$_4$-
∅$_5$-	'to him (her, it)', 'for him (her, it)'	∅$_5$-
∅$_{1p}$-	'we'	∅$_{1p}$-
∅$_{2p}$-	'you (pl.)'	∅$_{2p}$-
∅$_{3p}$-	'they'	∅$_{3p}$-
∅$_{4p}$-	'them'	∅$_{4p}$-
∅$_{5p}$-	'to them', 'for them'	∅$_{5p}$-

7.6.8.1. DEPENDENT PERSONAL PRONOUN SUBJECTS.

SUBJECT PERSON AND NUMBER). (Subjects of intransitives [= objects of transitives?].)

7.6.8.1.1. HUASTEC INDEX (ORDERED BY

Classical		Glosses	Modern	Examples (in McQuown 1982)
(1 sg.)				
[* ʔan- :]	ʔin₁-	'I'	ʔin₁-	(1)
	∅₁-	'I'	∅₁-	(2)
(2 sg. informal)				
[* ʔat- :]	ʔit-	'(thou); you'	ʔit-	(3)
	∅₂ⁱ-	'(thou); you'	∅₂ⁱ-	(4)
(2 sg. formal)				
[* ʔaš- :]	ʔiš-	'you'		(5)
	∅₂ᶠ-	'you'		(6)
(3 sg.)				
	ʔi₁-	'he (she, it)'	ʔi₁-	(7a)
	ʔu₁-	'he (she, it)'	ʔu₁-	(7b)
	wa₁-	'he (she, it)'	ʔu₁-	(7c)
	ya₁-	'he (she, it)'	ʔi₁-	(7d)
[*∅₄- :]	∅₃-	'he (she, it)'	∅₃-	(8)
(1 pl.)				
	ʔu₂-	'we'	ʔu₂-	(9a)
[* ʔaw(a)- :]	wa₂-	'we'	ʔu₂-	(9b)
[* [t]aw(a)- :]	[t]uw(a)-	'(in that) we'	[t]u₂-	(9c)
	∅₁ₚ-	'we'	∅₁ₚ-(...-čik)	(10)
(2 pl. informal)				
[* ʔat-...-čik :]	ʔit-...-čik	'you (pl.)'	ʔit-...-čik	(11)
	∅₂ₚⁱ-...-čik	'you (pl.)'	∅₂ₚⁱ-...-čik	(12)
(2 pl. formal)				
[* ʔaš- :]	ʔiš-(...-čik)	'you (pl.)'		(13a)
[* [t]aš(i)- :]	[t]aš(i)-	'(in that) you (pl.)'		(13b)
	∅₂ₚᶠ-...-čik	'you (pl.)'	∅₂ₚᶠ-...-čik	(14)
(3 pl.)				
	ʔi₁-...-čik	'they'	ʔi₁-...-čik	(15a)
	ʔu₁-...-čik	'they'	ʔu₁-...-čik	(15b)
	wa₁-...-čik	'they'	ʔu₁-...-čik	(15c)
	ya₁-...-čik	'they'	ʔi₁-...-čik	(15d)
[*∅₄-...-čik :]	∅₃ₚ-...-čik	'they'	∅₃ₚ-...-čik	(16)

7.6.8.1.2. HUASTEC INDEX (ORDERED BY [THIRD PERSON OBJECT WITH] SUBJECT PER- SON AND NUMBER). (Subjects of transitives [= possessor particles?].)

Classical	Glosses	Modern	Examples (in McQuown 1982)
(1 sg.)			
$ʔu_3$-	'(him …) I'	$ʔu_3$-	(17)
$\emptyset_1$-	'(him …) I'	$\emptyset_1$-	(18)
(2 sg. informal)			
$ʔa_1{}^i$-	'(him …) (thou); you'	$ʔa_1$-	(19a)
[* $ʔana\cdot(ʔ\neq ʔ)a_1{}^i$- :] $ʔana\cdot_1{}^i$-	'(that one …) (thou); you'		(19b)
*$ya_4{}^i$-	'(him …) (thou); you'	$ʔa_1$-	(19c)
$\emptyset_2{}^i$-	'(him …) (thou); you'	$\emptyset_2{}^i$-	(20a)
[* $ʔana\cdot ʔ\neq\emptyset_2{}^i$- :] $ʔana\cdot ʔ\neq\emptyset_2{}^i$	'(that one …) (thou); you'		(20b)
(2 sg. formal)			
$ʔa_f{}^f$-	'(him …) you'	$ʔa_f$-	(21a)
[* $ʔana\cdot(ʔ\neq ʔ)a_f{}^f$- :]	'(that one …) you'		(21b)
*$ya_4{}^f$-	'(him …) you'	$ʔa_f$-	(21c)
$\emptyset_2{}^f$-	'(him …) you'	$\emptyset_2{}^f$-	(22a)
[* $ʔana\cdot ʔ\neq\emptyset_2{}^f$- :] $ʔana\cdot ʔ\neq\emptyset_2{}^f$-	'(him …) you'		(22b)
(3 sg.)			
$ʔin_2$-	'(him …) he'	$ʔin_2$-	(23)
$\emptyset_3$-	'(him …) he (she, it)'	$\emptyset_3$-	(24)
(1 pl.)			
ya_2-	'(him …) we'	$ʔi_2$-	(25a)
* $ʔiya_7$-	'(him …) we'	$ʔi_2$-	(25b)
* $ʔi_2$-	'(him …) we'	$ʔi_2$-(…-čik)	(25c)
$\emptyset_{1p}$-	'(him …) we'	$\emptyset_{1p}$-	(26)
(2 pl. informal)			
$ʔa_1{}^i$-…-čik	'(him …) (ye); you (pl.)'	$ʔa_1$-…-čik	(27a)
[* $ʔana\cdot(ʔ\neq ʔ)a_1{}^i$-…-čik :] $ʔana\cdot_1{}^i$-…-čik	'(that one …) (ye); you (pl.)'		(27b)
$ya_4{}^i$-…-čik	'(him …) (ye); you (pl.)'	$ʔa_1{}^i$-…-čik	(27c)
$\emptyset_{2p}{}^i$-…-čik	'(him …) (ye); you (pl.)'	$\emptyset_{2p}{}^i$-…-čik	(28a)
[* $ʔana\cdot ʔ\neq\emptyset_{2p}{}^i$-…-čik :] $ʔana\cdot ʔ\neq\emptyset_{2p}{}^i$-…-čik	'(that one …) (ye); you (pl.)'		(28b)
(2 pl. formal)			
$ʔa_f{}^f$-…-čik	'(him …) you (pl.)'	$ʔa_f$-…-čik	(29a)

Classical	Glosses	Modern	Examples (in McQuown 1982)
[* ʔana·(ʔ≠ʔ)a ʄ-...-čik :] ʔana·ʄ-...-čik	'(that one ...) you (pl.)'		(29b)
ya₄ʄ-(...-čik)	'(him ...) you (pl.)'	ʔa ʄ-...-čik	(29c)
Ø₂ₚʄ-...-čik	'(him ...) you (pl.)'	Ø₂ₚʄ-...-čik	(30a)
[* ʔana·ʔ≠Ø₂ₚʄ-...-čik :] ʔana·ʔ≠Ø₂ₚʄ-...-čik	'(that one ...) you (pl.)'	Ø₂ₚʄ-...-čik	(30b)
(3 pl.)			
ʔin₂...-čik	'(him ...) they'	ʔin₂-...-čik	(31)
Ø₃ₚ-...-čik	'(him ...) they'	Ø₃ₚ-...-čik	(32)

7.6.8.2. DEPENDENT PERSONAL PRONOUN OBJECTS.

7.6.8.2.0. ENGLISH INDEX (ORDERED BY OBJECT PERSON AND NUMBER).

Glosses	Classical	Modern
(1 sg.)		
'me'	ʔan-	ʔin₄-
(2 sg.)		
'you (... he)'	ʔat-	[t]i₄-
'you (... I)'	[t]i₅-	[t]i₅-
'you (... I)'	ʔat-	[t]u₅-
(3 sg.)		
'it (... you)'	ʔan-	Ø₄-
'that one (... you)'	ʔana·(ʔ)-	Ø₄-
'him (her, it)'	Ø₄-	Ø₄-
'to (for) him (her, it)'	Ø₅-	Ø₅-
(1 pl.)		
'us'	ʔaw-	[t]u₅ₚ-
(2 pl.)		
'you (pl.) (... he)'	ʔaš-	[t]i₄-...-čik
'you (pl.) (... I)'	[t]i₅-...-čik	[t]i₅-...-čik
'you (pl.) (... I)'	ʔaš-	[t]u₅-...-čik
(3 pl.)		
'them (... you)'	ʔan-...-čik	Ø₄-...-čik
'those (... you)'	ʔana·(ʔ)-...-čik	Ø₄-...-čik
'them'	Ø₄-...-čik	Ø₄-...-čik
'to (for) them'	Ø₅-...-čik	Ø₅-...-čik

TABLE 5-4. Object/Subject Combinations: Classical

	Objects		Subjects 'I'	'you'	'he'	'we'
(1)	'me'	$\emptyset_4$-	ʔu$_3$-			
(2)	'me'	ʔan-		ʔa$_1$-/ya$_4$-		
(3)	'me'	ʔan-			ʔin$_2$-	
(4)	'me'	ʔan-				ya$_2$-/ʔiya$_7$-/ʔi$_2$-
(5)	'you (sg.)'	ʔat-/ʔi$_5$-	ʔu$_3$-			
(6)	'you (sg.)'	$\emptyset_4$-		ʔa$_1$-/ya$_4$-		
(7)	'you (sg.)'	ʔat-			ʔi(n$_2$)-	
(8)	'you (sg.)'	ʔat-				ya$_2$-/ʔiya$_7$-/ʔi$_2$-
(9)	'him'	$\emptyset_4$-	ʔu$_3$-			
(10)	'him'	$\emptyset_4$-		ʔa$_1$-/ya$_4$-		
(11)	'him'	$\emptyset_4$-			ʔin$_2$-	
(12)	'him'	$\emptyset_4$-				ya$_2$-/ʔiya$_7$-/ʔi$_2$-
(13)	'us'	ʔaw-	ʔu$_3$-			
(14)	'us'	ʔaw-		ʔa$_1$-		
(15)	'us'	ʔaw-			ʔi(n$_2$)-	
(16)	'us'	$\emptyset_4$-				ya$_2$-/ʔiya$_7$-/ʔi$_2$-
(17)	'you (pl.)'	ʔaš-/ʔi$_5$-	ʔu$_3$-			
(18)	'you (pl.)'	$\emptyset_4$-		ʔa$_1$-/ya$_4$-		
(19)	'you (pl.)'	ʔaš-			ʔi(n$_2$)-	
(20)	'you (pl.)'					ya$_2$-/ʔiya$_7$-/ʔi$_2$-
(21)	'them'	$\emptyset_4$-	ʔu$_3$-			
(22)	'them'	$\emptyset_4$-		ʔa$_1$-/ya$_4$-		
(23)	'them'	$\emptyset_4$-			ʔin$_2$-	
(24)	'them'	$\emptyset_4$-				ya$_2$-/ʔiya$_7$-/ʔi$_2$-

Combinations				Reflexives
'me'	*'you'*	*'him'*	*'us'*	
		$ʔu_3$-		$(t \neq (ʔ)u_4 \neq ba \cdot ʔ)$
[t]ana_1-/[t]anya_4- *[t]anin_2-* *[t]anya_2-/[t]aniya_7-/* *[t]ani_2-*	*[t]atu_3-/[t]i_5-*			
		$ʔa_1$-/ya_4-		$(t \neq (ʔ)a_2 \neq ba \cdot ʔ)$ $(t \neq ya_5 \neq ba \cdot ʔ)$
	[t]ati_{Ø3}- *[t]atya_2-/[t]atiya_7-* *[t]ati_2-*			
		$ʔu_3$- $ʔa_1$-/ya_4- $ʔin_2$- ya_2-/$ʔiya_7$-/$ʔi_2$-		$(t \neq (ʔ)im_3 \neq ba \cdot ʔ)$
			[t]awu_3- *[t]awa_1-* *[t]awi_{Ø3}-*	
		ya_2-/$ʔiya_7$-/$ʔi_2$-		$(t \neq ya_3 \neq ba \cdot ʔ)$ $(t \neq (ʔ)i_3 \neq ba \cdot ʔ)$
	[t]ašu_3-/[t]i_5-			
		$ʔa_1$-/ya_4-		$(t \neq (ʔ)a_2 \neq ba \cdot ʔčik)$ $(t \neq ya_5 \neq ba \cdot ʔčik)$
	[t]aši_{Ø3}- *[t]ašya_2-/[t]ašiya_7-/* *[t]aši_2-*			
		$ʔu_3$-...-čik $ʔa_1$-...-čik/ya_4-...-čik $ʔin_2$-...-čik ya_2-...-čik/ $ʔiya_7$-...-čik/ $ʔi_2$-...-čik		$(t \neq (ʔ)im_3 \neq ba \cdot ʔčik)$

113

TABLE 5-5. Object/Subject Combinations: Modern

Objects		Subjects 'I'	'you'	'he'	'we'	Combinations 'me'	'you'	'him'	'us'	Reflexives
(1) 'me'	∅$_4$-							ʔu$_3$-		(t≠(ʔ)u$_4$≠ba·ʔ)
(2) 'me'	ʔin$_4$-		ʔa$_1$-			[t]in$_5$-				
(3) 'me'	ʔin$_4$-			ʔin$_2$-		[t]in$_4$-				
(4) 'me'	ʔin$_4$-				ʔi$_2$-	[t]in$_6$-				
(5) 'you (sg.)'	ʔu$_5$-/ʔi$_5$-	ʔu$_3$-					[t]u$_6$-/[t]i$_5$-	ʔa$_1$-		(t≠(ʔ)a$_2$≠ba·ʔ)
(6) 'you (sg.)'	∅$_4$-									
(7) 'you (sg.)'	ʔi$_4$-			ʔi(n$_2$)-			[t]i$_4$-			
(8) 'you (sg.)'	ʔu$_5$-				ʔi$_2$-		[t]u$_7$-			
(9) 'him'	∅$_4$-							ʔu$_3$-		(t≠(ʔ)im$_3$≠ba·ʔ)
(10) 'him'	∅$_4$-							ʔa$_1$-		
(11) 'him'	∅$_4$-							ʔin$_2$-		
(12) 'him'	∅$_4$-							ʔi$_2$-		
(13) 'us'	ʔu$_{5p}$-								[t]u$_8$-	(t≠(ʔ)i$_3$≠ba·ʔ)
(14) 'us'	ʔu$_{5p}$-								[t]u$_9$-	
(15) 'us'	ʔu$_{5p}$-								[t]u$_{10}$-	
(16) 'us'	∅$_4$-							ʔi$_2$-		
(17) 'you (pl.)'	ʔu$_5$-/ʔi$_5$-						[t]u$_6$-...-čik/[t]i$_5$-...-čik	ʔa$_1$-...-čik		(t≠(ʔ)a$_2$≠ba·ʔ·ʔčik)
(18) 'you (pl.)'	∅$_4$-							ʔu$_3$-...-čik		
(19) 'you (pl.)'	ʔi$_4$-						[t]i$_4$-...-čik	ʔa$_1$-...-čik		
(20) 'you (pl.)'	ʔu$_5$-						[t]u$_7$-...-čik			
(21) 'them'	∅$_4$-									(t≠(ʔ)im$_3$≠ba·ʔčik)
(22) 'them'	∅$_4$-							ʔin$_2$-...-čik		
(23) 'them'	∅$_4$-							ʔi$_2$-...-čik		
(24) 'them'	∅$_4$-									

7.6.8.2.1. HUASTEC INDEX (OF OBJECT AND SUBJECT COMBINATIONS). (Ordered by object [person and number] and subject [person and number] [including reflexives].) See Tables 5-4 and 5-5.

7.6.8.2.2. ENGLISH INDEX (OF OBJECT AND SUBJECT COMBINATIONS). (Ordered by object [person and number], followed, with each such object, by subjects [ordered, in turn, by person and number], including reflexives.)

Glosses	Classical	Modern
(1 sg.)		
'me ... I'	$*\emptyset_4 ... ?u_3$	
	$?u_3$	$?u_3$ (refl.)
'me ... I'	$*\emptyset_4 ... \emptyset_1$	
	$\emptyset_1$	$\emptyset_1$ (refl.)
'me ... you (2 sg.^{i})'	$*[t]an...(?)a_1{}^i$	
	$[t]ana_1{}^i$	$[t]in_5$
'me ... you (2 sg.^{i})'	$*[t]an...ya_4{}^i$	
	$[t]anya_4{}^i$	$[t]in_5$
'me ... you (2 sg.^{i})'	$*[t]an...\emptyset_2{}^i$	
	$*[t]an_{\emptyset 2}{}^i$	$[t]in_5$
'me ... you (2 sg.^{f})'	$*[t]an...(?)a_1{}^f$	
	$[t]ana_1{}^f$	$[t]in_5$
'me ... you (2 sg.^{f})'	$*[t]an...ya_4{}^f$	
	$[t]anya_4{}^f$	$[t]in_5$
'me ... you (2 sg.^{f})'	$*[t]an...\emptyset_2{}^f$	
	$*[t]an_{\emptyset 2}{}^f$	$[t]in_5$
'me ... he'	$*[t]an...(?)in_2$	
	$[t]anin_2$	$[t]in_4$
'me ... he'	$*[t]an...\emptyset_3$	
	$*[t]an_{\emptyset 3}$	$[t]in_4$
'me ... we'	$*[t]an...ya_2$	
	$[t]anya_2$	$[t]in_6$
'me ... we'	$*[t]an...(?)iya_7$	
	$[t]aniya_6$	$[t]in_6$
'me ... we'	$*[t]an...(?)i_2$	
	$[t]ani_2$	$[t]in_6$
'me ... we'	$*[t]an...\emptyset_{1p}$	
	$*[t]an_{\emptyset 1p}$	$[t]in_6$
'me ... you (2 pl.^{i})'	$*[t]an...(?)a_1{}^i...čik$	
	$[t]ana_1{}^i...čik$	$[t]in_5...čik$
'me ... you (2 pl.^{i})'	$*[t]an...ya_4{}^i...čik$	
	$[t]anya_4{}^i...čik$	$[t]in_5...čik$
'me ... you (2 pl.^{i})'	$*[t]an...\emptyset_{2p}{}^i...čik$	
	$*[t]an_{\emptyset 2p}{}^i...čik$	$[t]in_5...čik$
'me ... you (2 pl.^{f})'	$*[t]an...(?a)_1{}^f...čik$	
	$[tana_1{}^f...čik$	$[t]in_5...čik$
'me ... you (2 pl.^{f})'	$*[t]an...ya_4{}^f...čik$	
	$[t]anya_4{}^f...čik$	$[t]in_5...čik$

115

Glosses	Classical	Modern
'me ... you (2 pl.^{f})'	*[t]an...Ø$_{2p}^{f}$...čik	
	*[t]an$_{\theta 2p}^{f}$...čik	[t]in$_5$...čik
'me ... they'	*[t]an...(ʔ)in$_2$...čik	
	[t]anin$_2$...čik	[t]in$_4$...čik
'me ... they'	*[t]an...Ø$_{3p}$...čik	
	*[t]an$_{\theta 3p}$...čik	[t]in$_4$...čik
(2 sg.)		
'you (sg.) ... I'	*[t]at...(ʔ)u$_3$	
	[t]atu$_3$	[t]atu$_3$, [t]utu$_3$
'you (sg.) ... I'	*[t]u$_5$...(ʔ)u$_3$	[t]u$_6$
'you (sg.) ... I'	*[t]ati$_5$...Ø$_1$	
	[t]ati$_{\theta 1}$	[t]i$_5$
'you (sg.) ... I'	*[t]at...Ø$_1$	
	*[t]at$_{\theta 1}$	[t]i$_5$
'you (sg.) ... you (2 sg.^{i})'	*Ø$_4$...ʔa$_1^{i}$	
	ʔa$_1^{i}$	ʔa$_1^{i}$ (refl.)
'you (sg.) ... you (2 sg.^{i})'	*Ø$_4$...ya$_4^{i}$	
	ya$_4^{i}$	ʔa$_1^{i}$ (refl.)
'you (sg.) ... you (2 sg.^{i})'	*Ø$_4$...Ø$_2^{i}$	
	Ø$_2^{i}$	Ø$_2^{i}$ (refl.)
'you (sg.) ... you (2 sg.^{f})'	*Ø$_4$...ʔa$_1^{f}$	
	ʔa$_1^{f}$	ʔa$_1^{f}$ (refl.)
'you (sg.) ... you (2 sg.^{f})'	*Ø$_4$...ya$_4^{f}$	
	ya$_4^{f}$	ʔa$_1^{f}$ (refl.)
'you (sg.) ... you (2 sg.^{f})'	*Ø$_4$...Ø$_2^{f}$	
	Ø$_2^{f}$	Ø$_2^{f}$ (refl.)
'you (sg.) ... he'	*[t]at...(ʔ)i(n$_2$)	
	*[t]ati$_{\theta 3}$	[t]iti$_{\theta 3}$, [t]i$_4$
'you (sg.) ... he'	*[t]at...Ø$_3$	
	*[t]at$_{\theta 3}$	[t]i$_4$
'you (sg.) ... we'	*[t]at...ya$_2$	
	[t]atya$_2$	[t]u$_7$
'you (sg.) ... we'	*[t]at...(ʔ)iya$_7$	
	[t]atiya$_7$	[t]u$_7$
'you (sg.) ... we'	*[t]at...(ʔ)i$_2$	
	[t]ati$_2$	[t]u$_7$
'you (sg.) ... we'	*[t]...(ʔ)u$_5$	[t]u$_7$
'you (sg.) ... we'	*[t]at...Ø$_{1p}$	
	*[t]at$_{\theta 1p}$	[t]u$_7$
'you (sg.) ... you (2 pl.^{i})'	*Ø$_4$...ʔa$_1^{i}$...čik	
	ʔa$_1^{i}$...čik	ʔa$_1^{i}$...čik (refl.)
'you (sg.) ... you (2 pl.^{i})'	*Ø$_4$...ya$_4^{i}$...čik	
	ya$_4^{i}$...čik	ʔa$_1^{i}$...čik (refl.)
'you (sg.) ... you (2 pl.^{i})'	*Ø$_4$...Ø$_2^{i}$...čik	
	Ø$_2^{i}$...čik	Ø$_2^{i}$...čik (refl.)

Glosses	Classical	Modern
'you (sg.) ... you (2 pl.^{f})'	$*Ø_4...ʔa_1{}^f...čik$ $ʔa_1{}^f...čik$	$ʔa_1{}^f...čik$ (refl.)
'you (sg.) ... you (2 pl.^{f})'	$*Ø_4...ya_4{}^f...čik$ $ya_4{}^f...čik$	$ʔa_1{}^f...čik$ (refl.)
'you (sg.) ... you (2 pl.^{f})'	$*Ø_4...Ø_2{}^f...čik$ $Ø_2{}^f...čik$	$Ø_2{}^f...čik$ (refl.)
'you (sg.) ... they'	$*[t]at...(ʔ)i(n_2)...čik$ $[t]ati_{Ø3}...čik$	$[t]iti_{Ø3}...čik$ $[t]i_4...čik$
'you (sg.) ... they'	$*[t]at...Ø_{3p}...čik$ $[t]at_{3p}...čik$	$[t]i_4...čik$
(3 sg.)		
'him ... I'	$*Ø_4...ʔu_3$ $ʔu_3$	$ʔu_3$
'him ... I'	$*Ø_4...Ø_1$ $Ø_1$	$Ø_1$
'him ... you (2 sg.^{i})'	$*Ø_4...ʔa_1{}^i$ $ʔa_1{}^i$	$ʔa_1{}^i$
'him ... you (2 sg.^{i})'	$*Ø_4...ya_4{}^i$ $ya_4{}^i$	$ʔa_1{}^i$
'him ... you (2 sg.^{i})'	$*Ø_4...Ø_2{}^i$ $Ø_2{}^i$	$Ø_2{}^i$
'him ... you (2 sg.^{f})'	$*Ø_4...ʔa_1{}^f$ $ʔa_1{}^f$	$ʔa_1{}^f$
'him ... you (2 sg.^{f})'	$*Ø_4...ya_4{}^f$ $ya_4{}^f$	$ʔa_1{}^f$
'him ... you (2 sg.^{f})'	$*Ø_4...Ø_2{}^f$ $Ø_2{}^f$	$Ø_2{}^f$
'him ... he'	$*Ø_4...ʔin_2$ $ʔin_2$	$ʔin_2$
'himself ... he'	$*Ø_4...ʔin_2$ $ʔin_2$	$ʔin_2$ (refl.)
'him ... he'	$*Ø_4...Ø_3$ $Ø_3$	$Ø_3$
'him ... we'	$*Ø_4...ya_2$ ya_2	$ʔi_2$
'him ... we'	$*Ø_4...ʔiya_7$ $ʔiya_7$	$ʔi_2$
'him ... we'	$*Ø_4...ʔi_2$ $ʔi_2$	$ʔi_2$
'him ... we'	$*Ø_4...Ø_{1p}$ $Ø_{1p}$	$Ø_{1p}$
'him ... you (2 pl.^{i})'	$*Ø_4...ʔa_1{}^i...čik$ $ʔa_1{}^i...čik$	$ʔa_1{}^i...čik$
'him ... you (2 pl.^{i})'	$*Ø_4...ya_4{}^i...čik$	

Glosses	Classical	Modern
	$ya_4{}^i...\check{c}ik$	$\eth a_1{}^i...\check{c}ik$
'him ... you (2 pl.^{i})'	$*\emptyset_4...\emptyset_{2p}{}^i...\check{c}ik$	
	$\emptyset_{2p}{}^i...\check{c}ik$	$\emptyset_{2p}{}^i...\check{c}ik$
'him ... you (2 pl.^{f})'	$*\emptyset_4...\eth a_1{}^f...\check{c}ik$	
	$\eth a_1{}^f...\check{c}ik$	$\eth a_1{}^f...\check{c}ik$
'him ... you (2 pl.^{f})'	$*\emptyset_4...ya_4{}^f...\check{c}ik$	
	$ya_4{}^f...\check{c}ik$	$\eth a_1{}^f...\check{c}ik$
'him ... you (2 pl.^{f})'	$*\emptyset_4...\emptyset_{2p}{}^f...\check{c}ik$	
	$\emptyset_{2p}{}^f...\check{c}ik$	$\emptyset_{2p}{}^f...\check{c}ik$
'him ... they'	$*\emptyset_4...\eth in_2...\check{c}ik$	
	$\eth in_2...\check{c}ik$	$\eth in_2...\check{c}ik$
'him ... they'	$*\emptyset_4...\emptyset_{3p}...\check{c}ik$	
	$\emptyset_{3p}...\check{c}ik$	$\emptyset_{3p}...\check{c}ik$
(1 pl.)		
'us ... I'	$*[t]aw...(\eth)u_3$	
	$[t]awu_3$	$[t]u_8$ (refl.)
'us ... I'	$*[t]u_{5p}...(\eth)u_3$	$[t]u_8$ (refl.)
'us ... I'	$*[t]aw...\emptyset_1$	
	$*[t]aw_{\emptyset 1}$	$[t]u_8$ (refl.)
'us ... you (2 sg.^{i})'	$*[t]aw...(\eth)a_1{}^i$	
	$[t]awa_1{}^i$	$[t]u_9$
'us ... you (2 sg.^{i})'	$*[t]u_{5p}...(\eth)a_1{}^i$	
	$[t]uwa_1{}^i$	$[t]u_9$
'us ... you (2 sg.^{i})'	$*[t]aw...\emptyset_2{}^i$	
	$[t]aw_{\emptyset 2}{}^i$	$[t]u_9$
'us ... you (2 sg.^{f})'	$*[t]aw...(\eth)a_1{}^f$	
	$[t]awa_1{}^f$	$[t]u_9$
'us ... you (2 sg.^{f})'	$*[t]u_{5p}...(\eth)a_1{}^f$	
	$[t]uwa_1{}^f$	$[t]u_9$
'us ... you (2 sg.^{f})'	$*[t]aw...\emptyset_2{}^f$	
	$*[t]aw_{\emptyset 2}{}^f$	$[t]u_9$
'us ... he'	$*[t]aw...(\eth)i(n_2)$	
	$[t]awi_{\emptyset 3}$	$[t]u_9$
'us ... he'	$*[t]aw...\emptyset_3$	
	$*[t]aw_{\emptyset 3}$	$[t]u_9$
'us ... we'	$*\emptyset_4...ya_2$	
	ya_2	$\eth i_2$ (refl.)
'us ... we'	$*\emptyset_4...\eth iya_7$	
	$\eth iya_7$	$\eth i_2$ (refl.)
'us ... we'	$*\emptyset_4...\eth i_2$	
	$\eth i_2$	$\eth i_2$ (refl.)
'us ... we'	$*\emptyset_4...\emptyset_{1p}$	
	$\emptyset_{1p}$	$\emptyset_{1p}$ (refl.)
'us ... you (2 pl.^{i})'	$*[t]aw...(\eth)a_1{}^i...\check{c}ik$	
	$[t]awa_1{}^i...\check{c}ik$	$[t]u_9...\check{c}ik$

Glosses	Classical	Modern
'us ... you (2 pl.^{i})'	*[t]u$_{5p}$...(ʔ)a$_1^i$...čik	
	[t]uwa$_1^i$...čik	[t]u$_9$...čik
'us ... you (2 pl.^{i})'	*[t]aw...∅$_{2p}^i$...čik	
	*[t]aw...∅$_{2p}^i$...čik	[t]u$_9$...čik
'us ... you (2 pl.^{f})'	*[t]aw...(ʔ)a$_1^f$...čik	
	[t]awa$_1^f$...čik	[t]u$_9$...čik
'us ... you (2 pl.^{f})'	*[t]u$_{5p}$...(ʔ)a^f...čik	
	[t]uwa$_1^f$...čik	[t]u$_9$...čik
'us ... you (2 pl.^{f})'	*[t]aw...∅$_{2p}^f$...čik	
	*[t]aw$_{∅2p}^f$...čik	[t]u$_9$...čik
'us ... they'	*[t]aw...(ʔ)i(n$_2$)...čik	
	[t]awi$_{∅3}$...čik	[t]u$_{10}$...čik
'us ... they'	*[t]aw...∅$_{3p}$...čik	
	*[t]aw$_{∅3p}$...čik	[t]u$_{10}$...čik

(2 pl.)

Glosses	Classical	Modern
'you (pl.) ... I'	*[t]aš...(ʔ)u$_3$(...čik)	
	[t]ašu$_3$(...čik)	[t]u$_6$...čik
'you (pl.) ... I'	*[t]u$_5$...(ʔ)u$_3$...čik	[t]u$_6$...čik
'you (pl.) ... I'	*[t]aši$_5$...∅$_1$(...čik)	
	[t]aši$_{∅1}$(...čik)	[t]i$_5$...čik
'you (pl.) ... I'	*[t]aš...∅$_1$(...čik)	
	*[t]aš$_{∅1}$(...čik)	[t]i$_5$...čik
'you (pl.) ... you (2 sg.^{i})'	*∅$_4$...ʔa$_1^i$...čik	
	ʔa$_1^i$...čik	ʔa$_1^i$...čik (refl.)
'you (pl.) ... you (2 sg.^{i})'	*∅$_4$...ya$_4^i$...čik	
	ya$_4^i$...čik	ʔa$_4^i$...čik (refl.)
'you (pl.) ... you (2 sg.^{i})'	*∅$_4$...∅$_2^i$...čik	
	∅$_2^i$...čik	∅$_2^i$...čik (refl.)
'you (pl.) ... you (2 sg.^{f})'	*∅$_4$...ʔa$_1^f$...čik	
	ʔa$_1^f$...čik	ʔa$_1^f$...čik (refl.)
'you (pl.) ... you (2 sg.^{f})'	*∅$_4$...ya$_4^f$...čik	
	ya$_4^f$...čik	ʔa$_1^f$...čik (refl.)
'you (pl.) ... you (2 sg.^{f})'	*∅$_4$...∅$_2^f$...čik	
	∅$_2^f$...čik	∅$_2^f$...čik (refl.)
'you (pl.) ... he'	*[t]aš...(ʔ)i(n$_2$)(...čik)	
	[t]aši$_{∅3}$(...čik)	[t]i$_4$...čik
'you (pl.) ... he'	*[t]aš...∅$_3$(...čik)	
	*[t]aš$_{∅3}$(...čik)	[t]i$_4$...čik
'you (pl.) ... we'	*[t]aš...ya$_2$(...čik)	
	[t]ašya$_2$(...čik)	[t]u$_7$...čik
'you (pl.) ... we'	*[t]aš...(ʔ)iya$_7$(...čik)	
	[t]ašiya$_7$(...čik)	[t]u$_7$...čik
'you (pl.) ... we'	*[t]aš...(ʔ)i$_2$(...čik)	
	[t]aši$_2$(...čik)	[t]u$_7$...čik
'you (pl.) ... we'	*[t]u$_5$...(ʔ)i$_2$...čik	[t]u$_7$...čik

Glosses	Classical	Modern
'you (pl.) … we'	* [t]aš…Ø$_{1p}$(…čik)	
	* [t]aš$_{Ø1p}$(…čik)	[t]u$_7$…čik
'you (pl.) … you (2 pl.^{i})'	*Ø$_4$…ʔa$_1$^{i}…čik	
	ʔa$_1$^{i}…čik	ʔa$_1$^{i}…čik (refl.)
'you (pl.) … you (2 pl.^{i})'	*Ø$_4$…ya$_4$^{i}…čik	
	ya$_4$^{i}…čik	ʔa$_1$^{i}…čik (refl.)
'you (pl.) … you (2 pl.^{i})'	*Ø$_4$…Ø$_{2p}$^{i}…čik	
	Ø$_{2p}$^{i}…čik	Ø$_{2p}$^{i}…čik (refl.)
'you (pl.) … you (2 pl.^{f})'	*Ø$_4$…ʔa$_1$^{f}…čik	
	ʔa$_1$^{f}…čik	ʔa$_1$^{f}…čik (refl.)
'you (pl.) … you (2 pl.^{f})'	*Ø$_4$…ya$_4$^{f}…čik	
	ya$_4$^{f}…čik	ʔa$_1$^{f}…čik (refl.)
'you (pl.) … you (2 pl.^{f})'	*Ø$_4$…Ø$_{2p}$^{f}…čik	
	Ø$_{2p}$^{f}…čik	Ø$_{2p}$^{f}…čik (refl.)
'you (pl.) … they'	* [t]aš…(ʔ)i(n$_2$)…čik	
	[t]aši$_{Ø3}$…čik	[t]i$_4$…čik
'you (pl.) … they'	* [t]aš…Ø$_{3p}$…čik	
	* [t]aš$_{Ø3p}$…čik	[t]i$_4$…čik
(3 pl.)		
'them … I'	*Ø$_4$…ʔu$_3$…čik	
	ʔu$_3$…čik	ʔu$_3$…čik
'them … I'	*Ø$_4$…Ø$_1$…čik	
	Ø$_1$…čik	Ø$_1$…čik
'them … you (2 sg.^{i})'	*Ø$_4$…ʔa$_1$^{i}…čik	
	ʔa$_1$^{i}…čik	ʔa$_1$^{i}…čik
'them … you (2 sg.^{i})'	*Ø$_4$…ya$_4$^{i}…čik	
	ya$_4$^{i}…čik	ʔa$_1$^{i}…čik
'them … you (2 sg.^{i})'	*Ø$_4$…Ø$_2$^{i}…čik	
	Ø$_2$^{i}…čik	Ø$_2$^{i}…čik
'them … you (2 sg.^{f})'	*Ø$_4$…ʔa$_1$^{f}…čik	
	ʔa$_1$^{f}…čik	ʔa$_1$^{f}…čik
'them … you (2 sg.^{f})'	*Ø$_4$…ya$_4$^{f}…čik	
	ya$_4$^{f}…čik	ʔa$_1$^{f}…čik
'them … you (2 sg.^{f})'	*Ø$_4$…Ø$_2$^{f}…čik	
	Ø$_2$^{f}…čik	Ø$_2$^{f}…čik
'them … he'	*Ø$_4$…ʔin$_2$…čik	
	ʔin$_2$…čik	ʔin$_2$…čik
'them … he'	*Ø$_4$…Ø$_3$…čik	
	Ø$_3$…čik	Ø$_3$…čik
'them … we'	*Ø$_4$…ya$_2$…čik	
	ya$_2$…čik	ʔi$_2$…čik
'them … we'	*Ø$_4$…ʔiya$_7$…čik	
	ʔiya$_7$…čik	ʔi$_2$…čik
'them … we'	*Ø$_4$…ʔi$_2$…čik	
	ʔi$_2$…čik	ʔi$_2$…čik

Glosses	Classical	Modern
'them ... we'	$*\emptyset_4...\emptyset_{1p}...\check{c}ik$	
	$\emptyset_{1p}...\check{c}ik$	$\emptyset_{1p}...\check{c}ik$
'them ... you (2 pl.^{i})'	$*\emptyset_4...\,{}^{\textstyle ?}a_1{}^i...\check{c}ik$	
	${}^{\textstyle ?}a_1{}^i...\check{c}ik$	${}^{\textstyle ?}a_1{}^i...\check{c}ik$
'them ... you (2 pl.^{i})'	$*\emptyset_4...ya_4{}^i...\check{c}ik$	
	$ya_4{}^i...\check{c}ik$	${}^{\textstyle ?}a_1{}^i...\check{c}ik$
'them ... you (2 pl.^{i})'	$*\emptyset_4...\emptyset_{2p}{}^i...\check{c}ik$	
	$\emptyset_{2p}{}^i...\check{c}ik$	$\emptyset_{2p}{}^i...\check{c}ik$
'them ... you (2 pl.^{f})'	$*\emptyset_4...\,{}^{\textstyle ?}a_1{}^f...\check{c}ik$	
	${}^{\textstyle ?}a_1{}^f...\check{c}ik$	${}^{\textstyle ?}a_1{}^f...\check{c}ik$
'them ... you (2 pl.^{f})'	$*\emptyset_4...ya_4{}^f...\check{c}ik$	
	$ya_4{}^f...\check{c}ik$	${}^{\textstyle ?}a_1{}^f...\check{c}ik$
'them ... you (2 pl.^{f})'	$*\emptyset_4...\emptyset_{2p}{}^f...\check{c}ik$	
	$\emptyset_{2p}{}^f...\check{c}ik$	$\emptyset_{2p}{}^f...\check{c}ik$
'them ... they'	$*\emptyset_4...\,{}^{\textstyle ?}in_2...\check{c}ik$	
	${}^{\textstyle ?}in_2...\check{c}ik$	${}^{\textstyle ?}in_2...\check{c}ik$
'themselves ... they'	$*\emptyset_4...\,{}^{\textstyle ?}in_2...\check{c}ik$	
	${}^{\textstyle ?}in_2...\check{c}ik$	${}^{\textstyle ?}in_2...\check{c}ik$ (refl.)
'them ... they'	$*\emptyset_4...\emptyset_{3p}...\check{c}ik$	
	$\emptyset_{3p}...\check{c}ik$	$\emptyset_{3p}...\check{c}ik$

7.6.8.2.3. ENGLISH INDEX (OF COMBINATIONS WITH INDIRECT OBJECT). With third person direct object only; ordered by object [person and number], with subjects [ordered by person and number]. See McQuown 1982.

A third person indirect object (since it is always $\emptyset_5$), preposed to any direct object, preposed in turn to any subject, has no effect on the resulting combinations.

An indirect object of any other person, if preposed to a third person direct object (since the latter is always $\emptyset_4$), has no effect on the resulting combinations.

Combinations of indirect object and direct object which involve persons other than third are not common, and, if ambiguous, will be disambiguated by the wider context.

7.6.9. SUBORDINATED DEPENDENT PERSONAL PRONOMINAL PARTICLES. A fair sampling of these (of some 848 examples), attested in Andrade's texts and in Tapia Zenteno, may be found in McQuown 1982.

7.6.9.1. WITH PREPOSED ti-.

7.6.9.1.1. OF INTRANSITIVES. These include sixteen examples of the basic forms.

7.6.9.1.2. OF TRANSITIVES. These include sixteen examples (with object 'him') with preposed ti-. In addition, the following combinations may occur (sixteen examples per combination: see McQuown 1982): with objects 'me,' 'you (sg.)', 'them', 'us', 'you (pl.)', 'for him ... me', 'for him ... you (sg.)', 'for him ... him', 'for him ... us', 'for him ... you (pl.)', 'for him ... them', 'for me ... it', 'for you (sg.)' ... it', 'for us ... it', 'for you (pl.) ... it'.

7.6.9.2. WITH PREPOSED ka-.

7.6.9.2.1. OF INTRANSITIVES. These include sixteen examples of the basic forms.

7.6.9.2.2. OF TRANSITIVES. These include sixteen examples (with object 'him') with preposed ka-. In addition, the following combinations may occur (sixteen examples per combination: see McQuown 1982): with objects 'me', 'you (sg.)', 'them', 'us', 'you (pl.)', 'for him ... me', 'for him ... you (sg.)', 'for him ... him', 'for him ... us', 'for him ... you (pl.)', 'for him ... them', 'for me ... it', 'for you (sg.) ... it', 'for us ... it', 'for you (pl.) ... it'.

7.6.9.3. WITH PREPOSED ti- FOLLOWED BY ka-.

7.6.9.3.1. OF INTRANSITIVES. These include sixteen examples of the basic forms.

7.6.9.3.2. OF TRANSITIVES. These include sixteen examples (with object 'him') with preposed *ti-* followed by preposed *ka-*. In addition, the following combinations may occur (sixteen examples per combination: see McQuown 1982): with objects 'me', 'you (sg.)', 'them', 'us', 'you (pl.)', 'for him … me', 'for him … you (sg.)', 'for him … him', 'for him … us', 'for him … you (pl.)', 'for him … them', 'for me … it', 'for you (sg.) … it', 'for us … it', 'for you (pl.) … it'.

7.6.10. DEPENDENT PRONOMINAL POSSESSOR PARTICLES. (= Subjects of transitive verbs?) (Ordered by person and number.)

Classical	Glosses	Modern	Examples
(1 sg.)			
$ʔu_4$-	'my'	$ʔu_4$-	(1)
(2 sg.)			
$ʔa_2$-	'your'	$ʔa_2$-	(2a)
$ʔana$-	'that … of yours'	$ʔa_2$-	(2b)
(3 sg.)			
$ʔin_3$-	'his (her, its)'	$ʔin_3$-	(3)
(1 pl.)			
wa_4-	'our'	$ʔi_3$-	(4a)
ya_3-	'our'	$ʔi_3$-	(4b)
$ʔi_3$-	'our'	$ʔi_3$-	(4c)
(2 pl.)			
ya_5-	'your (pl.)'	$ʔa_2$-…-čik	(5a)
* $ʔa_2$-…-čik	'your (pl.)'	$ʔa_2$-…-čik	(5b)
(3 pl.)			
$ʔin_3$-…-čik	'their'	$ʔin_3$-…-čik	(6)

Examples: (1) #$ʔu_4$≠$ʔi·šal$# 'my wife' (Cl); (2a) #$ʔa_2$≠$ʔakan$# 'your foot'; (2b) #$ʔana$≠$ʔi·šal$# 'that wife of yours' (Cl); (3) #$ʔin_3$≠$ʔi·šal$# 'his wife' (Cl); (4a) #t≠wa_4≠$ba·ʔ$# 'our selves' (Cl); (4b) #ya_3≠$ʔaha·tik$≠$(ʔ)a_3$≠$diyo·s$≠ 'our Lord God…' (Cl); (4c) #$ʔi_3$≠$ʔaha·tik$≠$(ʔ)a_3$≠$hesukri·stoh$# 'our Lord Jesus Christ' (Cl); (5a) #$ʔa_2$≠$t'aha·l$≠t≠ya_5≠ $ba·ʔ$# 'you (pl.) make yourselves' (Cl); (5b) #$ʔa_2$≠$ʔalwaʔtalčik$# 'your (pl.) goodness'; (6) #$ʔin_3$≠$k'ima·ʔčik$≠$haha·ʔ$# 'their house'.

7.6.11. DEPENDENT PERSONAL PRONOUN POSSESSORS (COMBINED WITH PERSONS POSSESSED). ('I am your …', etc., i.e., 'you possess me', etc.)

Possessed		Possessor	Combination	Glosses	Examples
tin_1-	…	tin_{02}-	[= tin_5-]	'I am your …'	(1)
tin_1-	…	tin_{03}-	[= tin_4-]	'I am his …'	(2)
$t[u]_{02}$-	…	tu_{01}-	[= tu_6-]	'you are my …'	(3)

122

Possessed		Possessor	Combination	Glosses	Examples
$t[i]_{02}$-	...	ti_{03}-	[= ti_4-]	'you are his ...'	(4)
tu_2-	...	$t[u]_{02}$-	[= tu_9-]	'we are your ...'	(5)
tu_2-	...	$t[u]_{03}$-	[= tu_{10}-]	'we are his ...'	(6)
*tu_1-	...	$t[u]_{01}$-	[= tu_3-]	'he is my ...'	(7)
*$t[a]_{03}$-	...	$t[a]_{02}$-	[= ta_1-]	'he is your ...'	(8)
*ti_{03}-	...	tin_{03}-	[= tin_2-]	'he is his ...'	(9)

Examples: (1) #tim₁≠(pe·l)≠tin₀₂≠tomki·l# 'I am your spouse'; (2) #tim₁≠(pe·l)≠tin₀₃ ≠tomki·l# 'I am her spouse'; (3) #tu₀₂≠(pe·l) ≠tu₀₁≠ʔiȼa·n# 'you are my uncle'; (4) #ti₀₂≠ (pe·l)≠ti₀₃≠ȼaka·mil# 'you are his child'; (5) #tu₂≠(pe·l)≠tu₀₂≠tolmiwa·l# 'we are your helpers'; (6) #tu₂≠(pe·l)≠tu₀₃≠tolmiwa·l# 'we are his helpers'.

7.6.12. INDEPENDENT POSSESSOR/POSSESSED PRONOMINAL PHRASES. (Ordered by person and number.)

7.6.12.1. *k'a·l* 'PROPERTY'.

Classical	Glosses	Modern	Examples
(1 sg.)			
ʔu₄≠k'a·l	'[it's] mine'	ʔu₄≠k'a·l	(1)
(2 sg.)			
ʔa₂≠k'a·l	'[it's] yours'	ʔa₂≠k'a·l	(2a)
ʔan≠(ʔ)a₂≠k'a·l	'that['s] yours'		(2b)
ʔana·ʔ≠(ʔ)a₂≠k'a·l	'that one [is] yours'		(2c)
(3 sg.)			
ʔin₃≠k'a·l	'[it's] his (hers) (its)'	ʔin₃≠k'a·l	(3)
(1 pl.)			
*wa₄≠k'a·l	'[it's] ours'	ʔi₃≠k'a·l	(4a)
*ya₃≠k'a·l	'[it's] ours'	ʔi₃≠k'a·l	(4b)
*ʔi₃≠k'a·l	'[it's] ours'	ʔi₃≠k'a·l	(4c)
(2 pl.)			
*ya₅≠k'a·l	'[it's] yours (pl.)'	ʔa₂≠k'a·lčik	(5a)
*ʔa₂≠k'a·lčik	'[it's] yours (pl.)'	ʔa₂≠k'a·lčik	(5b)
(3 pl.)			
*ʔin₃≠k'a·lčik	'[it's] theirs'	ʔin₃≠k'a·lčik	(6)

Examples: (1) #nana·ʔ≠(ʔ)u₄≠k'a·l# 'as for me, [it's] mine' (Cl); (2a) #tata·ʔ≠(ʔ)a₂≠ k'a·l# 'as for you, [it's] yours' (Cl); (2c) #tata·ʔ#ʔana·ʔ≠(ʔ)a₂≠k'a·l# 'as for you, that one [is] yours' (Cl); (3) #baba·ʔ≠(ʔ)in₃≠ k'a·l# 'as for him, [it's] his' (Cl); (3) #hitam≠ (ʔ)in₃≠k'a·l#ʔana·ʔ# 'whose (its property) [is] that?' (Cl); (4) #ʔi₃≠k'a·l# '[it's] ours'; (5b) #tat≠(ʔ)a₂≠k'a·lčik# 'as for you, [it's] yours (pl.)'; (6) #hah≠(ʔ)in₃≠k'a·lčik# 'as for them, [it's] theirs'.

7.6.12.2. *ba·ʔ* 'SELF'.

Classical	Glosses	Modern	Examples
(1 sg.)			
[t]≠(ʔ)u₄≠ba·ʔ	'(as) my self'	[t]u₄≠ba·ʔ	(1)
(2 sg.)			
[t]≠(ʔ)a₂≠ba·ʔ	'(as) your self'	[t]a₂≠ba·ʔ	(2)
(3 sg.)			
[t]≠(ʔ)im₃≠ba·ʔ	'(as) his self'	[t]im₃≠ba·ʔ	(3)
(1 pl.)			
[t]≠wa₄≠ba·ʔ	'(as) our selves'	[t]i₃≠ba·ʔ	(4a)
[t]≠ya₃≠ba·ʔ	'(as) our selves'	[t]i₃≠ba·ʔ	(4b)
*[t]≠(ʔ)i₃≠ba·ʔ	'(as) our selves'	[t]i₃≠ba·ʔ	(4c)
(2 pl.)			
[t]≠ya₅≠ba·ʔ	'(as) your selves'	[t]a₂≠ba·ʔčik	(5a)
*[t]≠(ʔ)a₂≠ba·ʔčik	'(as) your selves'	[t]a₂≠ba·ʔčik	(5b)
(3 pl.)			
[t]≠(ʔ)im₃≠ba·ʔčik	'(as) their selves'	[t]im₃≠ba·ʔčik	(6)

Examples: (1) #ku₃≠tamkuy≠ne(h)≠tu₄≠ba·ʔ# 'that I may join, I, myself'; (2) ≠ka₂≠tolmiy≠ta₂≠ba·ʔ# 'that you may help yourself'; (3) ≠kin₂≠loʔonči(h)≠tim₃≠ba·ʔ# 'that he may introduce it into himself'; (4c) ≠(ʔ)i₂≠belθa·l≠ti₃≠ba·ʔ# 'we conduct ourselves'; (5) ≠ka₁≠kʼaθatnaʔčik≠ta₂≠ba·ʔ# 'that you (pl.) may elevate yourselves'; (6) ≠hantʼuθaʔ≠tikin₂≠wilaʔ≠tim₃≠ba·ʔ# 'how they may develop themselves'.

7.6.12.3. *ʔe·b* 'PERSON'.

Classical	Glosses	Modern	Examples
(1 sg.)			
*[t]≠(ʔ)u₄≠ʔe·b	'(in) my person'	*[t]u₄≠ʔe·b	(1)
(2 sg.)			
*[t]≠(ʔ)a₂≠ʔe·b	'(in) your person'	*[t]a₂≠ʔe·b	(2)
(3 sg.)			
[t]≠(ʔ)in₃≠ʔe·b	'(in) his (her) (its) person'	[t]in₃≠ʔe·b	(3a)
[t]≠(ʔ)i₀₃≠ʔe·b	'(in) [his] person'	[t]i₀₃≠ʔe·b	(3b)
(1 pl.)			
[t]≠(ʔ)i₃≠ʔe·b	'(in) our persons'	[t]i₃≠ʔe·b	(4)

Classical	Glosses	Modern	Examples
(2 pl.)			
*[t]≠(ʔ)a₂≠ʔe·bčik	'(in) your (pl.) persons'	[t]a₂≠ʔe·bčik	(5)
(3 pl.)			
[t]≠(ʔ)in₃≠ʔe·bčik	'(in) their persons'	[t]in₃≠ʔe·bčik	(6)

Examples: (3a) #maš≠hunkaš≠tin₃≠ʔe·b# 'if (there is) one in (its) person'; (3b) #pʷes ≠kʷete·m≠hunkaš≠ti≠ʔe·b# 'so only one in person'; (4) #wawa·ʔ≠¢a·b≠ti₃≠ʔe·b# 'we two (in our persons)'; (5) #tata·ʔčik#¢a·b≠ ta₂≠ʔe·b# 'you (pl.) two in your persons'; (6) #haha·ʔčik#¢a·b≠tin₃≠ʔe·b# 'they two in their persons'.

7.6.12.4. kʷete·m 'ALONE'.

Classical	Glosses	Modern	Examples
(1 sg.)			
ʔu₄≠kʷete·m	'I alone'	ʔu₄≠kʷete·m	(1a)
ʔu₄≠kʷete·mniʔ	'I all alone'		(1b)
(2 sg.)			
ʔa₂≠kʷete·m	'you alone'	ʔa₂≠kʷete·m	(2)
(3 sg.)			
ʔin₃≠kʷete·m	'he (she) (it) alone'	ʔin₃≠kʷete·m	(3a)
Ø₃≠kʷete·m	'[he] alone'	Ø₃≠kʷete·m	(3b)
Ø₃≠kʷete·mniʔ	'[he] all alone'	Ø₃≠kʷete·m	(3c)
(1 pl.)			
*ʔi₃≠kʷete·m	'we alone'	ʔi₃≠kʷete·m	(4)
(2 pl.)			
*ʔa₂≠kʷete·mčik	'you (pl.) alone'	*ʔa₂≠kʷete·mčik	(5)
(3 pl.)			
*in₃≠kʷete·mčik	'they alone'	*ʔin₃≠kʷete·mčik	(6)

Examples: (1a) #ʔu₄≠kʷete·m≠na·ʔ# 'I alone' (Cl); (2) #ʔa₂≠kʷete·m≠ta·ʔ# 'you alone' (Cl); (3a) #ʔin₃≠kʷete·m≠ha·ʔ# 'he alone'; (3c) #Ø₃≠Ø≠kʷete·m# '(he's) alone' (Cl, Mn); (4) #tehe·ʔ≠ti≠wawa·ʔ≠ʔi₃≠ kʷete·m≠ʔi₃≠bičowil# 'here among us, we alone, our town'.

8. PARTICLES. We present the full range of particles and particle-combinations, both simple and complex (including such secondary uses of verbal and nominal stems as are appropriate to the particle category). All examples are in McQuown (1982), correspondingly ordered.

8.1. RELATIVE.

Classical	Glosses	Modern
(Manner)		
ʔantiʔaniʔ	'as, like'	šant'in
nuʔantiʔaniʔ	'as, like'	šant'iniʔ
	'as, like'	ʔehti·l
	'as, like'	ʔuθ
(Time)		
tam	'when'	tam
tam≠ti	'when ...'	tam≠ti
	'when ...'	tam≠ka
hayk'iʔ	'when'	hayk'iʔ
(Place)		
	'there where ...'	šan≠ti
	'there where ...'	šon≠ti(h)
	'there where ...'	hon≠ti(h)
	'there where ...'	hun≠ti(n)
(Cause)		
	'whereas'	hant'
(Quantity)		
	'what amount'	ha·y

8.2. INTERROGATIVE(-RELATIVE).

Classical	Glosses	Modern
(Manner)		
hat'amtiʔaniʔ	'in what manner?'	
hat'amt'o(h)	'in what manner?'	
	'how?'	hant'in
	'how [is it that]?'	hant'iniʔ
	'how?'	hant'oθ
	'how [is it that]?'	hant'oθaʔ
	'how?'	hant'uθ
	'how [is it that]?'	hant'uθaʔ
	'how [is it that]?'	hant'iʔuθaʔ
(Time)		
šayk'iʔ	'when?'	
hayk'iʔ	'when?'	hayk'iʔ
(Place)		
	'where?'	huʔta·(h)
	'where?'	huʔta(h)

Classical	Glosses	Modern
	'there where …'	huʔta(h)≠ti
	'where?'	huʔt
huʔtaˑm	'where?'	huʔtaˑm
	'where?'	huʔtam
	'there where …'	huʔtaˑm≠ti
huʔtaˑm≠ka	'where?'	*huʔtaˑm≠ka
	'where?'	huʔtaˑmaʔ
huʔwataˑm	'where?'	
huʔwataˑm≠tam	'where [is it] that …?'	
huʔwaˑn≠ti	'where [is it] that …?'	
(Cause)		
haʔtaˑmleʔ	'why?'	
	'[that it is] because …'	ʔabal
	'because'	haleʔ
	'[that it is] because'	ʔabal≠haleʔ
(Quantity)		
haˑy	'how much?' 'how many?'	haˑy
haˑyiˑl	'how many times?'	haˑyiˑl

8.3. MODAL.

Classical	Glosses	Modern
(Manner)		
ʔaniʔ	'thus'	ʔaniʔ
	'thus'	ʔahnaˑʔ
ʔan¢anaˑʔ	'thus'	ʔan¢anaˑʔ
	'thus'	ʔan¢eˑʔ
	'thus'	ʔuθ
(Time)		
	'[all] at once'	t'ah
(Place)		
	'separate'	piˑl
	'together'	hunaš
	'all together'	hununuˑl
(Cause)		
	'[it's not] for nothing'	ʔalk'iθ
(Quantity)		
hat'waʔ	'[it's only] a little'	hat'waʔ
	'a little'	weˑʔ
	'very [highly]'	tekeθ

Classical	Glosses	Modern
	'very [rightly]'	*winat*
	'very [much]'	*leh*
([Un]certainty)		
belamni?	'perhaps'	
	'who knows?'	*¢o?o·b*
	'perhaps'	*w(al)a·m*
	'perhaps'	*le·ki¢k'eh*
	'[not] really'	*huntam(ana?)*
čubaš	'surely'	*čubaš*
	'securely'	*šanah*
	'effectively'	*huntam*
	'certainly'	*wa·y*
([Non]addition)		
tokat	'just, only'	*tokat*
tokatni?	'alone'	
	'just, only'	*tokot*
	'only'	*?ešpiθ*
(Additionally)		
?anih	'and'	*?anih*
	'likewise'	*?ana·h*
hayeh	'also'	*hayeh*

8.4. TEMPORAL.

Classical	Glosses	Modern
(Units)		
	'one morning'	$hu·n \neq (?)i_6 \neq \theta ahuw$
	'one day'	*hunk'i·ča·h*
	'every day'	$putat \neq k'i·ča·h$
	'for two months'	$¢a·b \neq (?)a_3 \neq ?i·¢'$
	'one year'	*huntamub*
(Relative times)		
šawe·?	'now; today'	*šowe·?*
	'today'	*šo·?*
tamana?	'then'	*tamana?*
	'then'	*ta·m*
	'immediately'	*tam*
	'afterward'	*taley*
	'recently'	*?i·teh*
	'[quite] recently'	$wihi¢ \neq ?i·t$
	'formerly'	*?ok'oš*
	'some time ago'	$ti \neq wi?i·h$
	'last week'	$ti \neq wat'ay \neq sema·nah$

Classical	Glosses	Modern
	'a long time ago'	biya·l
ʔeȼ'ey	'continually'	ʔeȼ'ey
	'on-going'	be·l
(Times of day)		
tamel	'last night'	
	'at dawn'	ti≠čuθey
	'at dawning'	ti≠čuθe·l
	'in the morning'	θahuw
k'ubat≠(ʔ)a₃≠k'i·ča·h	'at noon'	ʔo·rah
wa·kal	'in the afternoon'	wa·kal
	'in the evening'	θamθu·l
ti≠ʔakal	'[at] night'	ʔakal
ti≠ȼ'ehel≠ʔakal	'[at] midnight'	ti≠ȼ'ehel≠(ʔ)i₆≠ʔakal
(Hours)		
	'at one o'clock'	ti≠hu·n≠(ʔ)i₆≠ʔo·rah
	'at nine'	ti≠bele·w-ʔo·rah
	'at noon'	ti≠ʔo·rah
(Relative days)		
ya·n≠(ʔ)i₆≠k'ih	'a long time ago'	
	'the other day'	ti≠ʔok'oš
ʔošk'iʔ	'three days ago'	
ʔošk'iwat	'on the third day'	
ti≠ȼabk'iʔ	'day-before-yesterday'	ti≠ȼabk'iʔ
ti≠weʔe·l	'yesterday'	ti≠weʔe·l
šawe·ʔ	'today'	šowe·ʔ
	'today'	šo·ʔ
kala·m	'tomorrow'	kala·m
ȼabk'iʔ	'day-after-tomorrow'	ȼabk'iʔ
ʔošk'iʔ	'three days hence'	
	'on whatever day'	hawaʔk'iʔ
holat≠(ʔ)i₆≠k'ih	'mid-week'	
	'it was a Sunday'	pe·l≠(ʔ)i₆≠domi·ngoh
(…-times) (cardinal)		
hu·ni·l	'once'	hu·ni·l
bo·ʔi·l	'five times'	bo·ʔi·l
	'nine times'	bele·wi·l
(…-times) (ordinal)		
	'for the first time'	k'aʔa·l
	'for the second time'	ȼabči·l
	'for the eighth time'	wašikči·l
(Distributive)		
hunčiki·l	'at times'	hunčiki·l
hunkaȼi·l	'at times'	

8.5. Local.

Classical	Glosses	Modern
(Relative)		
("Here")		
tiʔaše·ʔ	'here'	
tiʔahe·ʔ	'here'	*tehe·ʔ/te·ʔ*
	'hither'	*heʔta·h*
	'hither'	*heʔta(h)*
	'hither'	*heʔta·m*
teʔtam	'hither'	*heʔtam*
	'hither'	*he·ʔ*
("There")		
tiwaʔ	'there; thither; thence'	*tiw[(a)ʔ]*
tiwaʔtam	'thither from afar'	
	'there; thither'	*tahaʔ*
	'there; thither'	*ta·ʔ*
	'there (nearby)'	*tana·ʔ*
	'there (nearby)'	*tan*
	'thither'	*nuwaʔ*
("Elsewhere")		
[ti≠]humpokʼeʔ	'on the other side'	*humpokʼeʔ*
	'inside; beneath'	*ʔalta·h*
	'outside'	*ʔele·b*
ʔeba·l	'above'	*ʔeba·l*
walkʼiʔ	'on top of'	*walkʼiʔ*
ʔala·l	'below'	*ʔala·l*
šoʔta·m	'somewhere'	
	'on the opposite side'	*hekʼat*
	'up to where …'	*ma≠ti…*
	'together'	*huntam*
	'right there'	*hu·niniʔ*
([Non-]distant)		
	'near'	*niwaʔ*
nahaʔ (kʼih)	'nearby'	
	'near'	*ʔutat*
ʔo·w	'far'	*ʔo·w*
	'long ago'	*ʔowatiȼ*
(Specific)		
tampa·mʔolom	'Tampamolón'	*tampa·mʔolom*
tamȼabtokʼo·y	'Huexotla'	*tamȼabtokʼo·y*
tamtoko·w	'[Ciudad de los] Valles'	*tamtoko·w*
[tam]la·bto·m	'Ciudad de México'	*la·bto·m*
	'Tancanhuitz'	*kʼanwiȼ*
	'Tantzanaco'	*tamȼanakʼʷ*

8.6. CAUSAL.

Classical	Glosses	Modern
$tin_3 \neq \textrm{?}e\cdot ba\cdot l$	'because of ...'	$tin_3 \neq \textrm{?}e\cdot ba\cdot l$
	'[that's] why'	hašta·m
	'[that's] why'	hu·nakiȼ

8.7. QUANTITATIVE.

Classical	Glosses	Modern
(Partitive)		
$\textrm{?}i_6$	'some (of) ...'	$\textrm{?}i_6$
?an	'a (certain) ...'	?an
(Collective)		
("A little")		
	'(a) little (bit)'	we·?
	'(a) small amount'	we·?čik
		wečik
		wačik
("A lot")		
ya·n	'a lot'	ya·n
	'much'	yantam
	'a lot of ...'	yantalam
	'a lot of ...'	yantolom
	'a measure-ful of ...'	maθab
("All")		
pataš	'all'	patal
patal	'all'	patal
putat	'the entire ...'	putat
kiθat	'complete'	kiθat
(Approximative)		
	'by halves'	ȼ'e·h(e)li·š
	'approximately ...'	hu·n≠(?)i_6≠ ...
(Numeral)		
hu·n	'one'	hu·n
hun-...	'one ...'	hun-...
ȼa·b	'two'	ȼa·b
ȼab-...	'two; again'	ȼab-...
?o·š	'three'	?o·š
?oš-...	'three ...'	?oš-...
ȼe·?	'four'	ȼe·?
ȼe?-...	'four ...'	ȼe?-...
bo·?	'five'	bo·?
bo?-...	'five ...'	bo?-...

Classical	Glosses	Modern
ʔakak	'six'	*ʔakak*
ʔakak-...	'six ...'	*ʔakak-...*
bu·k	'seven'	*bu·k*
* buk-...	'seven ...'	** buk-...*
wašik	'eight'	*wašik*
wašik-...	'eight ...'	*wašik-...*
bele·w	'nine'	*bele·w*
bele·w-...	'nine ...'	*bele·w-...*
la·huh	'ten'	*la·huh*
lahuh-...	'ten ...'	*lahuh-...*
lahuhu·n	'eleven'	*lahuhu·n*
lahuhun-...	'eleven ...'	*lahuhun-...*
lahuȼa·b	'twelve'	*lahuȼa·b*
lahuȼab-...	'twelve ...'	*lahuȼab-...*
lahuʔo·š	'thirteen'	*lahuʔo·š*
lahuȼe·ʔ	'fourteen'	*lahuȼe·ʔ*
lahubo·ʔ	'fifteen'	*lahubo·ʔ*
lahuʔakak	'sixteen'	*lahuʔakak*
la·hu(h)≠k'al≠bu·k	'seventeen'	*lahubu·k*
la·hu(h)≠tin₃≠k'a·l≠bu·k	'seventeen'	
lahuwašik	'eighteen'	*lahuwašik*
lahubele·w	'nineteen'	*lahubele·w*
hunʔinik	'twenty'	*hunʔinik*
	'twenty-three'	*hunʔinik≠k'al≠ʔo·š*
	'twenty-five'	*hunʔinikbo·ʔ*
	'thirty'	*hunʔinik≠k'al≠la·huh*
	'thirty'	*ʔo·š≠(ʔ)i₆≠la·huh*
hunʔinikla·huh	'thirty'	*hunʔinikla·huh*
ȼabʔinik	'forty'	*ȼabʔinik*
ȼabʔinikla·huh	'fifty'	*ȼabʔinikla·huh*
	'fifty'	*ȼabʔinik≠k'al≠la·huh*
ʔošʔinik	'sixty'	*ʔošʔinik*
ʔošʔinik≠k'al≠la·huh	'seventy'	
ȼeʔʔinik	'eighty'	*ȼeʔʔinik*
ȼeʔʔinikla·huh	'ninety'	
boʔʔinik	'one hundred'	*boʔʔinik*
	'one hundred'	*hunsiye·ntoh*
	'one hundred thirty'	*hunsiye·nto(h)≠k'al≠ʔo·š≠* *(ʔ)i₆≠la·huh*
ȼabboʔʔinik	'two hundred'	
	'two hundred'	*ȼa·b≠(ʔ)i₆≠boʔčikʔinik*
	'two hundred'	*la·huh≠(ʔ)i₆≠hunčikʔinik*
	'two hundred'	*lahuʔinik*
ʔošboʔʔinik	'three hundred'	
	'three hundred'	*ʔo·š≠(ʔ)i₆≠boʔʔinik*
	'four hundred'	*ȼe·ʔ≠(ʔ)i₆≠boʔčikʔinik*

Classical	Glosses	Modern
	'four hundred'	$¢e\cdot{}^?\ne({}^?)i_6\ne bo\,{}^{??}inik\check{c}ik$
$bo\,{}^?bo\,{}^{??}inik$	'five hundred'	$bo\cdot{}^?\ne({}^?)i_6\ne bo\,{}^{??}inik$
	'five hundred'	$bo\cdot{}^?\ne({}^?)i_6\ne bo\,{}^{??}inik\check{c}ik$
$\check{s}i{}^?$	'one thousand'	
$hun\check{s}i{}^?$	'one thousand'	
	'one thousand'	$la\cdot huh\ne({}^?)i_6\ne bo\,{}^{??}inik\check{c}ik$
$¢ab\check{s}i{}^?$	'two thousand'	
${}^?o\check{s}\check{s}i{}^?$	'three thousand'	

([Numbered] classes of nouns)

	Glosses	Modern
	'a piece'	$humpeha\check{c}$
	'a slice'	$humpok{}^\cdot e{}^?$
	'a year'	$huntamub$
	'a job'	$hunt{}^\cdot ahat$
	'a drop'	$hunt{}^\cdot ukub$
	'a swallow'	$hunk{}^\cdot utub$
	'a handful'	$humboye\,{}^?\ne({}^?)i_6\ldots$
	'a branch'	$humboye\,{}^?\ne({}^?)an\ldots$
	'a step'	$hun\check{s}akab$
	'a glance'	$hunmet{}^\cdot a\theta$
	'a pot'	$hunmul\ne({}^?)i_6\ldots$
	'a ball'	$hunmule\,{}^?\ne({}^?)i_6\ldots$

8.8. PREPOSITIONAL.

Classical	Glosses	Modern
ti	'as', 'at', 'during', 'for', 'from', 'in', 'into', 'like', 'of', 'to', 'through'	ti
	'at the foot of …'	$ti\ne{}^?akan$
	'at the foot of …'	$tin_3\ne{}^?akan\ne ti\ldots$
	'in the middle of …'	$¢{}^\cdot ehel\ldots$
	'behind'	$ku\cdot\check{s}$
	'in', 'with', 'by'	$k{}^\cdot al$
	'with the …'	$k{}^\cdot al\ne({}^?)an/k{}^\cdot an$
	'above'	${}^?eba\cdot l$
	'for (to) …'	${}^?abal$
	'toward …'	${}^?abal\ne ti$
	'as'	${}^?abal\ne tin_3\ldots$
${}^?an\ne ti\ldots$	'as for …'	
	'among', 'in'	${}^?a\cdot l$
	'in'	$ti\ne{}^?a\cdot l$
	'among …'	$tin_3\ne{}^?a\cdot l$
	'in(to)'	$ba\cdot{}^?$
	'along'	$nake\cdot l$

8.9. NEGATIVE.

Classical	Glosses	Modern
(Manner)		
	'no'	ʔi·h
	'of course!'	kum ≠ ʔi·h
	'no!'	ʔabaʔi·h
	'no!'	ʔi·ba·h
ʔi·b	'no, not'	ʔi·b
	'no longer'	ʔi·biȼ
	'no longer'	ʔi·ba·ȼ
	'not yet'	ʔi·ba·yeh
ʔi·b...ʔohniʔ	'not ... rather ...'	
	'[it's] not so'	ʔišanaʔ
	'[it's] not so'	ʔišanah
	'[not] in any way at all'	šanťiniʔ
	'not even ...'	ni...
	'in no way'	nihanťin
	'in no manner'	nihanťoθ
tokatniʔ≠wa	'[not] only but rather'	
	'not!'	yabaʔ
	'not'	yab
(Time)		
	'not ever'	ʔi·ba·(h) ≠ hayk'iʔ
ʔi·b ≠...≠ šayk'iʔ≠wa	'not ... ever'	
	'no longer, already'	ʔiȼwa·ȼ
	'no longer'	ʔiȼwa·h
	'surely still not'	ʔi·ba·wa·yeh
	'at no time'	nihayk'iʔ
	'never, ever, they say'	nihayk'iʔuθkʷaʔ
	'not, already'	yabiȼ
	'not any more'	yaba·ȼ
	'not yet'	yabayeh
	'not ever'	yab ≠ hayk'iʔ
(Place)		
	'nowhere'	nihuʔtat
(Cause)		
	'not on that account'	yab ≠ tin₃ ≠ ʔe·ba·l
(Quantity)		
	'with nothing'	maptal

8.10. Conjunctional.

Classical	Glosses	Modern
(Coordinating)		
(Connective)		
	'and'	ʔan
		ʔani(h)
		ʔanih
	'and in that ...'	ʔan≠ti
	'and when'	ʔani(h)≠ti
	'and then ...'	ʔan≠ti≠kʼal
	'and'	ʔi(h)
	'... (and) ...' [appositional]	∅
(Alternating)		
(Positive)		
	'or'	ši
	'or'	∅
	'or'	ʔo(h)
	'either ... or ...'	ma...ma
(Negative)		
	'neither'	ni
(Subordinating)		
(Manner)		
(Modal)		
* ʔaniʔ	'thus'	ʔaniy≠
	'thus (they are)'	ʔančik
(Concessive)		
	'if ... perhaps'	maš
	'if that ... perhaps'	maš≠ti
	'if that ... perhaps'	maš≠ka
	'although'	ʔab
ʔabaʔ	'although'	
	'albeit'	ʔabaʔaniʔ
	'however it might have been'	ʔabahantʼoθakiȼ
	'although'	ʔebal
	'so ...'	pos
	'so ...'	poˑs
	'so ...'	pʷeˑs
	'even'	ma
	'even'	sikeˑrah
	'since ...'	kom...
	'since ...'	kum...
	'since ...'	komoh
(Time)		
("When")		
	'when'	ti
	'when'	tam

135

Classical	Glosses	Modern
	'when ...'	tam≠ti
	'when ...'	tam≠ka
tam≠wa	'when ...'	
("Then")		
	'then'	ta·m
	'then'	tamanaʔ
	'then'	tamnaʔ
	'then'	ti≠tamnaʔ
	'then'	ti≠k'aleh
	'then'	ʔento·ns
	'later'	ta·lbe·l
(Place)		
("Up to")		
	'up to ...'	ma...
	'as far as ...'	ma...
(Cause/purpose)		
(Adversative)		
	'but'	peroh
	'but'	pe·roh
(Causal)		
	'because'	ʔab
	'because'	ʔabal
	'because'	porkeh
	'since ...'	porke(h)≠ʔabal
haʔta·m	'for which reason'	
	'because'	haleʔ
	'and so ...'	ʔan≠ti≠k'al
	'nevertheless'	ʔabaʔaniʔ
	'nevertheless'	huntam
	'nevertheless'	be·l
(Purposive)		
	'so that ...'	ʔebal
	'so that ...'	ʔab
	'... that'	ʔabal
	'in order to ...'	ʔabal≠ti
	'so that ...'	ʔabal≠ka
	'so that ...'	por≠ka
	'let's see what ...'	ʔa≠ber
(Quantity)		
	'inasmuch as ...'	ʔen≠kʷa·nto(h)≠ke(h)
(Interrogative)		
ma...	'perchance ...?'	
ma...maš...	'whether ... or ...?'	
ma...≠wa...	'whether ... or perhaps ...?'	
ma≠wa...	'whether perhaps ...?'	

Classical	Glosses	Modern
(Dependentizing)		
	'that ...'	*ke(h)≠ ...*
	'that ...'	*ʔab*
	'the fact that ...'	*ʔabal*
	'as if ...'	*ʔabal*

8.11. REVERENTIAL.

Classical	Glosses	Modern
	'the sun'	*ʔa₃≠k'i·ča·h*
	'the moon'	*ʔa₃≠ ʔi·ȼ'*
	'the month'	*ʔa₃≠ ʔi·ȼ'*
	'May'	*ʔa₃≠ma·yoh*
	'God'	*ʔa₃≠diyo·s*
	'St. James'	*ʔa₃≠santiya·goh*
	'Vidal'	*ʔa₃≠bida·l*
	'Alexander'	*ʔa₃≠ ʔelisa·ndroh*

8.12. DERIVED PARTICLE STEMS. In position (1) in the particle complex occur the (derived) particle-*roots* (*-stems*); in position (2), the *anterior-modal* marker; in position (3), the *plural* marker; and in position (4), the *ad-verbial clitics*, found with the other major form-classes, the verbals and the nominals (some of which, as stems, have passed into the particle-stem form-class).

Not surprisingly, positions (2) and (3), as well as positions (2) and (4), are interchangeable, as are positions (3) and (4), as the focus shifts from restricted core (1), to anterior-modally marked core—(1) and (2)—to plurally marked core—(1) through (3).

The ad-verbial clitics in position (4) occur (with respect to each other) (except for *-iȼ* and *-eh* which are mutually exclusive) in the order presented below.

Examples:

(1) *Roots:* ʔuθ 'as, like', *tam* 'when', *ha·y* 'what amount', *we·ʔ* 'a little', *leh* 'very'; *stems:* ʔeh-t-i·l 'as, like', *hay-k'i·ʔ* 'when', *han-t'* 'whereas', *han-t'-in* 'how?' *huʔ-t-a·h* 'where?', ʔab-al 'because', *hal-eʔ* 'since', *ha·y-i·l* 'how

many times?', ʔab-a(ʔ)-ʔan-iʔ 'albeit', *tam-an-aʔ* 'then', *hun-tam* 'nevertheless'.

(2) *Anterior-modal marker -ak* (hypothetical): #ʔaš≠θ₃≠θ≠te·ʔ-ak# 'that one would [be] here'; ≠tam≠θ₃≠θ≠ta·lbe·l-ak-iȼ# 'then, already, [it] would [be] later'.

(3) *Plural marker -čik* (plurality [or collectivity]): ≠ši≠θ₃≠θ≠ȼe·ʔ-čik≠(ʔ)in₃≠ ʔakan# '(those) of which four (are) their feet'.

(4) *Ad-verbial clitics:* [1] *-iȼ* (*-iš*) 'already': #ʔan(ih≠ ʔ)u₁≠hayk'iʔ-iȼ≠ne ʔeȼ# 'and, whenever, already, it's going to ,...'; [1] *-eh* 'still; yet': #ʔani(h)≠ ʔi·ba·(h)wa·yeh≠(ʔ)in₂≠k'atuw ≠šanah# 'and surely not, still, had he bitten it securely'; [2] *-(i)k'ih[-(i)k'eh]* 'indeed': #tana·ʔ-k'i(h)≠tin≠ ʔeba·lil≠ 'there, indeed, on top of it ,...'; [3] *-kʷaʔ* 'it is said; they say': #ta·m-kʷaʔ≠tin₂≠k'aθbaʔ-kʷaʔ≠(ʔ)an ≠ȼa·h# 'then, they say, she got it up, they say, the rope'; [4] *-anaʔ* 'in fact': #ʔanih-anaʔ ≠k'eʔat≠bu·k≠...# 'and, in fact, another seven ...'.

8.13. COMPARATIVE(-SUPERLATIVE).

ʔok'oš 'prior' *kawi·l* 'more' *ma·s* 'more'
Examples: #ʔalwaʔ≠ ʔinik≠(ʔ)a≠hwa·n#

leh≠ ʔok'oš≠ ʔalwaʔ≠ ʔinik≠pe·droh# 'a good man is John; a very much better man is Peter' (Cl); *#kawi·l≠ ʔalwaʔ≠ ʔana·ʔ#* 'a better one is that one' (Cl); *≠yabaʔ≠hant'o(h) ≠ma·s≠* 'not anything more!' (Mn); *≠ma·s≠ke(h)≠* '(no) more than ...' (Mn).

8.14. INTERJECTIONAL.

Classical	Glosses	Modern
(Connective)		
	'oh, ...'	*ʔa(h)*
	'ah, ...'	*ʔa·(h)*
(Affirmative)		
	'yes'	*ʔohniʔ*
	'unh'	*ʔēh*
	'anh'	*ʔā·h*
	'uhuh'	*ʔahah*
	'anhanh'	*ʔāhāh*
	'mhmm'	*ʔmʔmʔm*
	'mm'	*ʔmh*
	'mmm'	*ʔm·h*
	'mhm'	*ʔmhʔm(·)h*
	'un'umh'	*ʔnʔmh*
	'hnh'	*hēh*
	'unhunh'	*hāʔāh*
	'good'	*bʷe·noh*
	'in effect'	*hunt'ahat*
	'of course'	*por≠supʷe·stoh*
(Interrogative)		
	'and that ...?'	*ʔi(h)≠niš≠tih#*
(Vetative)		
	'take care lest ...'	*kʷe·nta(h)*
	'take care how ...'	*kʷe·nta(h)≠kom...*
(Dubitative)		
	'it's possible that ...'	*ʔa·wil*
(Hesitating)		
	[hesitation form]	*ʔaʔ*
(Laughing)		
	'ha ... ha!'	*ha≠ha≠ha≠ha≠ha≠ha≠ha≠hah*
(Salutatory)		
	'man ...!'	*ʔo·mbreh*
	'good morning!'	*tahk'ane·nek*
	'good afternoon!'	*waklane·nek*
	'good night!'	*θamk'une·nek*

A fair sample of sentences containing examples of these particles will be found in Mc-Quown (1982).

9. SYNTACTIC CONSTRUCTIONS.

9.1. PARATACTIC:

#hu·n≠(ʔ)i₆≠θahal#ʔin₂≠to·k'oyal≠(ʔ)an ≠¢'e·n# 'a shout—the hill answers : an echo';

#hu·n≠(ʔ)i₆≠ʔinik#puli·l≠(ʔ'in₃≠ku·š# 'a person—curved his back : a hunchback';

¢ablam#ʔin₃≠ʔoko·b# 'a pair—its arms : it has two wings'.

9.2. SUBORDINATING.

(Relativizing)

#ʔan≠¢'ik'a·č#ʔaš≠(ʔ)u₃≠kulbe·tna·l# 'the girl whom I love'; *"#ʔan≠ši ʔi·l≠(ʔ)an≠ʔankel#" #ha·¢≠(ʔ)an≠wi¢#ʔaši≠Ø₃≠Ø≠leh≠ bi·nal≠ya·n≠(ʔ)an≠¢i ʔi·m#* '"angel's hair" (is) a flower which gives lots of honey'.

(Modificational)

(Compounding)

(Modifier + modified)

ʔušum-pik'oʔ '(female dog) bitch'; *¢akam-ʔe·yištala·b* 'small instrument', *ʔalwa ʔpihčiθ* 'well fed'.

(Modified + modifier)

to·m-ʔata·h '(straw + house) house-straw'; *t'uʔlek-ʔi¢a·mal* '(meat + deer) deer-meat'; *ʔat-k'ima·θ* '(fellow + house) house-mate'; *ʔat-¢eʔʔakan* '(fellow + quadruped) fellow quadruped'; *θabal-¢ik'a·č* '(owner + girl) girl-owner(s)'.

(Attributive)

(Modified + modifier)

¢abal≠kiθa·b '(earth + bad) bad earth'; *wi¢≠manunu·l* '(flower + yellow) yellow flower'.

(Deictic + modified + modifier)

ʔan≠wi¢≠¢akni ʔ '(a certain + flower + red) a certain red flower'.

(Numeral + partitive + modified + modifier)

hu·n≠(ʔ)i₆≠ʔinik≠yehnek '(one + some + person + tall) one tall person'.

(Modifier + modified [possessor + possessed])

patal≠(ʔ)a₂≠ʔiči·č 'all your heart'.

(Partitive)

(Numeral + partitive + noun)

hu·n≠(ʔ)i₆≠ho ʔčal 'one (of) canyon(s)'.

(Numeral + noun classifier + partitive + noun)

hun-k'utub≠(ʔ)i₆≠bi·nuh 'a swallow of liquor'.

(Possessive)

(Casual)

ʔin₃≠huhu·l≠(ʔ)an≠ʔata·h '(its hair the house) thatch'; *ʔin₃≠t'uʔu·l≠(ʔ)an≠θimalo·n-ʔolom* '(its meat the wild pig) boar meat'.

(Enduring)

ʔin₃≠pamta·ʔ≠(ʔ)u₄≠ʔakan '(its calf my leg) my calf'; *ʔin₃≠huhu·l≠(ʔ)u₄≠wal* '(its hair my face) my brows'.

(Possession of a possessed form)

ʔim₃≠paha·b≠(ʔ)a₂≠k'ubak '(its palm your hand) your palm'; *ʔim₃≠paha·b≠(ʔ)in₃≠ʔakan* '(its palm his foot) his sole'.

9.3. EQUATIONAL VERBAL (involving the copula [Ø]). *#Ø₃≠Ø≠pu·lik≠(ʔ)an≠t'uhub#* '[it's] large a certain stone'; *#pe·l≠hay-(eh)≠(ʔ)in₁≠te·nek#* '(being) also I [am] Huastec'; *#yaba ʔ≠kit≠Ø≠to·ntoh#* 'do *not* you [be] (a) fool!'

9.4. NARRATIVE VERBAL (involving other verbs).

(Simple)

#maš≠(ʔ)u₁≠k'apa·bakčik≠(ʔ)a₃≠ʔi·¢'#ʔan-ih≠(ʔ)a₃≠k'i·ča·h# 'if they were eaten, the moon and the sun'; *#ʔin₁≠ʔešo·bla·maθ≠ hu·n≠(ʔ)i₆≠we·ʔ#* 'I have studied a bit'; *#ʔan≠¢akam#Ø₃≠ne ʔe¢≠ka₈₃≠wa ʔ¢in#* 'the small one will grow'; *#haha·ʔ#Ø₃≠k'ʷah-at≠tim₂≠pakuwal#* 'he is breaking it up'; *#ʔu₃≠mukuyal≠(ʔ)an≠toltom#* 'I am dyeing the clothes'; *#ʔim₂≠bikla ʔ≠¢aba·l#* 'he tumbled it to the ground'; *#tata·ʔčik#tu₉≠ ʔuča ʔ≠wawa·ʔ#* 'you (pl.) said it to *us*'.

(Compound)

#ʔin₁≠¢'aybe·l-k'ak'e·l# 'I have chills and fever.'

9.5. VERBAL WITH ADJUNCTS.

(Single-argument)

#ʔit≠leh≠¢ekenek# 'you have gotten very tired'; #Q₃≠konoyat# 'he was asked'; #Q₁≠ k'ʷahat≠tin₁≠ʔahum# 'I am singing'; #Q₃≠ šeʔeš≠ti≠Q₃≠ʔalim≠toʔol# 'he is going about catching—fish'.

(Double-argument)

#tam≠kit≠holčat≠(ʔ)an≠to·m# 'when to you straw is emptied out'; #porkeh#ʔi·b≠(ʔ)u₃ ≠t'aya·mal#ʔan≠ʔe·m# 'because I have not sowed it, the corn-field'.

(Triple-argument)

#nan≠(ʔ)an≠¢alap≠tu₆≠piθa·l# 'I, certain advice (it is) that I give you'; #ka≠Q₂≠ šikʷčih≠(ʔ)in₃≠we·w# 'you pinch his tail on him!'; #ʔin₂≠ʔuča ʔ≠(ʔ)am≠bu·roh# 'he said it to the donkey'; #ʔin₂≠ʔuča ʔ≠(ʔ)am≠ bu·roh# 'to him the donkey said it'; #ʔin²≠ čikčih≠(ʔ)an≠ʔata·h≠(ʔ)an≠¢'ehwanta·l-ʔin- ik# 'they burned the house on the poor man'; #tam≠tikin₅≠ʔayči(h)≠ti≠ʔali·la·b# 'then so that you await [my arrival] for me in the cornfield'.

(With appositional complements)

#ʔi(h)≠šowe·ʔ≠Q₃≠kʷaʔali¢≠(ʔ)an≠¢akam #ʔin₃≠t'a·m# 'and now she has it, already, the little one—her offspring'.

(With circumstantial complements)

#Q₁ₚ≠neʔeš≠tu₂≠k'apul≠ti≠ʔo·rah# 'we are going to eat **at mid-day**'; #ʔin₁≠t'elelela·¢ ≠(ʔ)u₄≠ʔiči·č# 'I trembled a lot, already, **(in) my heart**'; #tam≠tin₁≠ʔulnekiš≠**tampi·koh**# 'when I had arrived, already, **(at) Tampico**'; #ʔim₁≠pitk'on≠**haha·ʔ**# 'I was abandoned **(with respect to) him**'; #Q₁≠k'ʷahiy≠tin₁≠ nu·hul≠θiʔ# 'I was selling **(with respect to) firewood**'; #ʔabal≠ti≠Q₃≠wak'lam≠k'al≠ (ʔ)i₆≠ʔat'aštala·b# 'so that he might dump **(with respect to) garbage**'; #ʔi(h)≠...#ʔin₂≠ čišiyal≠**hu·ni·l**# 'and ... he was felling it **again**'; #Q₁≠neʔ≠tu₆≠halbiy#ʔakak≠tumi·n ≠ta₃≠k'i·ča·h# 'I'm going to pay you **six bits a day**'; #yab≠tikin₅≠t'ah(aʔ)≠**tin₁≠Q**≠ **to·ntoh**# 'don't make me [to be] (a) **fool**!'; #Q₁≠neʔ≠tin₁≠keθmaš≠**bičim**# 'I'm going to be driving **[with respect to] horses**'.

140

(Normal)

VSO: #ʔin₂≠ʔučaʔ≠(ʔ)am≠bu·roh≠(ʔ)an≠ we·yeš# 'he said it to him—the donkey to the ox'

(High-lighted)
(Fronted)
SOV: #nan≠(ʔ)an≠¢alap≠tu₆≠piθa·l# 'I, advice, I give it to you'
OSV: #ma≠k'eʔat≠(ʔ)i₆≠labaštala·b≠(ʔ)a₁≠ bela·mal# 'in other supernatural signs have you believed?' (Cl)
OSV + anti-passivization: #θimalo·n-ʔolom# niše·ʔ≠hay(eh≠ʔ)i₂≠keθkom# 'wild pig, that one, too, we chase'
Preposed possessor: #ʔan≠ʔalwaʔčik≠kris- tiya·nos#ʔin₃≠ʔa·nimah# 'of good Chris- tians, their souls' (Cl)
Preposed adverbial goal: #ti≠ʔa₃≠ʔe·b#ka_Q₃ₚ ≠na·¢# 'to heaven, they will go' (Cl)
(Topicalized)
#ʔan≠ʔalwaʔčik≠kristiya·nos#ʔin₃≠ʔa·ni- mah#huʔwata·m≠ka_Q₃ₚ≠na·¢#tam≠ka_Q₃ₚ ≠¢eme¢#ʔin₃≠ʔiniktal# 'the good Chris- tians, their souls₁, where will they₁ go, when they₂ die, their₂ bodies?' (Cl)
#ʔam≠bu·roh#tokat≠(ʔ)in₂≠ʔe·yanθa·l# 'the donkey₂, he₁ just employed him₂'
#ʔan≠ʔe·m#ma≠yabayeh≠(ʔ)i₂≠ʔak'ya· mal# 'the maize, we have not even har- vested it'.
(Plural-marked)
#komo(h)≠Q₃≠¢eme¢i¢≠(ʔ)u₄≠mi·m#patal ≠(ʔ)u₄≠ʔi¢ak'čik≠(ʔ)an(ih)≠(ʔ)u₄≠ ʔiša·m#yabaʔ≠hayk'iʔ≠Q₃≠k'apul#ʔab ≠(ʔ)u₃≠¢e·mančal≠ku₃≠ʔalči(h)≠we·ʔ- čik≠(ʔ)an≠k'apne·l# 'since she died, al- ready, my mother, all my nephews, and my sister-in-law, they did not ever eat, although I tried to find a little (for **them**) some food'.

(Low-lighted)
(Obliqued)
#komoh≠(ʔ)an≠ʔa·mo(h)≠Q₃≠piθač≠k'al ≠(ʔ)a₃≠diyo·s# 'since [to] the master was given by God'
#Q₃≠konoy**at**≠(ʔ)an≠we·yeš≠k'al≠(ʔ)am

≠bu·roh# 'he was asked, the ox by the donkey'

#Ɵ₃ ≠ ʔučan≠k'al≠(ʔ)in₃≠k'ima·θil# '[to] him it was said by his wife'

#ta·m≠nan≠(ʔ)in₁≠kʷeʔčin≠hu·n≠(ʔ)u₄ ≠šeke·t# 'then [from] me was stolen a jacket of mine'

≠tin₁≠keθmaš≠k'al≠(ʔ)am≠bičim# 'in that I was driving [with respect to] horses'

#ʔan≠le·¢ah≠ʔabal≠kim₂≠pihčišnaʔ#k'al ≠(ʔ)in₃≠¢aka·mil# 'the milk, so that she might feed him₁, [with respect to] her youngster₁'.
(Gapped)

#u₃≠ ʔihka·l≠ʔu₃≠¢aʔuwal#ʔi(h)≠Ɵ₁≠ θa·ʔiyal# "I tumbled it, I mashed it, [I] flattened [it]'

#tan≠(ʔ)it≠t'o·hon#hanči(h)≠Ɵ₂≠t'aha·l #Ɵ₂≠ ʔak'iš≠k'a(l≠ʔa)n≠ʔe·m# 'there you worked; in what [you] did, [you] were clearing with respect to the cornfield'

#tan≠(ʔ)in₁≠k'ʷahiy≠tin₁≠keθmaš≠ k'al≠(ʔ)am≠bičim#Ɵ₁≠leh≠ʔu¢'a·lak≠ (ʔ)an≠θuhal# 'there I was driving— horses; [I] used to drink liquor a lot'

#kim₂≠paʔbaʔčik≠(ʔ)i₆≠sa·ntoh#Ɵ≠Ɵ₃ ≠paʔbaʔčik≠yantam≠(ʔ)i₆≠ʔalwaʔčik# 'may he bring down some saints; [may he] bring down lots of good things!'

#yaba·¢≠(ʔ)in₁≠k'al(eh)#kom≠Ɵ₁≠ʔa¢'- (aʔ≠ʔ)it≠k'ʷahat≠tit≠k'apul# 'I no longer came, since [I] heard you were eating'

#yab≠(ʔ)in₁≠leh≠wayal#kom≠tamanaʔ≠ Ɵ₁≠kʷaʔal≠ya·n≠(ʔ)an≠¢alap# 'I didn't sleep much, since then (I) had a lot of worry'

#tamanaʔ≠nan≠(ʔ)u₃≠ʔuča·l#Ɵ₁≠neʔe¢≠ kin₁≠ʔayin#porke(h)≠komo(h)≠Ɵ₁≠ ʔabči·¢≠(ʔ)an≠ʔu·w#ʔu₄≠ʔata·tal≠ti≠ wiʔi·h# 'then (it is) I (who) say to him, I'm going to go back, inasmuch as (I) sent off, already, a letter (to) my brother, a while ago'

#yaba·¢≠(ʔ)u₃≠k'ayaʔ#Ɵ₁≠ʔuhnaʔ≠ma- θab# 'no longer did I suffer it; (I) got used to a lot'

#ta·m≠yabi¢≠tu₁₀≠t'aha·l≠tu₁₀≠Ɵ≠ kʷe·ntah# 'then no longer do they do it to us, do they [pay] attention to us'.

(Anticipatorily gapped)

#Ɵ₁ₚ≠le·ʔ≠ki₂≠ ʔuluw≠Ɵ≠(ʔ)i₂≠k'aniθa·l # '[we] want to say (that) we appreciate him'

#Ɵ₁≠kʷahat≠Ɵ₁≠le·ʔ≠ku₃≠¢'at'aʔ≠hu·n ≠(ʔ)i₆≠bakan# '[I] am wanting to beat out a maize griddle cake'. (Contrast: #ʔan(ih)≠tin₁≠kʷahat≠tu₃≠le·ʔ≠ku₃≠ tah(aʔ≠ʔ)an≠ʔalmuθa·l# 'and I am wanting to make lunch'.)

(Gapped)(with resumed marking)

#tokot≠tin₂≠nuhuwal≠ ʔabal≠ʔabal≠ka₈₃ ≠k'ʷahiy#haha·ʔ≠Ɵ₃≠leh≠wilel≠ʔi(h)≠ leh≠putat≠(ʔ)in₂≠t'aha·l# 'just in that he is selling it so...so that [he] may be very drunk, and the very whole thing he does'.

(Gapped)(but with a change of subject)

#tu₆≠nuhčal≠(ʔ)u₄≠pa·kašil#bʷe·noh#Ɵ₂ ≠¢'ayʔčal# 'I'll sell you my cow; will [you] buy it from [me]?'

#maš≠yab≠(ʔ)a₁≠¢uʔu·mal...#ʔi·ba·(h)≠ Ɵ₁≠¢uʔu·mal# 'have you not perhaps seen it? [I] have not seen it!'

ACKNOWLEDGMENTS

The following institutional entities were involved in the gathering of the modern Huastec materials (or in their subsequent processing): Carnegie Institution of Washington (1930's, 1946–1947), National Science Foundation ("Maya Linguistics" GS 1332: 10/1/65–9/30/70; "Huastec" GS 40461: 10/1/73–9/30/75), University of Chicago: Department of Anthropology (Lichtstern Research Fund: 1971–1981), and University of Chicago (Computation Center: 1970–1981). Their aid is gratefully acknowledged.

Special thanks are due to Raymond S. Larsen and his assistant from Aquismón, to Benjamín Hernández from Tamarindo (Pequetzén), to Víctor Saldaña from San Antonio, to Ignacio Aguilar Altamirano from Tamaletón, to Enrique Santos Concepción from Tampamolón, to José Miguel Hernández from Tancoltzi, and to various bilinguals in Tancanhuitz (most particularly to Rafael Espinosa, fluent in Huastec, although his mother tongue is Spanish).

BIBLIOGRAPHY

ALEJANDRE, MARCELO
1890 *Cartilla huasteca*. Mexico City: Secretaría de Fomento.

ANDRADE, MANUEL
1946 Materials on the Huastec Language. Microfilm Collection of Manuscript Materials on Middle American Cultural Anthropology, Series 2, No. 9. Chicago: University of Chicago Library.
1975 Huastec Texts. Microfilm Collection of Manuscripts on Cultural Anthropology, Series 31, No. 165. Chicago: University of Chicago Library.

ANDREWS, J. RICHARD
1975 *Introduction to Classical Nahuatl*. Austin: University of Texas Press.

ANGULO, JAIME DE
1933 The Chichimeco Language (Central Mexico). *International Journal of American Linguistics* 7:152–194.

ASCHMANN, HERMAN PEDRO
1962 *Vocabulario totonaco de la Sierra*. Serie de Vocabularios y Diccionarios Indígenas Mariano Silva y Aceves, No. 7. Mexico City: Instituto Lingüístico de Verano.
1975 *Diccionario totonaco de Papantla, Veracruz*. Serie de Vocabularios y Diccionarios Indígenas Mariano Silva y Aceves,

No. 16. Mexico City: Instituto Lingüístico de Verano.

BERENDT, KARL H.
1876 Arte en lengua choltí . . . nuevamento copiado por C. H. Berendt. MS, Brinton Collection, University of Pennsylvania Library. Philadelphia.

BRINTON, DANIEL G.
1869 Notice of Some Manuscripts in Central American Languages. *American Journal of Science and Arts*, Series 2, 47: 222–230.

CRAWFORD, JOHN C.
1963 *Totontepec Mixe Phonotagmemics*. Summer Institute of Linguistics of the University of Oklahoma, Pub. No. 8. Norman.

CRUZ, JUAN DE LA
1571 *Doctrina christiana en la lengua guasteca*. Mexico City: P. Ocharte. Copy in John Carter Brown Library, Brown University, Providence.

DIXON, R. M. W.
1972 *The Dyirbal Language of North Queensland*. Cambridge Studies in Linguistics 9. London: Cambridge University Press.

DRIVER, HAROLD E., AND WILHEMINE DRIVER
1963 *Ethnography and Acculturation of the Chichimeca-Jonaz of Northeast Mexico*.

Indiana University Research Center in Anthropology, Folklore, and Linguistics, Pub. 26. The Hague: Mouton.

ELSON, BENJAMIN F.

1960 *Gramática del Popoluca de la Sierra*. Biblioteca de la Facultad de Filosofía y Letras, No. 6. Xalapa, Mexico: Universidad Veracruzana.

1967 Sierra Popoluca. In *Handbook of Middle American Indians*, vol. 5, edited by Robert Wauchope and Norman A. McQuown, pp. 269–290. Austin: University of Texas Press.

FOSTER, MARY L.

1969 *The Tarascan Language*. Berkeley and Los Angeles: University of California Press.

FOUGHT, JOHN G.

1973 Chortí Semantics: Some Properties of Roots and Affixes. In *Meaning in Mayan Languages: Ethnolinguistic Studies*, edited by Munro S. Edmonson, pp. 59–83. The Hague: Mouton.

FREEMAN, JOHN F.

1966 *A Guide to Manuscripts Relating to the American Indian in the Library of the American Philosophical Society*. Philadelphia: American Philosophical Society.

FRIEDRICH, PAUL

1969a Metaphor-like Relations between Referential Subsets. *Lingua* 24:1–10.

1969b *On the Meaning of the Tarascan Suffixes of Space*. International Journal of American Linguistics, Memoir 23. Chicago: University of Chicago Press.

1970 Shape in Grammar. *Language* 46:379–407.

1971a Dialectical Variation in Tarascan Phonology. *International Journal of American Linguistics* 37:164–187.

1971b Distinctive Features and Functional Groups in Tarascan Phonology. *Language* 47:849–865.

1971c *The Tarascan Suffixes of Locative Space: Meaning and Morphotactics*. Indiana University Publications, Language Research Monograph, vol. 9. The Hague: Mouton.

1974a From Distinctive Feature of "Unique" Phonemic Rule. In Festschrift for Clarence Parmenter, edited by Eric Hamp. MS, Department of Anthropology, University of Chicago.

1974b *On Aspect Theory and Homeric Aspect*. International Journal of American Linguistics, Memoir 28. Chicago: University of Chicago Press.

1975 *A Phonology of Tarascan*. Series in Social, Cultural, and Linguistic Anthropology, University of Chicago Studies in Anthropology, No. 4. Chicago.

1979 *Language, Context, and the Imagination*. Stanford: Stanford University Press.

GATES, WILLIAM E.

1935 (ed.) *Arte y diccionario en lengua choltí: A Manuscript Copied from the Libro Grande of Father Pedro Morán of about 1625*. Maya Society Pub. No. 9. Baltimore.

GILBERTI, MATURINO DE

1559 *Diccionario de la lengua tarasca o de Michoacán*. (1901 ed. edited by Antonio Peñafiel. Mexico City: Tipografía de la Oficina Impresora de Estampillas.)

GOSSEN, GARY H.

1974 To Speak with a Heated Heart: Chamula Canons of Style and Good Performance. In *Explorations in the Ethnography of Speaking*, edited by Richard Bauman and Joel Sherzer, pp. 389–413. London: Cambridge University Press.

GREENBERG, JOSEPH H.

1963 Some Universals of Grammar with Particular Reference to the Order of Meaningful Elements. In *Universals of Language*, edited by Joseph H. Greenberg, pp. 58–85. Cambridge: M.I.T. Press.

GUITERAS HOLMES, CALIXTA

1948 Sistema de parentesco huasteco. *Acta Americana* 6:152–172.

HARRISON, W. ROY, AND MARGARITA B. HARRISON

1948 *Diccionario zoque*. Mexico City: Instituto Lingüístico de Verano.

HENDERSON, EUGENIE

1960 *Tiddim Chin*. Oxford: Oxford University Press.

HOIJER, HARRY, et al.

1945 *Linguistic Structures of Native North America*. Viking Fund Publications in Anthropology, No. 6. New York.

HOOGSHAGEN, SEARLE

1959 Three Contrastive Vowel Lengths in Mixe. *Zeitschrift für Phonetik* 12:111–115.

1974 Estructura de la cláusula en Mixe de

Coatlán. *Summer Institute of Linguistics Workpapers* 1:31–44. Mexico City.

KEY, HAROLD, AND MARY RITCHIE KEY
1953 *Vocabulario mejicano de la Sierra de Zacapoaxtla, Puebla*. Mexico City: Instituto Lingüístico de Verano.

LaFARGE, OLIVER, AND ERNEST NOYES
1929– Transcripts and Correspondence on
1933 Cholti. MS, Peabody Museum, Harvard University, Cambridge.

LARSEN, KAY
1949 Huasteco Baby Talk. *El México Antiguo* 7:295–298.

LARSEN, RAYMOND S.
1955 *Vocabulario huasteco del Estado de San Luis Potosí*. Mexico City: Instituto Lingüístico de Verano. (Also, Microfilm Collection of Manuscripts on Cultural Anthropology, Series 31, Nos. 168, 169. Chicago: University of Chicago Library.)
1971 *An it jilchith cau c'al i Ajatic Jesucristo: El Nuevo Testamento del Nuestro Señor Jesu Cristo: Huasteco de San Luis Potosí*. Mexico City: Biblioteca Mexicana del Hogar.
1972 *Hablemos español y huasteco*. Mexico City: Instituto Lingüístico de Verano.

LARSEN, RAYMOND S., AND EUNICE V. PIKE
1949 Huasteco Intonations and Phonemes. *Language* 25:268–277.

LASTRA DE SUÁREZ, YOLANDA
1969 Notas sobre algunos aspectos sintácticos del chichimeco-jonaz. *Anales de Antropología del Instituto de Investigaciones Históricas* 6:109–114. Mexico City: Universidad Nacional Autónoma de México.
1971 Dos fiestas chichimecas. *Anales de Antropología del Instituto de Investigaciones Históricas* 8:203–212. Mexico City: Universidad Nacional Autónoma de México.

LETHROP, LISA AND MAX
1960 *Jimbani Eiatsperakua Tata Kristueri: El Nuevo Testamento de Nuestro Señor Jesucristo*. Mexico City: Sociedad Bíblica de México.

LORENZANA, SERAPIO D.
1896 *Un intérprete huasteco*. Mexico City: Secretaría de Fomento.

LYON, DON D.
1967 Tlahuitoltepec Mixe Verb Syntagmemes. *International Journal of American Linguistics* 33:34–45.

LYON, SHIRLEY
1967 Tlahuitoltepec Mixe Clause Structure. *International Journal of American Linguistics* 33:25–33.

McQUOWN, NORMAN A.
1967 (vol. ed.) *Linguistics*. Vol. 5 of *Handbook of Middle American Indians*, edited by Robert Wauchope. Austin: University of Texas Press.
1974 Sobre un diccionario totonaco de Papantla, Veracruz. *Notas Antropológicas* 1:73–81.
1976a A Huastec Autobiographical Text. In *Mayan Texts I*, edited by Louanna Furbee-Losee. Native American Texts Series 1(1):3–20. Chicago: International Journal of American Linguistics.
1976b Huastec Morpheme List. Microfilm Collection of Manuscripts on Cultural Anthropology, Series 31, No. 167. Chicago: University of Chicago Library.
1980 San Luis Potosí Huastec Grammar. Microfilm Collection of Manuscripts on Cultural Anthropology, Series 17, No. 102. Chicago: University of Chicago Library.
1982 Gramática del huasteco potosino (1727–1949). Microfilm Collection of Manuscripts on Cultural Anthropology. Chicago: University of Chicago Library.

MOLINA, ALONSO DE
1571 *Vocabulario en lengua castellana y mexicana*. Mexico City: Antonio de Spinosa.

NORDELL, NORMAN
1962 On the Status of Popoluca in Zoque-Mixe. *International Journal of American Linguistics* 28:146–149.

NOYES, ERNEST
1957 Grammar and Lexicon of Black Carib and Lexicon of Cholti and Chorti. Microfilm Collection of Manuscripts on Middle American Indian Cultural Anthropology, Series 7, No. 39. Chicago: University of Chicago Library.

PICKETT, VELMA B.
1969 Isthmus Zapotec. In *Handbook of Middle American Indians*, vol. 5, edited by Robert Wauchope and Norman A. McQuown, pp. 291–310. Austin: University of Texas Press.

PICKETT, VELMA B., et al.
1959 *Vocabulario zapateco del Istmo: Castellano-zapateco y zapateco-castellano*. 1st

ed. Serie de Vocabularios Indígenas Mariano Silva y Aceves, No. 3. Mexico City: Instituto Lingüístico del Verano.

REDD, JAMES G.

1975 Huastec Text Word-Concordance. Microfilm Collection of Manuscripts on Cultural Anthropology, Series 31, No. 166. Chicago: University of Chicago Library.

ROMERO CASTILLO, MOISÉS

1960 Los fonemas del chichimeco-jonaz. *Anales del Instituto Nacional de Antropología e Historia* 11(1957–1958): 289–299.

SCHOENHALS, ALVIN

1962 A Grammatical Classification of Totontepec Mixe Verbs. MA thesis, Department of Linguistics, University of Texas, Austin.

1979 Totontepec Mixe Stage and Event Clauses. *Discourse Processes* 2:57–72.

SCHOENHALS, ALVIN, AND LOUISE C. SCHOENHALS

1965 *Vocabulario mixe de Totontepec: Mixe-castellano, castellano-mixe*. Serie de Vocabularios Indígenas Mariano Silva y Aceves, No. 14. Mexico City: Instituto Lingüístico de Verano.

SOUSTELLE, JACQUES

1937 *La Famille otomi-pame du Mexique central*. Travaux et Mémoires de l'Institut d'Ethnologie 26. Paris: Université de Paris.

SWADESH, MORRIS

1966 Porhé y Maya. *Anales de Antropología del Instituto de Investigaciones Históricas* 3:173–204. Mexico City: Universidad Nacional Autónoma de México.

1969 *Elementos del tarasco antiguo*. Serie Antropológica, Instituto de Investigaciones Históricas, 11. Mexico City: Universidad Nacional Autónoma de México.

TAPIA ZENTENO, CARLOS DE

1727 Paradigma apologético de la huasteca potosina . . . MS in Ayer Collection, Newberry Library, Chicago.

1767 *Noticia de la lengua huasteca*. Mexico City: Bibliotheca Mexicana.

1967 Noticia de la lengua huasteca (potosina). Edited by Terrence S. Kaufman. MS on file, Department of Anthropology, University of Pittsburgh.

VAN HAITSMA, JULIA D., AND WILLARD VAN HAITSMA

1976 *A Hierarchical Sketch of Mixe as Spoken in San José El Paraíso*. Summer Institute of Linguistics of the University of Oklahoma, Pub. No. 44. Norman.

VELÁZQUEZ GALLARDO, PABLO

1978 *Diccionario de la lengua phorhépecha: Español-phorhépecha, phorhépecha-español*. Mexico City: Fondo de Cultura Económica.

WARES, ALAN C.

1956 Suffixation in Tarascan. M.A. thesis, Department of Linguistics, Indiana University, Bloomington.

WEST, ROBERT C.

1948 *Cultural Geography of the Modern Tarascan Area*. Smithsonian Institution, Institute of Social Anthropology, Pub. No. 7. Washington, D.C.

WONDERLY, WILLIAM L.

1951 Zoque II: Phonemes and Morphophonemes. *International Journal of American Linguistics* 17:105–123.